My Life with

BARBRA

My Life with

BARBRA

A Love Story

BARRY DENNEN

Prometheus Books

59 John Glenn Drive
Amherst, New York 14228-2197

Published 1997 by Prometheus Books

01 00 99 98 97   5 4 3 2 1

Library of Congress Cataloging-in-Publication Data

Dennen, Barry.
    My life with Barbra : a love story / Barry Dennen.
        p.   cm.
    ISBN 1–57392–160–2 (cloth)
        1. Streisand, Barbra. 2. Singers—United States—Biography. 3. Dennen, Barry.
I. Title.
ML420.S915D46   1997
782.42164'092—dc21
[B]   97–24796
                                                                         CIP

Printed in the United States of America on acid-free paper

To my beloved James McGachy, who stood by me through thick and thicker.

"If you are born with a voice, it's against God not to exercise it. And if you are born as part of history, your own or others, it is against God not to leave a record of it."

Giovanni Batista
nineteenth-century bel-canto vocal teacher

"Keep a diary and some day it'll keep you."

Mae West

Contents

CONTENTS

Foreword

I like the past; I live part of my life there. But the past is a far-off and partially imagined country that, as I try to approach and recollect it, seems to retreat faster the closer I get.

I'm hardly Mr. Memory, the prodigiously gifted memorizer in Hitchcock's *Thirty-Nine Steps,* nor am I the eponymous victim of total recall in Jorge Luis Borges's story "Funes the Memorious."

Funes was forced to spend his life in a darkened room because he was overwhelmed with a reminiscence so rich that he could remember sharply each detail from every moment on any given day in his life, down to the precise shape of the cloud formations in the sky or the exact pattern of cracks in the wall.

This book is not an exercise in memory. Of course I could never recall exactly who said what in every conversation Barbra and I had thirty-seven years ago.

But I have gone back to my letters and diaries, and questioned the friends who were witnesses, and I've tried to re-create the truth of what happened as sharply as I can. Everyone remembers the same things differently. This is my version.

Many years ago my friend Paul, a film director, told me he ran into Barbra and her manager, Marty Erlichman, at a private showing at the Museum of Modern Art.

"Paul!" Barbra exclaimed. "What are *you* doing here?"

Paul, somewhat offended, managed to reply, "Well, Barbra, actually I was invited here tonight."

"Oh, yeah?" she said. "Are you still making those crazy little movies?"

"Yes," said Paul, fuming quietly, "as a matter of fact, I am."

"Marty," said Barbra, "this is my friend Paul. I know him from way back when."

"Hi, Paul," Marty said, then immediately turned back to her. "Hey, Barbra, what was it like when you were just starting out?"

Barbra slowly turned her head and shot Marty a piercing look.

"I don't know, Marty," she said slowly and emphatically. "I *just . . . don't . . . remember.*"

Of course Barbra couldn't remember. Barbra has always wanted to go forward and never look back.

And ultimately, all memory is sad. If you rummage around in the attic too long, you wind up feeling tired and melancholic, with dusty hands.

But in the end, our recollected lives are the repository of our history, the way we were . . . and who we are.

1

A Blast from the Past

*O*ne late, otherwise unremarkable January afternoon in 1992, in my home in the Hollywood Hills in Los Angeles, I was lying on the sofa, scratching my dog's tummy and watching the news with my boyfriend, when the phone rang. I stood up and strolled out to the kitchen to answer it.

"Hello, Barry? This is Barbra."

I felt a loud thump in my chest. God. There it was again. The Voice. I hadn't seen Barbra in, what?... maybe twenty-four years.

And suddenly there we were, leaning over some sheet music, her hair brushing my arm as we argued over the lyrics, having a $1.35 dinner at the Pam Pam Coffee Shop in the Village, and she was sneaking a bite of baked potato off my plate and I was laughing... and then we were falling back on our bed, exhausted, Vaughan Williams' *The Lark Ascending* soaring on the hi-fi.

Then I popped back into the present, back into my kitchen, in Hollywood in 1992. I was standing there, holding the telephone, and on the other end was The Biggest Star in the World. There was a long pause, and I took a big breath.

13

"Barbra *Who?*" I asked.

The phone crackled at me irritably, as if, on the other end, its cord were being swooshed around the room.

"Barbra *Streisand*, who do you think?" the Voice exclaimed.

Naw, it wasn't The Biggest Star. It was just my Barb. I suppressed a smile.

"I just wanted to make sure," I said as nonchalantly as I could, while I nervously yanked open the refrigerator door. Nothing to nosh on! I shut the fridge, grabbed a glass from the cupboard and hauled open the freezer compartment.

"So...how are ya?" Barbra asked.

"I'm fine, Barb. Long time no hear. How are *you?*" I asked, filling my tumbler with ice cubes. She wants something, I thought. But what could she possibly want from me?

"Fine. Tired. Busy."

She's in terse mode, I decided. Gotta warm her up...but how?

"Yeah," I offered unhelpfully, a little at a loss for words. "I've been busy, too."

There was another awkward pause, bordering on dead air space, while we each regrouped. Well, if I was having a little trouble getting going here, so was she.

"So what's that clinking I'm hearing?" she asked. "I hear water running. Are you in the bath?"

"No, no, I'm in the kitchen. I'm just having a glass of ice water," I explained.

"Oh, yeah. Ice water. It's hot today. Sure, sure," she said.

"Don't you hate it when people eat in your ear?" I asked philosophically. "Practically everyone you call, they eat and drink, right in your ear."

"Yeah, I hate that," she agreed. "Even my therapist does that. It's very L.A."

"You still go to a therapist?" I asked.

14

"Sure," Barbra stated flatly. "Doesn't everyone?"

"Um...could be," I said. "So, whatever happened to you?" I asked, trying to make an off-the-wall joke, as if she'd vanished without a trace since I last saw her instead of becoming the most watched celebrity on the planet, but the leaden silence on the other end told me my little attempt didn't go over too well. Barbra had always been basically a very serious person. I knew that, but I hadn't been around her for so long I didn't really know who she was these days. It's hard to pick up on old relationships, harder still when there used to be a lot of feeling between the two of you, and you parted badly.

I tried to pull the conversation back from the brink. "So, what have you been up to?" I asked.

"Oh, please. Stop," she said. "Movies, records. Everything. You?"

"I'm keeping busy. I'm writing," I told her.

"That's good, that's good. Hey, remember way back when? When we used to live together, on 9th Street?" she asked.

"Of course I remember," I said.

"It seems like such a long time ago," she said.

"God, it *was* a long time ago. It was nearly...uh...thirty-two years ago," I said. "Hey, listen, since we're talking and all, there's something I've always wanted to say to you. You remember how we broke up, and everything..."

"Sure," she said, a little too fast, as if it happened five minutes ago.

"Well, what I wanted to say was...I mean...despite every-thing that happened, and all the arguments and upset feelings and everything...oh, God, I don't know how to say this..." I bumbled, running out of steam.

"Go ahead," she said. "I think I know anyway," she added, her voice sounding mellow and full of memory.

"Well, the thing is...I mean, back when we were together..." I faltered, then pressed on. "I mean, I know I hurt your feelings, and behaved really … really bad. But … the thing is, I honestly and truly did love you, you know, in spite of everything. I want you to know how I felt. I've always wanted you to know that I really did care."

"I know that," she said simply. "Hey," she added, "we were just kids. What did we know? We did the best we could."

"Yeah, I guess that's true," I said, relieved I'd finally gotten something off my chest that I'd wanted to say thirty years ago.

"Listen, I wanna ask you something," she went on, in an artfully off-handed tone of voice.

"Sure, go ahead," I offered. "Anything."

Here we go, I thought to myself, the roller coaster inside my head having clanked up to the top of the first hill, and ready for the drop. I waited. Don't say anything, I thought.

"Why do people hate me?" Barbra blurted out, sounding genuinely hurt, confused, and a little resentful as well. The question hung in the air, suspended in the miles of fiber-optic telephone wires between us. I could hear her soft breathing on the other end of the line, waiting for me to answer, to say something, to explain to her. I felt her insecurity, her vulnerability.

Obviously she had thought a lot and for a long time about asking someone this, and now, finally, that someone was me. It was an act of courage on her part, and I instinctively held back from saying anything that might hurt her. Still, she was opening herself up to me, asking sincerely, and, as always, Barbra demanded the truth.

Of course, I'd heard stories about how some people in Hollywood were less than fond of Barbra: how difficult she was, how unrelentingly meticulous, such a perfectionist, such a pain in the butt. Only a year earlier, Barbra's legendary manager, Marty Erlichman, took me out to dinner and told me stories about Barbra's two-o'clock-in-the-morning phone calls to him, early in their relationship. He called them her "How Come" calls: How

Come Elizabeth Taylor has a bigger dressing room than me? How Come Eydie Gorme makes more money a week than I do? How Come Ann-Margret has a Jacuzzi in her bathroom and I don't? It was enough to make anyone, even someone who loved her a lot, impatient, especially at two in the morning.

But my working relationship with Barbra had been early on, and I'd never witnessed her firsthand since she'd become a star. I had no way of knowing whether her professional behavior was appropriate, or impossible.

"Who do you think hates you?" I asked. "Your fellow workers? Your colleagues?"

"No, no, no," she replied impatiently. "I get along with them fine, despite what they say in the *Enquirer*. It's my *fans*. My fans are my biggest foes!" she exclaimed.

I snorted. "I'm sorry," I said, "but that just doesn't make sense. Your fans adore you."

"Some of them," she commented darkly. "First of all, first of all," she demanded, "I wanna ask your opinion on something." She took a big, dramatic pause. Then she said, "Do I owe my fans anything?"

"Well, of course," I replied.

"No, I don't!" she snapped back defiantly. "They never gave *me* anything!"

"Barbra," I started off carefully, "your voice comes into their homes, into their cars, it's in every corner of their lives. They buy your records, your tapes, your CDs. They plunk down their money to go see your movies. They feel invested in you, like they know you. Your fans give you interest and energy and love and money, and it's inevitable that they want a piece of you back."

"But that's *me*, the real me, it's personal. It's private. It doesn't belong to anyone but *me*," she finished, her voice trembling with feeling.

"Well, that's how *you* feel," I said, "but clearly *they* feel like you

17

owe them something. That's the price of fame. That's the Deal," I finished.

"The *Deal*?" she snapped. "*What* Deal?"

"The Fame Deal," I said. "You can't put yourself out there in front of the public, saying love me, love me, love me, make me rich and famous, and then when they do, insist that 'all I vant iss to be left... alone!' That's not how it works. You traded in your privacy."

There was a muffled sputtering of indignation on the other end of the line. "Barry," she said pointedly, "the last time I was in a crowd they tried to rip the clothes off me. I was terrified!" she said.

"The more you pull away from the public, the hungrier they get to sink their claws in you," I insisted.

"Yeah," she mused, conceding the point. "I got this Japanese philosopher gentleman who calls me from time to time. He calls them My Loyal Enemies. They love me so much, they hate me."

"My Loyal Enemies," I repeated. "That's perfect."

"See, this is what's getting me so crazy. This is what I absolutely don't understand..." She stopped.

"What?" I prodded gently.

"Well, I'm..." she started almost shyly, "...I'm a nice person. Why do people have such horrible feelings about me?"

"What did you imagine people felt about you?" I asked gently.

Barbra sighed wistfully. "I thought..." she let it float in the air. "I thought...I was beloved," she said sadly, pronouncing it like a rabbi at a Jewish funeral: Be-*love*-ed. "But now, I'm afraid to go out of the house, I'm afraid to go shopping. I imagine all sorts of bad things are going to happen to me. People just don't understand..." her voice trailed off.

I felt so sad about what she was saying. Barbra used to be a prize-winning Champion Shopper. I remembered her whoop of triumph as she plucked a marvelous, bulky burgundy cardigan off the bargain rack in Macy's basement.

"Look at this!" she beamed. "Seven dollars...and it's real wool!"

Or how she burst with pride the day she introduced me to the cut-price glories of Cost Less Drugs, where she stocked up on half a dozen boxes of black currant throat pastilles, two bottles of nail polish remover, a cake of cerulean blue eye shadow, and an electric vaporizer.

"Look at all this stuff—and for less than ten bucks!" she had exclaimed in the checkout line.

And now here she was, breaking my heart, telling me she was a prisoner in her own house and she felt unloved. I wanted to say something that would make her feel appreciated, and special, the way I felt about her.

"Maybe it's your enormous talent," I offered. "People are intimidated by that."

"Intimidated?" she protested, incredulous.

"Barbra, please," I said. "You're one of the greatest popular singers who ever lived..."

"Oh, stop," she interjected.

"You're a wonderful actor, director, producer. I mean, come on, what do you expect?" I said. "By the way, I loved *Yentl*," I added parenthetically.

"Thanks," she said.

"Okay, so they're intimidated and overwhelmed. But they also want a piece of you. Like the warriors who kill the lion so they can eat its heart and share in its strength," I said.

"Yeah, right, share its strength. If they only knew!" she said. "I'm so insecure, I'm so nervous. I worry about everything all the time."

"What are you worried about?" I asked.

"What, are you kidding? My life, my career, my image. I'm always at the doctors. I got phobias and psychosomatic illnesses. And I'm constantly worried about money..." she trailed off.

"Wait a minute. I'm talking to one of the richest women in the world, with houses in Malibu and Beverly Hills and New York, and you're telling me..."

"Yeah, yeah, yeah," she said. "My money is all tied up. The taxes are killing me. I've got these cash flow problems. I got no cash!" she exclaimed.

"Why don't you sell one of the houses?" I asked.

"I tried," she answered gloomily. "I put it on the market. Nobody can afford it."

An idea popped into my head.

"Listen," I said. "I bet I know how you can make a lot of money, real fast."

There was a pause. I could hear the gears cranking.

"Oh, yeah?" she said dubiously. "How?"

"Concertize," I said.

"Oh, Barry, please," she protested.

"Come on, Barbra. Do concerts! Everybody is *dying* to hear you sing live again. They'd flock by the thousands...and they'd pay a *lot* of money for the privilege."

"Do concerts, huh?" Barbra mused. "Yeah, a lotta people have told me that over the years. Marty Erlichman* is always going on at me to do concerts, do concerts."

"How long has it been since you sang in public?" I asked her.

Barbra sighed. "I dunno," she said thoughtfully. "Twenty-two years, maybe..."

"So?" I said. "It's about time."

---

*Marty Erlichman is still Barbra's manager. He's been faithfully by her side almost since the beginning, except for a long hiatus when Jon Peters took over. A few years ago, over dinner, I asked Marty how the two of them got back together again. He explained that Barbra had called and asked him how would he like to come back and manage her? There was a pause, then Marty told her that he'd have to think about it. After another pause Barbra replied, "That's not the answer I expected."

"I can't," she said. "I . . . can't do it."

"Why not?" I pressed.

"I'm scared. I'm scared somebody would try to kill me."

"Oh!" I said, and thought about that. "You know, that's a real fear. There probably is some crackpot out there who wants to be The Person Who Killed Barbra Streisand, like that guy with John Lennon."

"Oy, a big chill just went down my back," her voice shivered.

"I'm sorry," I said. "I'm not trying to scare you."

"Oh, really?" she countered. "Well, you're doing a pretty good job."

"But listen," I said, "it doesn't have to be like that. You'll install check points, you know, metal detectors, like they have at the airports. You'll have guards, policemen, security, all over the place. Nobody will be able to get anywhere near you with a weapon."

"Metal detectors?" she said. "Like at the airports? Huh! I never thought of that!" she mused.

"It'll be great," I insisted.

"No," she pleaded. "I get stage fright, Barry, when I sing in public. Awful, crippling stage fright. It's debilitating. I get clenched. I get paralyzed. I can't go to the bathroom. I get so that I can't even walk!" she wailed.

"Listen, Barb," I said, "you *will* have stage fright."

"What?" she said, shocked.

"No, wait," I went on. "You'll be standing in the wings, and you'll have butterflies in your tummy, and your palms will be sweating like crazy. And then the music will start, and you'll hear the orchestra, and there'll be *violins*!" I said.

"Please, please, stop!" she pleaded. "Just talking about this is making me nauseous!"

"And then you'll walk out on the stage, and this wave of applause and intensity and love will wash over you, and you'll take

21

a deep breath, and the first notes will come out, and all the nervousness and fear will fall away."

I listened. There was nothing.

Finally Barbra said, in a little voice, "Go on."

"Okay," I said. "And you'll be *so* glad you decided to do this, *so* glad to be singing in public again, you'll feel absolutely terrific, and you'll do concert after concert, and you'll have lots and lots of money and you'll pay off all your bills. Happy Ending. The End."

There was nothing on the other end of the line but another silence.

"Hello, Barb?" I said. "Are you there?"

"Yeah. Yeah. Sure I'm here. I'm thinking," she replied. "Maybe. I dunno. It's possible. Maybe."

"You can do it," I said. "You *know* you can do it. You'll love it. If you don't love it, you can call me up and say: Barry, I didn't love it."

"Bar?" Barbra's voice on the other end of the phone was sharp and clear. "Listen, I gotta go," she said. "I'll call you. 'Bye."

And that was it. The phone went dead and the moment evaporated, as if the whole conversation had never happened.

As I hung up the receiver I thought: Oh, God. Isn't this where I came in?

For the next hour, I wandered around the house, looking at my things. Was there anything left of my life with Barbra, any memento, any souvenir? Yes, there was the Tiffany lamp from our apartment, with its embedded red glass cherries, golden peaches, and clusters of shiny purple grapes now hanging over my dining room table. And the blue glass pitcher on which, when you filled it with milk, baby Shirley Temple's picture appeared.

And tucked away in my bank vault, the tapes I made of her so long ago at the Bon Soir, the tapes that caused so many problems between us.

All the rest of that day, my mind was sent shunting back through the corridors of memory. And through the days and weeks that followed, I found myself recalling things I hadn't thought of for a long, long time—moments, thoughts, and feelings that had been stored away like fragile glass Christmas tree ornaments packed in tissue paper in an old trunk. And in my mind, as I unwrapped each glittering souvenir, I found myself being unexpectedly surprised and delighted and moved.

From the moment I met her, I thought Barbra was original and unique and luminously talented, but it never occurred to me that millions of people would someday think so, too.

And so I've decided to tell the story of Barbra and Barry, about our life together when we were just starting out and everything seemed possible and, amazingly, everything was.

I want to take you into the special world Barbra and I shared three decades ago...privately and intimately...together.

2

Butterflies

The first time I saw Barbara Streisand, she was madly running around an empty theater stage, desperately and ditzily flapping a pair of cloth butterfly wings stuck to her shoulders. I watched as she moved through the shafts of afternoon sunlight, her dancing shoes kicking up motes of dust from the wooden floorboards into the air. It was one of the most magical moments of my life.

I had just wheezed my way to the top of a long, creaky, wooden flight of stairs in the Czech National Hall, inconveniently located on 73rd Street between First and Second Avenues, in New York City. "The Hall" was a kind of elaborately tacky ballroom with a stage at one end. There were clouds painted on the ceiling and a mirror ball, probably installed for some unimaginable series of Czechoslovakian proms, weddings, and cocktail parties.

The cast of *The Insect Comedy* had been in rehearsal for almost two weeks when an actor left and I got roped into joining the group. They hadn't even given me a script yet; all I knew was I was supposed to show up at "The Hall."

The voices of the rehearsing actors ricocheted off the walls with an unflattering, tinny quality; the whole room was drafty, dingy, and grim, just the place to rehearse a comedy.

"Hi," I said.

"Hi, I'm Barbara," she said, gasping for breath. "Barbara Streisand."

She shook my hand and swayed, catching her balance. I grabbed a hand to steady her and she looked up at me with azure-blue eyes, so electric and sharp they crackled. There were two thick trails of black eyeliner ringing her eyelids, and even though it was the middle of a hot spring day, she wore a heavy base of makeup. Her beautifully shaped mouth had no lipstick, just a sheen of shiny, clear gloss on those sensuous lips. She had what my acting teacher called "The Actor's Mask": a face dramatically distinctive, with sculptured, carved features that demanded, "Look at me, look at me!" on the stage.

Barbara was wearing a black leotard, tights, and dance shoes, and as she struggled to catch her breath, her breasts pushed out in tiny points beneath the leotard top. Her cloth wings, which had been hand-painted on flimsy, translucent fabric, hung sadly by her sides and drooped on the ground. She wasn't tall, about five feet five. Her long, dark brown hair was pinned up, and on top lay a round, braided hairpiece that unfortunately resembled a prune Danish. The flailing, flapping butterfly dance she had been practicing had shifted it a little, and now it was hanging on for dear life. To me, she looked vulnerable, and brave, and incredibly young. She was only seventeen.

"I'm having trouble with my wings. I keep stepping on them," she admitted. Then she giggled up the scale in an arpeggio. "They're neat, though, huh?" she added, giving them one final flap.

"Why don't you tilt your head back when you make those turns. And lift the *shmatas*,* those painted wing things, a little higher," I suggested.

"Higher, yeah, yeah." Barbara seemed unconvinced. The wings could wait, she seemed to be saying; she'd worry about them later. She shifted her weight from foot to foot impatiently. Her body language was all angular, knees and elbows poking out. It was as if there were something inside her struggling to get free, her own butterfly pushing out of its chrysalis, a chick impatiently pecking its way out of the shell.

"Think of Loie Fuller," I suggested.

"Louie *Who?*" she asked.

"Loie Fuller, with the wings. The dancer. In the Toulouse-Lautrec posters." She looked at me blankly, like I was speaking Hindustani. "Never mind," I said.

"So, what's your name?" Barbara asked, squinting quizzically at me.

"I'm Barre," I said.

"Barry, huh? That's a funny name. No, wait a minute, I don't mean funny, like *funny.* I mean, like, unusual. It's not an everyday kind of a name, ya know what I mean, like Lennie, or Bernie. I mean, ya don't meet many Barrys. At least I never did. Until now," she muttered, seeming to run out of steam.

Barbara was kibitzing with me in that Brooklynese patois she had perfected, verbally piling up brick upon brick, her talk jerking forward like a car with a bad clutch. I realized later that even at this young age, at our first meeting, the way she moved right into your face with her talking was a direct extension of the force of her budding personality. She was, in her speech as in her life, thrashing around, trying on ideas for size, turning things over and over, exam-

---

*For the Yiddish-impaired, literally "rags."

ining, questioning, searching, pushing forward, retreating, heatedly coming to conclusions at the same time she was skeptically doubting everything. She bubbled with life and its contradictions.

"I don't like the name Barre," I admitted. "I never did."

"Barry," she said. "It's not so bad."

"No, see, just to make my life miserable, my mother spelled it B-A-R-R-E. With an *accent aigu*," I slashed my finger from left to right, "over the E. It's on my birth certificate."

"Barre," she thought about it. "With an E! That's some name."

"Right," I said. "My mother wanted me to be different, you know, to be special. Special," I explained, "like getting the shit beat out of you in the playground."

"Yeah," Barbara said, and her eyes clouded over for a moment. "You have a hard time in school?"

"Oh, sure," I said. "With a name like that, I wasn't very popular."

"Uh-huh," she said, looking at me closely. "Me too. Even without a name like that." Her voice immediately lost its street-tough quality, and a lost, puzzled look filmed over her eyes, as if the indignities and hurt feelings from her young past were again engulfing her. Barbara switched gears so quickly, from brash wise-cracking to the most delicate sensitivity; she whirled her feelings in a verbal Cuisinart.

We had both been jabbering away like a couple of mynah birds, but suddenly we seemed to have run out of things to say. She was staring at me. I hoped she didn't think I was too skinny. At twenty-one I was pale with pitch black hair, about three inches taller than Barbara. A friend said my eyes looked like they had ten thousand years of Jewish suffering in them. Hopefully she'd think I was intense and interesting, a look I'd tried like mad to cultivate in college.

I noticed that her complexion was lightly pitted and bumpy, and the thick makeup was a raw attempt to cover it over. She was so young she was still having problems with oily skin, and the merest suggestion of baby fat slightly rounded her cheeks. She was what my father would have called "kooky," in the sense that she wasn't conventionally pretty. So why was I thinking, my God, this girl is *beautiful.* What was it that was so compelling about her, so striking? She was so painfully thin, so earnest, so yearning. I decided that she looked . . . hungry.

"You know, when I was young," I told her, "these mean kids on my block used to rub all the powder off a butterfly's wings. Then they'd put the butterfly on a clothesline and make it walk along. They'd twang the string with their finger and laugh when it tried to hold on."

"So why didn't it fly away?" she asked.

"It couldn't. That's why they rubbed all the powder off," I explained.

"A butterfly who can't fly. That's good. I can use that image, ya know? Listen," she added, lowering her voice conspiratorially, "I'm really glad you're here. I've just been going along with all this stuff, but I don't think these people really know what they're doing. Listen," she pleaded, "will you just give me a hand saying these lines? I just don't understand what I'm supposed to be saying here. I don't get it."

"Sure," I said. "But I don't even have a script yet. Show me yours."

She walked me over to the side of the stage to a couple of wooden chairs near the makeshift wings. Her chair back was draped with a wool cardigan.

"How come you brought that?" I asked, pointing to the sweater. "It's *boiling* out."

"You never know!" Barbara said ominously, removing a small stack of magazines piled up on the seat and placing them next to a large brown paper shopping bag on the floor.

We both plopped down. Barbara hoisted the shopping bag onto her lap and started to forage through it. It was chock full of clothing, makeup, costume jewelry, cosmetics, aspirin, and other bottles and jars—a whole bunch of *stuff*. Clearly Barbara made her own little nest, staked out her own little world around herself wherever she went, even if it was just a wooden chair in a rehearsal hall. As she rummaged around she looked fondly at her shopping bag as if it were some kind of pet.

"My initials are B.S.," she said. "Backwards, that's S.B.: Shopping Bag.* This bag is my entire *life*. Everything I own or want or need is in this bag."

"It looks like you could carry around your own Kleig light in there," I said.

"Kleig light?" she said, suddenly sitting up straight. "What's a Kleig light?"

Oh Lord, I thought, this girl doesn't know anything.

"A Kleig light," I told her, "is this real bright, hot spotlight. They use it in the movies, you know, like at premieres."

As she nodded she finally found her Samuel French copy of *The Insect Comedy* and, somewhat nervously, gave me the dog-eared, tattered script. She looked as though she was afraid I was going to scold her for its frayed condition. I opened it. Her speeches were all underlined in red pencil, and scribbled notes and questions filled the margins. I skimmed down the page with growing astonishment and horror.

"Oh, my God, this dialogue!" I whispered. "It's very…uh…

---

*Ironically, I was reminded of this dialogue a couple of years ago, when Barbra appeared on TV with a magnificent suite of Art Nouveau furniture that she was putting up for auction. The original owner had been Sarah Bernhardt.

"S.B. and B.S.," Barbra said, pointing out an embroidered detail. "We both have the same initials."

Baby, I thought, you've come a long way from Shopping Bags.

expressionistic," I said numbly, flipping through the pages to the last scene.

"And that ain't all!" Barbara added tartly.

"Listen to this," I said. "This is the part where the Chrysalis gets born. The stage direction says, 'She bends her husk and leaps forth as a moth, upstage center, swaying over the lights.'"

I glanced over at Barbara, who was looking at me dubiously. "What *is* this?" I inquired.

"Go on," Barbara said with a hint of practiced nonchalance. "You just got here. I've had weeks of this stuff. Nothing would surprise me."

"O-kay," I said, and read aloud: "'Oh, oh, oh! I enjoin creation. The whole of life surged up to bring me forth, and it burst in its throes.'" I looked up at Barbara. "Oh, oh, brother!" I commented.

"More," she encouraged me. "Read some more."

I sighed heavily and turned the page. "'Harken! O, Harken! I proclaim immense tidings!'" I shook my head in stunned disbelief and looked up at her again. "This is really dreadful!" I stammered. "Mind-bogglingly awful."

"Ya think so?" Barbara snorted. "Keep reading. It gets worse."

I took a deep breath and plowed on. "Let's see," I said. "The Chrysalis has been born, I guess, because now she's whirling on a glass platform and, uh...emoting, and I suppose everyone's all harkening like she wanted them to, because she goes on, 'I bear a mighty mission. Silence, silence! I will utter great words!' Then the stage direction says, 'The Chrysalis drops dead, center.' I looked up at her, stunned. "Is this a weird joke? Are we supposed to say this dialogue with a straight face?"

"Yeah, right," she said, nodding her head as if she were blaming me for getting her into this. Then Barbara looked down at her middle fingernail, rubbed it with her thumb and frowned. "Ya see what I mean?" she added, with the smug wisdom of someone who'd been warning me about this play for years and I just wouldn't listen.

I picked up the script as though it had turned into some kind of alien thing in my lap. "Then somebody named 'The Vagrant' comes up and stands over her," I informed Barbara, my voice cracking a little. "Who's 'The Vagrant'?" I asked, fearing the worst.

"That's Vasek," Barbara said, pulling an emery board out of her shopping bag and giving her snagged nail a little buff. "He's the lead. The only problem is, Vasek can't speak English very well."

"Yeah. I know Vasek. We went to UCLA together. 'The Vagrant' says, 'Rise up, moth. See, she's dead. Oh, God, why must it die? What is this fearful lack of meaning?' " I stopped reading, appalled, and weakly let the play script fall back into my lap.

"So, whaddya think?" Barbara asked with a naughty little smile, tossing the nail file back into her shopping bag.

"My God," I said, feeling a little panicky, "I didn't know what I was getting into when I said I'd do this thing. I mean, we're all playing *insects*."

"Of course," Barbara said. "That's why it's called *The Insect Comedy*. It's a comedy about insects."

"A comedy about insects?" I shot back. "I'm not sure insects are intrinsically funny. Jesus," I fumed, "this is like something out of *Auntie Mame*."

Barbara fixed me with a blank stare. "Auntie *Who*?"

"Never mind," I said. I couldn't believe she'd never heard of *Auntie Mame*. The book had been a huge hit just a few years back.

"No, no, tell me. I like to learn things," she begged.

"*Auntie Mame*. Right. It's this really funny book by Patrick Dennis, about this wonderful, outrageous woman who has all these wacky escapades..."

"Hold on," Barbara exclaimed, "I know about this. It was a movie with Rosalind Russell. I saw it."

"It wasn't as good as the book," I said dismissively. "Well, anyway, there's this stupid Broadway show that's a terrible fiasco where everything falls apart and—"

"Wait a minute, wait a minute," Barbara pleaded. She impatiently uncrossed her legs, then crossed them the other way. "What's a *fiasco*? It sounds like a flavor of Italian ice cream."

I sighed. "It's something where everything goes all wrong. I mean, we're going to wind up playing three performances to an all-Czech audience, who may or may not understand English. They're going to have to run Czechoslovakian subtitles along the stage floor on a huge paper roll, like a foreign movie."

She scrunched up her face and studied me. "You're great," she said. "I never met anybody like you. You want some gum?" she asked me carefully, offering me the Doublemint pack as though my answer was going to be some kind of litmus test.

"No, thanks. God, I can't believe this," I said, shaking my head. "I can't believe I'm really going to be running around a stage with antennae on my head, playing a butterfly!"

"Well, actually, *I'm* the butterfly," Barbara explained thoughtfully, carefully unfolding the foil wrapper and loading the stick of gum into her mouth. "*You're* the moth."

At the end of the day, after a chaotic, disorganized rehearsal and everyone else had gone home, Barbara and I sat on the wooden steps that led up to the stage. The hall was empty and darkening. The heat of the day hung heavily in the room, and through the large, open windows the cries of kids playing and the chatter of women's voices in an exotic Eastern European dialect floated up from the street.

Barbara sat on the top of the steps looking down at me, her knees curled up against her chest. A red and blue neon sign outside washed a colored shadow across her cheek, her eyes glowed warmly in the dark. I lit up a Parliament and we talked about our parts.

"Ya know, Bar," she said, "I'm really kinda worried about this thing. I mean, I know it's a stupid play and everything, but somebody said the critics are gonna get invited, and if we're gonna get seen, I really want to be good," she explained, a tone of aching, sweet sincerity suffusing her voice.

"Would you like me to help you?" I offered. "We could rehearse late, ya know, work out some interesting business, make it as good as we can."

Even in the dusk I could see the little flash in her eyes.

"Yeah. Yeah," she enthused. "That would be terrific, just great," she said. "Hey, I mean, it's fine running around the stage, flapping your wings, ya know, and doing all the *choreography* and everything, if that's what you call it. But we've gotta talk about our characters, their emotions, what they're *feeling*! Their inner *lives*!"

"Barbara, how can we talk about the emotional inner life of these characters?" I asked her. "They're *bugs*."

"So?" she countered loftily. "Bugs are people, too." A barely concealed smile formed at the corners of her mouth. I smiled back.

Hmm, I thought. I bet somebody's been filling her head with Actors Studio mumbo-jumbo. "Hey, by any chance are you taking acting classes?" I asked her ingenuously.

"Yeah," she admitted. "From my friend Allan."

"What does he teach?" I persisted. "Method Acting?"

"Kinda," she said grudgingly. "Kinda Methody."

"I see," I said.

Barbara sat bolt upright. "Whatsa matter? You don't believe in The Method?" she demanded incredulously, as if I'd told her I didn't believe in Santa Claus or God or something.

"Stanislavsky's great," I admitted carefully. "A real bright teacher, and obviously he must have been a very talented actor. And he worked out a way to put emotional truth into acting that in those days must have put the Broadway actors to shame."

"Right," Barbara agreed, nodding her head decisively.

"But you know, Barb, Stanislavsky wasn't infallible. Chekhov thought he directed *The Seagull* all wrong. Too…serious. Too…heavy."

Barbara scrooched around uncomfortably as if I were preaching some seditious religious heresy. "At the dress rehearsal," I persisted, "Chekhov kept running up the aisle to him and pleading, 'Konstantin, it's a *comedy!*'"

Barbara was staring at me as if I were some kind of exotic animal she'd never seen before. "Really?" she said disbelievingly.

"Yeah," I said. "There's this little movie theater in L.A. that shows these great old flicks. About a year ago they showed this Russian movie with excerpts of the Moscow Art Theater in their plays. Olga Knipper, doing that famous letter scene from *The Cherry Orchard*…"

"Oh, yeah?" Barbara said, sounding impressed, and then added, "Who's Olga Knipper?"

"Chekhov's wife," I said. "She was pretty good. Very concentrated. Oh, and there was a wonderful, long sequence from *The Lower Depths* with this really terrific older guy who played a down-at-the-heels count—I can't remember the actor's name. Moskvein, maybe? Something. Anyway, the point is, the first Method actors were good, but they weren't any better than any other good actors."

"Huh!" Barbara humphed.

"Anyway, I have a feeling maybe the American actors who went over to Russia in the 1920s to study with Stanislavsky kinda got it wrong," I said.

Barbara sat upright and glared at me.

"Some of it," I amended hastily.

Barbara shrugged one shoulder, as if to indicate that was closer to the right answer.

"But the thing is, Barb," I went on, blowing out a thin, gray stream of smoke, "about this scene: I think maybe you should just play your character like a young girl with a crush, you know, burning up with love. Forget about all the butterfly business. She's just *consumed* with sex and passion, all she wants to do is get it on with this guy. That's what's going on here."

She fixed me with those stunning, cornflower-blue eyes. Her left one, a little wonky from tiredness, was slowly gliding in toward her nose. I wanted to put my arms around her, protect her.

A little shiver ran through Barbara's body. And then she leaned forward to speak and at the same time touched my kneecap with one long fingernail, and I felt as though somebody had put a hand under my stomach and pushed up slightly, as though a jolt of electricity had sprung from my center and shot up my spine. It was thrilling and unexpectedly erotic.

"Ya know, Bar," Barbara said, "I think you've got something there. Yeah, yeah," she reasoned with growing excitement, tapping her nail on my knee. "I get it. She just wants to get laid. And then she does get laid. And then they all die."

We stared at each other. There was a breathless silence, loaded with promise. Neither one of us seemed to want to move. She laughed softly and put her hands back around her legs, and then a far-off look moved across her face, as if she were pulling back inside herself, drawing a curtain. She lowered her head for a long moment, staring down into her lap. The silence was deafening, palpable.

Then suddenly Barbara looked up at me, straightened her back. There she was: pulled together, focused, ready to do battle with the city, the streets, and anything the New York subway system might throw at her.

"Well," she said, and cleared her throat. "I gotta get going. Thanks, Bar. You been a *lotta* help. See ya tomorrow."

3

It's a Wonderful Town

$\mathcal{T}$he screaming headline hit me right between the eyeballs:
BILLIE HOLIDAY DEAD OF DRUG OVERDOSE.

I stood in traumatized disbelief, staring at the piles of late edition papers on my corner neighborhood newsstand in New York City's then unfashionable Upper West Side.

I was wearing my gorgeous new black suit from the most elegant men's clothier in Los Angeles, which my dad had bought me as my going-away gift, along with a luxurious selection of new shirts, ties, and shoes.

Yes, I was an expensively dressed, know-it-all newcomer, a Beverly Hills brat, and yes, I had been spoiled; according to my mother, who had a mouth on her, I had been "brought up like a rich bitch." So sayeth Rose L. Dennen.

We hadn't always been so well off. Only a few years earlier we had left Chicago, where my brother, Lyle, and I were born, under a black cloud. My father never really talked about it, but I got the impression that he owed somebody powerful and vindictive an

37

awful lot of money. So one cold winter afternoon in 1952, he bundled my mother, my brother and me, and our black cocker spaniel, Chucky, a dog whose singular talent was biting, into the car for the long trek to California.

When we got to Los Angeles my dad borrowed a considerable amount of cash from a rich relative, and with it he bought a large venetian blind factory on La Cienega Boulevard. My mother pitched in as his secretary, and even I worked there one summer, rescuing blinds that were being ground up and mauled inside the ancient, gigantic, clanking venetian blind washing machine. Those were the heady days when California was blossoming physically and financially. New schools were popping up everywhere in rapidly expanding neighborhoods like San Bernardino and Anaheim. My father bid on and won many big contracts to install thousands of window coverings in the new facilities. He made a lot of money, and soon we were living in a big house on Coldwater Canyon, one of Beverly Hills' most exclusive, expensive enclaves.

Over the last four years as an honor student in the theater department at UCLA I'd carved out a reputation for myself as a red-hot actor and writer, someone who was going to go places. Immediately after graduation my dad asked me what I wanted to do with my life. I told him that more than anything, I wanted to move to the East Coast and act on the Broadway stage. To my utter surprise and amazement he didn't try to talk me out of it. In fact, he gave me his blessing and offered to give me a helping hand financially for a year or so, until I got on my feet.

So two weeks later I found myself in American Airlines' loving arms, on a plane headed straight for Manhattan, to spread my wings and soar like an eagle over the Great White Way.

That was two weeks ago. And now here I was, standing on the corner of Broadway and 86th Street in New York City, New York. It was July 1959, and God, was it hot!

Remember 1959? Maybe you're too young, or maybe you don't want to.

Eisenhower and Nixon were running the country. A new car cost $2,850, gas was thirty-one cents a gallon, a pound loaf of bread twenty cents. Lurid orange Formica slabs in free-form shapes like giant dysentery amoebas were the latest rage in coffee tables.

Bright plastic radios everywhere were blasting Bobby Darin's "Mack the Knife." Hollywood was throwing 3-D movies right into the audience's faces in an attempt to win them back, as film attendance slumped and Uncle Miltie kept viewers glued to their sofas on Tuesday nights. The U.S. Postmaster General banned the mailing of *Lady Chatterley's Lover* as obscene.

On Broadway that season, Ethel Merman was knockin' 'em dead in *Gypsy*, Lucille Ball tore things up in *Redhead,* and Jackie Gleason clowned around in *Take Me Along.* At the clubs, Tony Martin was crooning at the Copacabana while Johnny Ray wailed at the Latin Quarter. Off Broadway, *Little Mary Sunshine* was a camp hit with a young Eileen Brennan and a newcomer named Carol Burnett was making a huge smash in *Once Upon a Mattress* over at the Phoenix.

In February, I'd had my twenty-first birthday.

And a month before that, in January of 1959, a gawky, offbeat-looking seventeen-year-old named Barbara Streisand had graduated from Erasmus Hall High School and made the momentous twenty-minute subway trip from Brooklyn to Times Square which, for her, was just as big a leap as mine was from California. In the sizzling summer I hit town, I believe Barbara was already ensconced on West 48th Street, babysitting her acting teacher's children in exchange for free classes.

The newspaper headlines had burned themselves into my stinging eyes, and the news vendor was beginning to look at me nervously. I'd been standing there so long, he was probably afraid

I was going to mug him. I could feel the sun scorching the top of my head as sweat ran in rivulets down my back, drenching my already damp shirt, my sticky armpits, my fried feet.

I had just crawled up out of the subway after another disappointing interview with yet another uninterested agent. And on top of everything, Billie Holiday was dead and nobody seemed to care. Aggressive pedestrians pushed past me, grabbed their papers, paid the newsman, melted back into the crowd. I still couldn't believe it. She was only forty-four.

Another great singer I missed the chance to hear sing live, I thought, as I turned and trudged uptown toward 89th Street, where "Geri," a cousin of a friend of my dad's, had arranged to sublet me her apartment for my first, special, sweltering summer in the city.

When I first got into town Chemical Bank had refused to give me immediate credit on my California check and put a hold on it until the funds cleared. I thought I might just squeak by, but the small amount of cash I had brought with me was nearly gone, and out of pride, I'd refused my dad's kind offer to let me run things up on his credit card. So here I was, stumbling up Broadway, wearing the nattiest men's clothes in the West Eighties and starving to death.

I staggered across Seventh Avenue, and at the corner, as I stepped up onto the curb, the toe of my beautiful, brand-new Italian shoe scraped the sidewalk, carving a long scar into the supple black leather. My shoe was gashed, and Billie Holiday was dead. New York was trying to crush my spirit, to scratch me, dehydrate me, besmirch me with soot and broil me to death. Limp and disconsolate, I schlepped down the side street toward my apartment building, feeling down in the dumps and a long way from home.

I was missing my music. I had no record player, no tape deck—I'd left everything behind in California. Since my earliest childhood I had always been passionately interested in music, particularly popular female personality and jazz vocalists, although I was blessed with wildly eclectic tastes. I'd amassed a huge record collection over the years, everything from Rachmaninoff to rock 'n' roll. This was a palmy time for collectors. The new long-playing record had just been introduced, and dealers everywhere were dumping their 78s to make room for the new LPs. I haunted the local record shops and picked up incredible treasures for little or nothing.

Suddenly I remembered the day less than a year ago when I'd dropped by a tiny Hollywood record shop, where I excitedly discovered a small cache of original, mint-condition Billie Holiday-Teddy Wilson records on the English Parlophone label. What a find!

> A bird with feathers of blue
> Is waiting for you
> Back in your own backyard...*

All that evening, Billie's sweet inimitable voice floated from the loudspeakers and out the windows of my little guest house behind my parents' place, onto the cool, eucalyptus-scented breeze where it bounced softly off the hillsides of Coldwater Canyon. And now it was a humid, sizzling 98 degrees Fahrenheit in New York City, and Lady Day was dead.

I wheezed up the endless flights of the airless and relentlessly cheerless stairwell and stood gasping for breath on the fourth-floor landing. The door of the apartment looked war-torn: scarred, dented, and battered. My fantasy was that every time I went out, a band of desperate but incompetent burglars suddenly appeared from nowhere and began systematically gouging it with crowbars and smashing it with sledgehammers, scurrying for

---

*Al Jolson, Billy Rose, and Dave Dreyer, "Back in Your Own Backyard." Copyright © 1927 by Bourne Co. and Larry Spier Inc. Copyright renewed. All rights reserved. International copyright secured. Reprinted by permission.

cover only when they heard me skirmish with the street door, then start my long, pitiful crawl up the landings at the end of every heavy, hot, impossible day.

Just getting into the apartment was unbelievably complicated, like everything else in New York seemed to be. I struggled with the large, clunky metal key ring to locate the three keys to the security lock and two dead bolts which, in partnership with the pair for the downstairs door and mailbox, plus the one for the laundry room in the basement, formed a lumpy, misshapen bulge when the whole damn thing was stuffed in my suit pants pocket.

The apartment itself was a paradigm of impersonality. Although the rooms were overcrowded with lamps, sofas, and chairs that looked like they had been bought on sale at a particularly poor branch of St. Vincent de Paul, the whole place felt irredeemably hollow, empty, and lifeless.

I hadn't met "Geri," the specter who normally haunted these halls, but if her sense of interior design was any reflection on her identity, she'd had a surgical operation to have her soul removed. There was no trace of her character or spirit anywhere in any room, except perhaps for the stolen, ugly ashtrays she'd strewn on the scarred, water-ringed tables ("Franny's Frolic Room," "Casa Del Pacifico," "Easy Credit Banks") and the paper Hawaiian flower leis, now depressingly faded, hanging listlessly from the doorknobs. It was like living inside a dull toothache, and I stayed away as much as possible.

I poured myself a glass of ice water from the fridge, collapsed on the couch, kicked off my shoes. Okay, I'd been in New York a few weeks and what had I accomplished? Well, I'd hawked my photographs around to several theatrical agents. Not surprisingly, all my interviews had been characterized by exactly the same, brief, monotonously repetitious slice of dialogue:

"What have you done in New York, kid?"

"Nothing, but…"

"Uh-huh. Come back when you've done something."

"Oh, before I go, uh, can I use the bathroom?"

I also had auditioned for an off-Broadway production of Bertolt Brecht's *Mother Courage*, which was being mounted as a starring vehicle for Katina Paxinou, the renowned Greek actress. I'd read for the role of Eileff, Courage's oldest son. He sings, he dances, he gets killed. I was praying for a callback.

I looked around at my hovel away from home—the bare colorless walls, the dusty sun-faded carpet, the water-stained parchment window shades. Lackadaisically I picked up an ashtray. Two Paisans From Palermo Pizza Parlor. "We Deliver." I wondered if the second statement was surrounded in deprecatory quotes, like "real" leather or "genuine" zircon. Maybe it meant they were just kidding—they really didn't deliver. I tossed the ashtray back on the end table where it jiggled for a moment with a plasticky clatter. Very shortly I had to move out of this dump. Miss Ghost was due to come back from her vacation any day now.

The telephone rang. Maybe it was my Mother Courage callback. I scrambled for the receiver.

"Dennen?" a female voice demanded.

"Yes," I replied.

"This is Patricia Sauers of America," a voice announced.

"Hi, Patty, how are you?" I said.

"Hot," she said.

"I'm hot, too," I said.

"You know how I feel about heat," she said. "It's nice weather for a suicide."

Patty was a funny, wonderful woman. We'd gone to UCLA together and moved to New York together. She'd just found herself a little studio apartment on West End and 87th.

"Anyway, listen," she went on, "I just passed a building that has

43

an apartment for rent. A garden, underlined, garden apartment," she emphasized.

I sat up. "Hey, that sounds good," I said.

"You bet, Mister," Patty said. "And if it works out, you owe me. Big time." I laughed, and she gave me the address on West 90th. "Get going, Dennen," she ordered, and hung up.

I quickly slid into jeans and a T-shirt, squeezed my swollen feet into a pair of sneakers and went through the Dance of the Keys with the door in reverse. When I got to the entrance hall I shouted upstairs, "I'm going out now, Mr. Burglars! Get a move on! Break that door down!" On the first-floor landing an apartment door cracked open but when I turned my head it quickly slammed shut. I bopped out onto the sidewalk and headed toward the river.

I found the building right where Patty said it was. A shaky hand had scratched "GARDEN" APT. FOR RENT in a childish scrawl on a piece of typing paper and Scotch-taped it to the glass front door of the building. I stared at the word "GARDEN" in a kind of frozen bemusement. Did everyone in New York specialize in "deprecatory" quotes, I wondered? Did they teach them in high school English classes here?

A creepy super ushered me down a long corridor and gave me a guided tour of this inimitable dwelling, which turned out to be a dark, oblong one-room cell, sunk halfway down below street level. Its main feature was a row of small, dingy barred windows at the back facing onto the "garden." The "garden" part was of a quality at least equal to the interior: a worn-out, scrubby, hard-scrabble patch of bare, blasted dirt nestled beneath a couple of parched, dusty, generic trees.

Further amenities included a wheezing behemoth of an air-conditioner, an ancient refrigerator, and a suspiciously damp-feeling sofa. Utilities were included and the rent was an affordable $120.

Then, as now, apartments in New York were exceptionally hard to find. This unique *pied-à-terre* at least had the advantage of being available.

The skulking super barged into my thoughts.

"Well, whaddya think?" he asked, flashing me a hideous smile with several black holes where teeth should have been.

"I've never seen anything like it," I said truthfully. "I'll take it."

I called home for cash and immediately plunked down a deposit. A few days later I moved out of "The Hovel" and into "The Cave."

Not much of anything important happened during my stay in this deluxe accommodation except I found myself cruising the embankment of Riverside Drive late at night, along with a collection of other desperately lonely looking men who looked away frightened when you tried to make eye contact.

A month after I moved in, Christine, a pretty and sweet-natured, laid-back brunette who'd been Patty's roommate at UCLA, dropped into New York for a short visit. The night she and I went out to dinner there was an extensive power failure that blithely crippled all of Manhattan from 59th Street up. It rained mistily, the streets were dark and spooky with candles burning in all the windows, and phantom shapes flitted in and out of shadows. Christine and I bumped around in the dark and finally I convinced her to stay the night.

Years later I was amused to read that there were a record number of births in the New York area nine months from the night of the Big Blackout.

In October my folks came to New York to visit me. Although I tried to keep them away, they insisted on looking at the place where I was living. When my father saw "The Roach Room," he turned ashen and looked like he needed to sit down but was afraid to touch the furniture. Over dinner that evening Dad convinced me to move into a nicer apartment and told me he'd cover the rent for me until I could establish myself. As we left the restaurant, he pressed a credit card into my hand.

These days, when applications to open yet another credit card account arrive with the regularity of junk mail, it's easy to forget how difficult it was to get a credit card in 1959, how few people had one, and what a special gift my father had given me.

My dad, Ernest, was a man who had a difficult time articulating his feelings to me or to my brother, Lyle, four years my junior. I don't think a direct expression of emotion was welcomed in his parents' family. You have to practice saying "I love you." Perhaps my father had never been taught how; in any case, the words just wouldn't come out. So he expressed his love in other ways: gifts, cash . . . credit cards.

My name was embossed on the Diner's Club card. My father had put me on his own, personal account. That meant he intended to pay for any charges I ran up. I looked up at him, stunned.

"Dad, I can't take this," I protested.

"I don't ever want you going hungry," he said, and winked.

"But Dad—" I began.

"Keep it," he said. "Put it away. You never know when you'll need it." I thanked him very much.

I had landed the understudy for the role of "Bub" Hicks in the off-Broadway revival of Jerome Kern and P. G. Wodehouse's *Leave It to Jane* at the Sheridan Square Playhouse. I loved being in the Village to rehearse, and when work was over found it hard to make myself get on the train to go back uptown. I still got a thrill just hanging out down there, browsing in a pharmacy that played Vivaldi as its shopping music; eating at Aldo's, a popular gay restaurant; or having a chic drink on the sidewalk cafe at O'Henry's.

While walking around I'd noticed a brand-new apartment building going up on the corner of Sixth Avenue and 9th Street:

69 West 9th. It seemed like such a good omen, all those sixes and nines. Very posh, doorman and everything. It was right across the street from a neat-looking little bar called The Lion. I took a peek at a studio apartment on the twelfth floor. It had parquet floors and a spectacular view of the South Village all the way down to the financial district. Before I had much time to think about it I was choosing the paint color for the kitchen and living room walls.

In the last week of November 1959, I made the big move from the Cave to my small, glamorous, parentally subsidized Greenwich Village apartment.

The first time I dropped in for a drink at The Lion, my jaw nearly fell off. It was Fairy Heaven, a gender-defying, denizen's den of vacuum-packed, wall-to-wall gay guys. Every winter evening they slid in from the slippery sidewalks to squeeze into this boisterous, boy-bursting bar. Once inside, amid puffs of smoke and overwrought laughter, everyone seemed to be half-drinking and half-bundling.

Not long ago, a female friend whose brother had just declared his homosexuality remarked to me, "I *love* it when men come out of the closet. There's so much more room for me to hang up my clothes!" But back in 1959, the Stonewall revolution was ten years away and the closet door was not only closed, it was padlocked shut. Few could afford to be publicly gay in those days; you risked your reputation, your livelihood, and sometimes your life. In self-defense, gay men donned discretion like a cloak of invisibility. The Lion was different—it was wide open. It was the first place I ever went where you could hear a waiter wailing, "Oh, Rock, I *want* you!" and come to the stunning, head-on realization that Rock Hudson was in all likelihood gay.

The Lion was not, as some reports would have it, a dive. It was very upscale, and all the men packed into the front bar wore jackets and ties. They had to, so as not to attract the undue attention of the police on the streets even though, on any given night, there was likely to be a cop in The Lion's rather nice dining room at the rear, cadging a free meal. On Tuesday nights, I discovered, they held a talent contest back there that was supposed to be a hoot.

At the piano bar, Paddy, the impossibly cute pianist who perched just below a brandy snifter stuffed with dollar bills, could play any show tune you challenged him with, in any key. From time to time he would set aside his Juilliard training and pound into a whorehouse piano rendition of "How Could Red Riding Hood," and for a brief moment, every frosty pose hit the floor as all the men in the bar raucously joined in singing:

> How could Red Riding Hood
> Have been so very good
> And still keep the wolf from her door?
> Now you may ask it—
> Who filled her basket?...

This would be punctuated by a deafening silence, immediately followed by hoots of laughter and applause. Then slowly the glacial veil of attitude would rise once again, bodies would shift away uneasily from each other, and the very serious business of not looking anyone else directly in the eye would begin anew.

It's hard to imagine today how truly dirty it felt to be gay in these United States in the early 1960s. Then we were perverts, inverts, deviates, degenerates, homos, fairies, faggots, cocksuckers, queers, and as far as the American Psychiatric Association was concerned, officially mentally ill. I didn't want to be gay. I didn't want it. But if I didn't want it so badly, what was I doing every night at The Lion?

My move into 69 West 9th Street coincided with the last gasp of the 1950s. An era was ending, not only for me but for the whole United States. Americans were on the threshold of the wildest

decade to hit our shores since the Roaring Twenties: the Psyche-
delic Sixties! The giddy, intoxicated joys of Flower Power, drugs,
discos, groovy gear, rock 'n' roll, and the despair and agony of
Vietnam. We were all about to take a giant step forward into a big,
noisy wonderful party, and I myself was about to step over a personal threshold into one of the most exciting, whirlwind periods
of my life.

It all began one evening when I was home alone, watching an
old movie on television, and the telephone rang.

"Dennen? Sauers."

"Hi, Patty, what's up?" I said.

"I'm calling from Command Central. What are you doing?"

"Well, as a matter of fact I'm watching *Mata Hari* on TV."

"*Mata Hari*? The old movie?" she asked incredulously.

"Precisely," I said. "It's got everything: Garbo, espionage, las-
civious dances, stolen formulas, firing squads, nuns, prisons, close-
ups, telephone calls. Why?"

There was a pause while she ostentatiously cleared her throat.
"Listen," she said finally, "how would you like to be in a *play*?"

I didn't know it, but I was about to meet Barbara Streisand.

4

Bugged

*W*hen it was first produced on the New York stage in 1922, *The Insect Comedy* (or *The World We Live In*, as it was subtitled with ham-fisted irony) caused a sensation. The original production boasted a cast of forty-five actors playing a mixed assortment of flies, crickets, ants, beetles, moths, and snails, plus a regiment of extras as the ant workers and armies.

One can imagine theatergoers in the early twenties, glutted with stale Belasco drawing-room comedies and Eugene O'Neill's long-winded dramatic endurance contests, being dazzled by the evocative lighting of the Linnebach projectors washing giant colored images of trees, flowers, and animals over the cyclorama and stage floor. And they were no doubt charmed by the play's exotically weird settings and strange dialogue, and intrigued by the insect-clad actors in their vibrant costumes as they swirled around on two-inch-thick glass platforms sunk in the floor, spotlights illuminating them from below.

One can picture the audience as they tumbled out onto the

51

sidewalk in front of the Jolson Theater after the second act, seriously discussing the "symbolism" of the lumpish, married-couple Beetles, arguing and insulting each other while pushing their enormous ball of dung up a hill.

And I bet many members of the audience took a quick snort of illicit bathtub gin from their hip flasks as fortification against Act Three.

And maybe those twenties vamps saw a reflection of themselves in the flighty, fickle flappers swirling through the pastel silk drapes in the butterfly boudoir. And perhaps the men in the audience were reminded of their relatives and buddies who had met bloody deaths only four years earlier in the War to End All Wars, by the battle scenes between the two enormous, opposing ant armies, swarming from their anthill trapdoors, clashing, killing, and dying in heaps on the stage.

In its day, *The Insect Comedy* must have been a wow, the literal bee's knees.

But that was on Broadway in 1922.

By comparison, in April of 1960, our raggle-taggle little group numbered thirteen, and only half our players spoke English as their first language. Our stage effects were limited to the lavish use of several wooden orange crates and a few cutout paper bushes that fell over when you walked past them. In truth, the production we mounted can only be described, and then somewhat overgenerously, as threadbare.

Our troupe of merry thespians called itself "The Actors' Co-op" (those joshing old deprecatory quotes again), to which some prescient wag had prophetically appended "A Non-Profit Group."

Vasek was our leader. He was a ramshackle contraption of a man with dishwater-blue, bloodshot eyes that always seemed to be searching for something on the ceiling. I remembered him from college as some sort of exchange student from a generic, unspecific, Eastern European country. During that time, Vasek was cast in several plays, in big roles with long, complicated, talky speeches. This was a source of ongoing amazement and mystification to me, for he spoke English in a thick-as-sour-cream accent which was virtually incomprehensible, a mushy goulash of swallowed vowels and catarrhal consonants.

I think Vasek conceived of himself as a grand but temporarily impoverished dramatic genius, the Max Reinhardt of the unemployment line. To himself he was the supreme performer, writer, director, producer, scenic artist, and lighting designer, and to us, his faithful subjects, an all-around, pervasive, theatrical pain in the tit.

For no discernible reason whatsoever Vasek would fly into a completely unwarranted temper tantrum, ranting in his mangled, unintelligible English, waving his stumpy arms through the air as he stomped around the rehearsal hall in mud-encrusted boots. Nevertheless, and despite all his overwrought, operatic, time-consuming Sturm und Drang, Vasek's volatile artistic temperament was entirely unsupported by his abilities: he was talent-free.

The first minute of the first day of my first rehearsal, I got into the first of a series of daily squabbles and skirmishes with Vasek. He was sitting in the auditorium on a wooden folding chair, watching the stage, muttering darkly, scribbling notes, occasionally sipping from an extra-large cardboard container of take-away coffee while never removing a smoldering, half-smoked cigarette that dangled from the corner of his mouth. The smoke curled up into his eyes; occasionally he brushed away the accumulations of gray flakes that fell in tiny flurries onto his shirt.

The company had already been in rehearsal for several weeks when I joined it; an actor had jumped ship (a very, very wise, or, as I came to realize shortly, a very, very lucky actor), and I was replacing him in his various roles. Vasek had previously staged the scene and I was being worked into the already established blocking, which is actors' slang for their movements: exactly when they are directed to sit, stand, or walk across the stage. In Act One, I was to play Felix, a vapid, pretentious butterfly-poet who writes over-heated romantic quatrains but has no real, practical experience of sex or lovemaking.

And so I found myself sitting on a couch, all the female but-terflies clustered around behind me and at my feet. They had been directed to flap their wings unceasingly and scream with delight, running their hands through my hair and over my shoul-ders and chest while I recited a stupendously stupid love poem. We tried it once, and I stopped everyone halfway through. This was truly bad directing: the moment was unfocused and confusing, the audience wouldn't know who to look at or what to listen to.

So I turned to the actresses and said, "Look, kids, when you land on the sofa after your little...dance over there, let's have you gather around and be very interested in my poem, you know, like you're doing. But let's have you listening to me, totally fascinated. You can slowly open and close your wings, the way butterflies do when they land on something they love..." I paused for effect, "...like a turd."

All my butterflies burst into naughty giggles. I took a quick glance at Barbara. She was enjoying this, smiling slightly, nodding her head in agreement. Silently she mouthed to me, "Go on, go on!"

In the auditorium, Vasek stopped writing and looked up at the stage, confused and suddenly alert, like a deer caught in a tank's headlights.

"But listen to what I'm saying, quiet and enraptured, okay?" I encouraged them. "You can sigh, and smile, and look at me ador-ingly. And then, when I get to the end of the first stanza and I say, 'Iris! Pure as fire is!' you can do a big burst of squeals and ap-plause, like Johnny Ray's fans."

"Noh, noh, noh!" Vasek screamed from the auditorium as he

lurched violently to his feet, knocking his wooden chair over backward to the floor with a clattering crash, and ostentatiously pretending not to notice.

"What's the matter, Vasek?" I asked him, unperturbed.

"I vant dem to be screamink all de time, and in cohnstant movemwent," Vasek gargled, and pumped his arms up and down energetically a few times. "Hup, down, hopen, close…flyink about on de wind, like bugs do!" He took a long, poisonous-looking drag on his cigarette, then flicked it to the floor and crushed it out mercilessly beneath the heel of his boot.

"Look, Vasek—" I began.

"Did you never see moths?" he interrupted, looking at me slyly out of the corner of his eye, as if he'd got me this time. All I could think about was Vasek's tongue, which seemed to be slipping its clutch, having a great deal of trouble getting a grip on the American "th" sound, so it came out something like "mawts."

"Moths?" I said.

"Yes! Did you never see *mawts?*" he repeated insistently, his bushy eyebrows rising with incredulity toward his hairline.

The room was dead quiet. I cleared my throat. "I have," I said, and that was all I could manage for the moment. Suddenly Vasek's tongue slippage seemed incredibly funny to me. I thought, if I speak I'm going to laugh. No, don't, I said to myself. Don't laugh. I took a deep, even breath, screwed the self-control knob a little tighter. "Yes. Yes, I have seen…moths," I said.

"Flep, flep, flep, dey keep movink!" Vasek persisted.

"No," I said.

Vasek opened his eyes even wider and glared at me, incensed and affronted. "*No?* Sooo?" he said.

"So," I repeated, "the girls can burst into little flurries of giggles and flap-flap-flaps," I went on, standing my ground. "But we have to figure out exactly when. It can't be all the time."

There was an uneasy rustling behind me. I turned around to find Barbara staring out into the auditorium at Vasek with a worried look on her face. She flicked a glance over to me and crossed her eyes. I snorted and turned back to face Herr Direktor.

I was getting the inescapable feeling that the rest of the cast was already fed up to the gumline with Vasek, but this was the first time anyone had actually had the nerve or effrontery to openly challenge him.

"Yes, yes, of course, ahl de time!" Vasek burbled, gesturing grandly, as a wavelet of coffee churned up over the rim of his paper cup and splattered on the floor, splashing up on his pants leg.

I heard Barbara sigh heavily as she hunkered down out of sight behind me, and felt the warm puffs of her breath on the back of my neck as she whispered pleadingly in my ear, "Barre, please, don't argue with him. It only makes things worse. He loses it real easy, ya know what I mean?"

I turned my head around to look at her. Her face was very close to mine. Without thinking, I gave her a little peck on the cheek. She smiled shyly. "Don't worry," I said softly, "I can stand up for myself."

"No, no, it's not that," she muttered, suddenly frowning. I could feel her searching for the right words to convey her concern to me. "He's just so totally paranoid, you wouldn't believe," she said.

"Believe me, I believe," I whispered.

Barbara gave a quick little look over my shoulder out into the house to see if Vasek was listening, then cupped her hand and whispered nervously through the side of her mouth. "Just don't get him worked up," she went on in rapid, urgent Brooklynese. "I mean, he goes totally nuts, completely crazy. It could take us hours to get him back on track."

This was the first time I experienced that peculiar sensation of Barbara being absolutely sincere and urgent, so overwhelmingly open and direct and earnest that there was something irresistibly funny about it.

Vasek was bent over, wiping his trouser cuff with a paper napkin. Suddenly he looked up warily, his nose twitching like a warthog sniffing the breeze. "Vhat are you two vhisperink about?" he asked in a strangely strangulated tone.

"Uh-oh," I heard Barbara say under her breath. I felt her stand up behind me and as she did, her hand brushed the back of my hair. It gave me an unexpected little thrill.

"Nothing, Vasek," I lied.

Vasek clunked down the aisle and glared up at me over the edge of the stage. "Vhy are you all talkink behind my bahk?" he inquired of the other actors, the floor, and the ceiling. I looked around. Everyone was staring nervously in a different direction.

"Vasek, we're not saying anything behind your back, it's just…" I began.

"Den vhy all dis vhisperink?" Vasek interrupted. "Vhy don't you just do the scene like I ahsk you to?" he said, his voice dropping down to a dangerous, quietly crazy tone. I wondered if he'd been taking Peter Lorre lessons.

"Because it doesn't work the way you want it," I said calmly. "It's nothing personal. Don't get paranoid."

I could feel Barbara's fingers digging a warning signal into my shoulder but it was too late. Vasek's eyes rolled around wildly in their sockets. I'm sure at that moment, if he'd been Rumplestilskin, he would have stamped through the floor and exploded in a violent puff of smoke.

"Ach!" he shrieked to the gods of an unfair universe, and clawed at the hair on his head. "Paranoid? *Paranoid*? What are you *sayink*? Vhat are you *implyink*? I am the Direktor of this play, the metteur en scene, The Leader! I cannot *vork*!" he ranted, stomping up and down, "I cannot *vork* under dese conditions!"

"Oh, come on, Vasek, don't get overdramatic," Barbara said, trying to coax him down from the ceiling.

"Overdramatick?" Vasek frothed. "You are not co-*vop*erating vit me!" he shouted, turning his back on his unco-voperative actors and clomping up the aisle.

"Vasek, please," Barbara pleaded, but to no avail.

"You, you, you, all! You are not co-*vop*erating!" he fumed, his emotions boiling up in a rich amalgam of furious, wounded and misunderstood, with a big dollop of crazy on the top. He schlepped heavily to the door of the rehearsal room, then turned back dramatically to face us all with what was meant to be one final, devastating, confrontational glare.

That did it. I rolled over on my stomach on the little sofa and tried to stifle my overwhelming, unstoppable laughter, but I was convulsed. I covered my face with my hands and squeezed, but tears of mirth streamed out through my fingers. Barbara stepped between me and Vasek's line of vision, but not soon enough.

With one final, world-shattering sniff, Vasek turned, slammed out the door, and pounded down the stairs.

It didn't take long to realize that this was, in the main, what the rest of the rehearsal sessions were going to be like: straightening out an endless series of psychotic power struggles and misunderstandings between Vasek and the rest of the company. And soon after that it became crystal clear that, in reality, Vasek didn't know what he was doing or what he wanted, but was determined to get it.

In any case, these schizophrenic delights all lay ahead of me. During the lunch break, Barbara introduced me to Terry Leong. He was exquisite: young, finely boned, softly spoken, immaculately polite, and as delicately attenuated as a Chinese rod puppet carved of linden wood. He had the grace, taste, and manners of a rarefied but approachable connoisseur.

Terry had met Barbara through her roommate, Marilyn, who

introduced them because Barbara needed clothes for auditions and for *The Insect Comedy* and she couldn't afford much. Terry, it seemed, had a way of finding things, of making things appear out of nowhere, of putting things together, that bordered on the magical.

It was very warm that day, but somehow Terry refused to perspire as he trudged upstairs with several shopping bags. (I began to wonder if, when you became a friend of Barbara's, you were issued a complimentary starter set of shopping bags as your basic kit.) After we'd said hello, he collapsed in one of the wooden auditorium chairs and pulled out a beautiful, rich-looking piece of fabric.

"Oh, my God, this is incredible!" Barbara exclaimed, running her fingers over this iridescent piece of sea-green silk. "Terry, where did you find this?" she marveled.

Terry shrugged and smiled slyly, a magician unwilling to reveal his tricks. "It turned up," he said, with a self-effacing smile.

"Terry's in the garment industry," Barbara explained.

"I find things," he said. "I shop around."

"It's gorgeous!" she exclaimed, holding it up to the light.

Terry's dark eyes sparkled. "Yeah," he said softly.

"How much do I owe you?" Barbara asked.

"Oh, never mind about that," Terry sloughed it off. We moved over to a panel of mirrors along the back wall. Terry took the fabric from Barbara, unfolded it and displayed its full length. "Uh, do you mind slipping out of your rehearsal clothes?" Terry asked her.

Barbara looked around the rehearsal hall, empty except for the three of us.

"I can run downstairs and have a cigarette," I offered, scooping up my pack of Parliaments and preparing to leave.

"No, don't bother," Barbara said. "I don't mind," she added, "I'm wearing a bra."

She wiggled out of her rehearsal top and to my surprise she

was wearing a shiny, satiny kind of brassiere with a line of black lace along the upper edge, the kind of thing you might wear with an evening gown. The swell of her bust was voluptuously round and curving, and I found myself wishing I could see the rest of it.

A fantasy formed in my head: I was standing behind Barbara, loosening her bra in back and sliding the straps carefully down her arms, so softly and slowly that a spray of goosebumps rose on her shoulders. Carefully I lifted the bra away and exposed her bare, beautiful breasts. I gently reached around and cupped my hands over her nipples, which contracted and hardened in my palms. I felt a sudden throb in my pants, scrabbled in my pocket for my sunglasses and slapped them on my face. God, what did I want? I'd had sex with boys and I'd had sex with girls. I still wanted to fool around with men, but I wasn't prepared to give up women. I didn't feel bisexual exactly. I didn't know what I was, except really confused.

My eyes lazily followed the line of lace across Barbara's chest as Terry murmured to her. "What I'd like to do with this is make a Chinese top," he said, producing a box of straight pins and draping the fabric like a shawl around Barbara's shoulders, which looked creamy and smooth in the slatted sunlight filtering in the windows.

"Chinese," Barbara pondered briefly. "Chinese could be good," she agreed. Suddenly she lifted her eyes to look at me and caught me looking at her breasts. I felt a rush of blood to my face. Barbara suppressed a sexy little smile, then added suggestively, "Why don't you take your sunglasses off indoors, Barre? You'll hurt your eyes."

With that, I took my glasses off very deliberately and stared openly and defiantly at her body, then looked into her eyes, straight and hard. This time Barbara looked away.

With a mouth full of straight pins, Terry continued to fold up a bottom hem, oblivious to anything going on above him. "Maybe with a very, very full skirt, which will take it into an American look, a fashion kind of look," Terry said, standing up. He smoothed the cloth over Barbara's shoulders then turned her around to face the mirror, holding the whole thing in place to give her an idea of the style he had in mind. "Take a look," he said.

"This is the most wonderful color," Barbara enthused.

"Celadon green," Terry extrapolated precisely. "It's so full and luscious. I see it maybe edged in a beige satin, with long sleeves, and a Chinese closing, right...here," he said, folding down an edge, carefully placing a straight pin right in the center of the front.

"This is a good color for me," Barbara said.

"You're right," Terry agreed, then lifted the fabric from her, folded it carefully and placed it back in his bag, saying, "Barbara has a very sharp sense of what looks good on her, what colors to wear."

"Oh, please," Barbara protested.

"And she's got a great body for clothes," Terry concluded.

"Yeah, and those long, elegant legs," I agreed, as she and I looked at each other's reflections in the mirror. Now it was Barbara's turn to blush.

"Oh, would you two *stop*? Terry does all his own sewing," she went on. I was interested to notice how smoothly she changed the subject.

"Really?" I said. "I learned how to run a machine and sew on a button in costume class, but I know I could never create a whole outfit from scratch."

"Oh, it's just a matter of making a design, and a paper pattern, and then..." his voice faded away as he searched for something in the second shopping bag.

"What have you got in there?" Barbara asked, leaning over curiously. "Terry finds the most wonderful stuff."

"I've got a surprise for you," he said, looking through the bag and fishing around.

"What?" Barbara cried impatiently. "What?"

I was aware that suddenly the whole mood had completely changed. With the possibility of an unexpected gift, sex and sexiness had gone right out the window.

From the bowels of the shopping bag, with an impressive dramatic flourish Terry produced a pair of amazing antique green velvet shoes with big buckles. He displayed them in front of us like Cinderella's glass slipper on a silken cushion.

"1910," he said. "Just wonderful."

"Oh, my God!" Barbara said breathlessly. "Where did you find these?"

"They just turned up," Terry said. "Try them on."

He placed them lovingly into Barbara's hands and prestidigiously produced a shoehorn from his pocket. She sank into a chair.

"Go on," he said.

Looking suddenly like a child staring at her own birthday cake, Barbara gazed at the shoes, her eyes glowing with wonder and delight. I found myself wishing that she would look at me like that, full of excitement and desire. Stepping out of her rehearsal shoes, she placed the green velvet beauties gingerly on the floor in front of her and slipped her feet inside.

She looked up with a gasp. They fit perfectly. She stood up and walked a few steps.

"They don't even pinch," she marveled. "They could have been made for me." She thrust out one of her beautiful legs and beveled the foot. "Perfect," she concluded.

"Terry," I said, impressed, "where *do* you find these things?"

"Thrift stores, mostly," he said, turning to me with a discreet but satisfied grin. "Neat, huh? Nobody knows about this stuff. Except us." He smiled sweetly at Barbara, who smiled back at him. They were like brother and sister, I thought, with secrets, and codes, and a language of shared experience.

"Well, Barbara," I said, "if the old shoe fits, wear it."

Then Terry stood up, whisked a cloth tape from his pocket, and began to take measurements of Barbara's upper body which he jotted down in ink in an immaculately neat, tiny handwriting.

"You buy thrift-store clothes?" I asked.

"Sure," she said, as if everybody else were crazy not to. "We find wonderful things. Even old underwear, beautiful lace slips, camisoles."

"I hope you send them to the dry cleaners first," I said, cringing a little.

"Well, of course!" she exclaimed, offended. "Listen, this stuff is all donated from rich women's closets. I mean, they're rich, they take baths, they gotta be clean, right?"

"I certainly hope so," I said.

"Oh, stop that," Barbara scolded. "This is really good stuff, ya know. Couture. I mean, like, thirty- or forty-year-old couture, but couture all the same!"

"It's incredible what you can find," Terry chimed in, still taking deft measurements and transcribing them swiftly onto paper.

"Hey, ya know what? I once picked up a three-thousand-dollar Fabiani original," Barbara said proudly. "Right off the rack."

"Stand still," Terry told a fidgeting Barbara as he took the measurement from her shoulder to her wrist.

"You've already got my measurements, Terry," Barbara complained.

"Yeah, but this is going to fit very neatly," Terry said softly, "so we're just going to double-check. Your arms have grown a *lot* longer," he said, looking up with surprise.

"What?!" an incensed Barbara sputtered.

"Just kidding," he grinned.

"Well, cut it out," Barbara said.

"Hey, I've got to get going," Terry said. "My lunch hour's almost over, and I've got to get back to the Tish Building."

"Terry works at MacGregor, designing men's shirts," Barbara explained. "How's that goin', Ter?"

"It's okay," he said, a little defeated wrinkle creasing his forehead. "I haven't really got a handle on it yet."

I could see why Terry loved devoting so much time to Barbara, shopping for remnants on Seventh Avenue with her, designing and making her clothes, bumming around the thrift shops together. He was crazy about her. And he was stuck in a job he didn't really like.

"So, you wanna come thrift-store shopping with us?" Barbara asked me. "Next weekend, maybe?"

"Are you kidding?" I said. "Count me in."

And so the three of us began to traipse around Manhattan together, pillaging the Ninth Avenue thrift shops where we picked up spectacular clothing bargains for Barbara, and haunting antique stores that we couldn't in any way afford. Terry had made friends with a volunteer saleswoman in one of the thrifts who pointed out incredible treasures and who saved things for us: a spectacular 1900 black beaded bodice that Terry designed a black velvet skirt to go with. An antique doily, cream colored, which Terry fashioned into the back of a dress, the corners coming forward into an empire waistline. A Juliet's cap made out of tiny rows of seed pearls.

Barbara was remarkably intuitive and astute about clothes, colors, and fabrics. Before anyone else in the world became aware of it, she appreciated that this rare, antique clothing was of a quality you simply couldn't find anywhere else.

"Look," she'd say, holding up a sequined Victorian top for my inspection. "See these incredibly tiny sequins? You can't find anything like them anymore. I guess they just stopped making them. And this delicate silk net they've sewn on? Boy, did we scout around for this stuff. You can only get it today in wedding veils—and then it's a special order!"

One day we were all in a thrift shop, each of us attacking a separate jam-packed rack. I would claw dresses out and hoist them up in the air for Barbara's approval or rejection.

"Yeah, pull that," she'd say, "I wanna try that on." Or, "Naw, too matronly," and I'd shove it back into its place in used-clothing limbo.

"Hey, Bar?" Barbara said, her fingers flying expertly through hanger after hanger, pulling clothes out, putting them back, examining everything with her eagle-eye.

"Yeah?"

"Ya know why I think women held their arms in to their sides in the nineteen thirties? Like this," she said, pulling her elbows into her waist and raising her hands gracefully like Ginger Rogers.

"Tell me," I said.

"Because they didn't have any deodorant," she speculated.

"What a theory! Style through lack of personal hygiene," I said.

"It could happen," Barbara said. Suddenly her voice dropped and in a tone of total awe she said, "Oh, my God, look at this."

Both Terry and I stopped what we were doing and moved over to her rack; Barbara had an infallible eye for the spectacular find.

She held up a full-length, lustrous fur coat, its pelts a mass of soft, tiny curls.

"What *is* this?" she wondered.

"That's a caracul coat," Terry said. "Wow, and double-wow."

"Uh, isn't there something creepy about caracul?" I asked squeamishly. "Like, it's made from unborn baby lamb or something?"

"Stop, stop," Barbara said. "I don't wanna know."

"My mom used to have a coat like that," I went on, "but I think she called it Persian Lamb."

"It's the same thing," Terry said. "Try it on, Barb."

65

We helped Barbara slip into the caracul coat, which fit her as though it had been hand-cut to her measurements.

"It's great," she said, looking at herself in the mirror, her eyes glowing with the triumph of the huntress. "Let's grab it!"

(Years later, Terry told me that Barbara had had the coat copied for the movie *Funny Girl*—in leopard! Now, this was just before the endangered species scare, when everyone began to be politically correct about wearing animal skins and where in some European cities, women wearing fur coats on the streets were being doused in buckets of animal blood by activists.

"Maybe it wasn't really leopard," I suggested.

"It looked like leopard to me," Terry replied.)

As week followed week you didn't have to be a genius to figure out that *The Insect Comedy* wasn't very good and probably wasn't going to get much better. Actors left in a huff and were magically replaced, fights erupted with monotonous regularity, and I came down with a horrible case of bronchitis. Throughout the whole hideous adventure Barbara and I clung closer and closer to each other, worked on our own scenes, and just tried to get through it.

Barbara struggled valiantly to find her character in the scenes we rehearsed together privately, secretly, at the end of the day after everyone else had gone. Finally, I said to her, "You know, it's odd, but these speeches of yours, they sound just like Mae West. You know who Mae West is, don't you?"

"Sure," Barbara said. "I think I've seen some of her old movies on television."

To me, Mae West was the high priestess of innuendo, comic timing, and really funny lines.

"Say that line about 'shameless creature' for me," I said. "But do it like Mae West."

66

" 'Oh, I hate you—you shameless creature,' " Barbara said, rolling her eyes and sashaying around the stage. It was fabulously funny.

"Do the other one."

" 'Oh! Oh!' " Barbara said, " 'you great, strong, handsome thing!' "

I burst out laughing. "That's it," I said. "Do that, it's great."

I sat down on the steps and lit a cigarette, and Barbara sat beside me. "You know, Mae West's autobiography just came out, and in it she tells a story about this diamond dealer she meets who has a black Sealyham dog named Benny. What she doesn't know is that his dog swallows the stones to smuggle them through customs."

"Oh, brother," Barbara said. "What a mean trick."

"Yeah, but funny. When Mae asks him if he can get a thirty-carat diamond, and makes a circle about the size of a nickel, the dog keels over on its back and groans."

"Oh, oh," Barbara said in perfect Mae Westish. "Whatsa matter with your animal?"

Whatsa matter with your animal. It became our password code phrase for whenever things were outrageous, confusing, or going completely, irretrievably off the rails.

My friend Paul came to sit through and endure the final dress rehearsal. Afterward I found him sitting alone in the rows of rickety seats, looking like he'd not just witnessed *The Insect Comedy,* but been stung by a nest of angry wasps in the process.

"Bar, I'll be kind," he said. "It's unspeakably awful. You'll be lucky if the critics don't flay you into julienne strips and serve you on cocktail toothpicks."

"Don't hold back, Paul," I said. "I can take it."

"Atrocious. Abominable. Worst thing I've ever seen."

"Tell me what you really think," I persisted.

"It stinks," Paul replied.

I gave him a long, deadpan stare.

"Be honest," I said.

At the end of the first week in May we played for three nights. Frank Aston in the *New York World Telegram and Sun* gave us our one and only notice, to the effect that, although no one in the company could be deemed anything like a pro, we had all *tried* very hard. Actually, there was one other review in a small neighborhood paper, no doubt to alert the locals to this rare extravaganza in their midst.

Barbara snatched up the *Tägliche Zeitung* and skimmed down the page. The whole thing was in German, which none of us could speak or read.

"Hey, listen to this," Barbara said, running her finger under the sentence as she read, " '*Die Barbara Streisand Vorstellung war ausgezeichnet.*'* *Ausgezeichnet!*" she repeated, smiling and looking proudly around the room. "Hey," she added, frowning suddenly, "what does that mean?"

---

*"Barbara Streisand's performance was outstanding."

5

A Plum from Blum

*O*ne day at rehearsal, Barbara rummaged around in her shopping bag and fished out a black-and-white eight-by-ten photograph to show me.

"Here, whaddya think of this?" she asked, sliding it under my nose. "I thought I'd use it as my picture in the lobby."

It was a picture of her, all right, but she was swathed in veils and scarves, with elaborate dangling earrings, many rings on several fingers, and a row of exotic bracelets that marched right up her arm. She was wearing extra-heavy makeup, dark dark lipstick, and she stared into the camera lens with eyes ringed in kohl circles. She looked about three hundred years old, give or take a century.

"Barb, where did you get this picture?" I asked her.

"Some photographer at a school took it . . . for free!" she said.

She waited for me to say something. I didn't know where to begin.

"So, whaddya think?" she prodded. "Interesting, huh?"

"Oh, absolutely," I replied. "Absolutely . . . interesting. Uh . . .

what parts are you looking to get cast for when you send out this picture?" I asked.

"Whaddya mean?" she fumed indignantly. "I'm an *ehktress*! I can play any part, any role, any character. Young girls, middle-aged, old women. Anything."

"Yeah," I said, wincing slightly but not wanting to make her feel bad. "But...ya see...the thing is...well, you look sort of like Scheherazade in the Garden of Allah here, you know what I mean? Kind of...Arabian-bazaar-camels-in-the-marketplace-looking. I mean, if they were casting a fortune teller or a gypsy, I'm sure you'd get called in right away," I finished weakly.

She snatched the picture back from me. "Yeah, well," she grumbled, "free is all I could afford. Anyway, Eddie Blum, in the Rogers and Hammerstein office, is casting a tour of *The Sound of Music*. I sent one of these to him."

I wondered what Eddie Blum, looking for children, nuns, and Nazis for that most wholesome of musicals, would make of Barbara's "Come to de Cazbah" photograph when it hit his desk.

A few days after *The Insect Comedy* crashed to the ground in flames, Barbara called me from a midtown pay phone.

"Hi, it's me!" she said, her voice full of excitement.

"Hi," I said. "What's up?"

"Guess what?" she said enthusiastically. "No, never mind guessing. You remember when I sent that picture to Eddie Blum?" she said.

"Sure," I said.

"Yeah, well, he called me and said I should come to his office. He said he was intrigued to see what kind of a kook would send out that weird picture." I could hear the smile in Barbara's voice.

"Yeah, so what happened?" I asked.

"Well, I spent the whole afternoon with him," she said. "He asked me all about myself, what parts I've done."

"That sounds good," I said.

"Yeah, yeah. Then he took me out to lunch, then we went back to his office, then he took me out to dinner…" her voice trailed off for a moment, then shot right to the point. "He wants to hear a tape of me singing."

"Singing?" I said. "I don't understand. Singing what?"

"Singing a song," she said. "Now listen, didn't you tell me you had a real good tape recorder or something?"

"Yes, I do," I said. "It's an Ampex stereo. It's great."

"Well, can I come down to your house and make a tape?" she asked.

"When?" I said.

"Why not right now?" she said. "You busy?"

"Well, no, I'm not busy but—"

"I've got Carl Esser and his guitar here with me. So whaddya think?" she pleaded.

"Sure, Barb," I said. "Come right over. I'll be here," I said.

Barbara and I had never even talked about singing, or songs, or anything like that. Nobody I knew had ever heard her sing. What in the world is she up to, I wondered. All I could think was that, desperate to break in anywhere, in any way, Barbara was having the *chutzpah*, the unmitigated gall, to present herself as a singer.

I went into the bathroom and splashed some cold water on my face. "Singing?" I said to my dripping reflection in the mirror. "Barbara, singing?" Hey, why not, I thought. Why not run away with the circus? Why not learn how to charm snakes?

In what seemed no time at all, Barbara and Carl turned up at my front door. Barbara looked like she was burning with excitement, like she had some incredibly special secret she was dying to tell me. I was really glad to see her, she looked so incandescent and sparkly.

"Hey, Barre, how are you?" Carl asked with an engaging grin. "Wow, what a neat pad!" he added, looking around at the apartment as he laid his guitar case down on the couch and took a seat next to it.

Carl Esser was a rubbery-faced fellow, tall and bean-pole thin, with an open smile and a goofy expression that I felt sure masked a highly overactive libido. At UCLA I'd acted in a funny, original musical for which he'd written the tunes, and in *The Insect Comedy* we'd appeared in tandem as Snails One and Two. I'd convinced Terry Leong we should be costumed in business suits and derbies, with attaché cases and accompanying English accents.

"Hi, Bar, how are ya?" Barbara asked as she parked her shopping bags and gave me a moist little peck on the cheek.

"I'm great," I said, already feeling a little nervous about what I was certain was the coming calamity. "You look terrific," I told her. Barbara was wearing a beautiful, flowered chiffon top with a gathered skirt. She looked fresh-faced and feisty. "Is that one of Terry's special numbers?" I asked.

"Yeah," Barbara said. "It's just a little something we whipped up."

We? I wondered. I'll bet over on Chrystie Street Terry Leong was up all night, flogging himself to "bobbin the bobbin and pedal the pedal," like Betty Hutton in her demented love song to the sewing machine in the movie *The Perils of Pauline*.

"Hey, did you hear about Vasek?" Barbara asked.

"No, what?" I said.

"There was a five-hundred-dollar light bill down at 'The Hall.' They want to make him pay it."

"Oh, brother," I replied. "Vasek doesn't have five zloties to rub together, let alone five hundred. I bet he books steerage on the next boat back to Serbo Ding-Dong Land."

"Listen, we'd better get going," Carl said, unsnapping his instrument case. "Hi, baby," he said parenthetically to his guitar and gave it a little kiss, then propped it on his knee and fiddled with the tuning. "I gotta be uptown by three-thirty," he explained.

Barbara plunked herself down in a chair and browsed through her shopping bag, eventually producing a piece of sheet music. I went to work, screwing the microphones onto their stands, uncoiling the cables and plugging them into the input jacks. Carl produced a soft red cloth and gave his guitar's sound box a little polish.

"This is exciting!" Barbara enthused, looking at me over the top of her music.

"Yeah, it's gonna be fun," I said, offering up a silent prayer that this wasn't going to be a totally excruciating embarrassment.

I adjusted the mikes' positions in front of each of them.

"I'm gonna sing 'Day by Day,'" she said, holding up the music.

"That's a pretty song," I said, hoping against hope it would all be over quickly.

"It's the only one we both know," she explained, smiling conspiratorially at Carl.

I fiddled around with the tape recorder controls. "Listen, I'm gonna add a little echo here so you'll be able to hear your voice coming out of the speakers," I explained to Barbara.

"Fine," she said, and cleared her throat.

Carl plucked a bell note. Barbara hummed it softly.

"You two ready?" I asked.

They both nodded their heads.

"Then let's try one," I said. I mentally crossed my fingers, and switched on the record button. The tape spun past the recording head through the capstan and wound around the takeup reel.

Carl played a jazzy little bossa nova introduction and then Barbara began to sing.

As the first few cool phrases of the song floated out of the speakers, I remember I blinked. And then something like a cold electric shock ran right up my spine from my heels to my head, like a letter opener up an envelope, until I felt like the hair on the

73

back of my neck was standing on end. As the song went on and her lovely voice filled the room, I thought, I am going crazy.

Now, when I look back at the up-and-down of our relationship, I believe that this is the exact moment when "Barbara" first began to metamorphose into "Barbra." This woman I thought I knew, this nutty little kook, had one of the most breathtaking voices I'd ever heard. My heart started to pound faster. Imagine hearing Barbra sing for the very first time! What a gorgeous, glorious, heavenly sound. When she finished and I turned off the machine, I needed a long moment before I dared look up at her.

"Barbara, you..." I stammered, "...you have an incredible voice."

"Oh, yeah?" she said. "Thanks."

"No, but I mean, really...amazing. You have a voice the microphone *loves*."

"Yeah, well," she smiled. "I enjoy singing."

"No, no, no. I mean, you *have* to sing. You *have* to." Ideas were flashing through my brain like an electrical storm in a summer sky.

"Oh, I dunno," Barbara said. "I don't want to be a singer. I'm an *ehktress*. That's really what I want to do."

I could feel her trying to slip away from me, but I wasn't going to let her. I took hold of her hands and led her over to the couch, where we both sat down, still looking at each other.

"Look," I said. "There's a place right across the street. The Lion. It's a bar. A gay bar. They have a talent contest every Tuesday night. If you go down there and sign up, I'll help you put together a nightclub act."

"But I don't wanna sing in a nightclub," she whined. "I don't like air conditioning, and drinking, and all that cigarette smoke. I wanna *act*!"

"You can still act," I explained. "Even if you were in a Broadway show right now, you could sing after it came down every night. And besides, you could make a little extra money. And it's something you could do when you weren't working in the theater. You know, in between things."

"But I wanna do plays," she said. "Play characters."

"I know that. We'll do each song like a little play," I said. "I'll help you choose the songs and direct you. We'll create characters and their inner life for each song. It'll be like five or six little plays in a row, only you'll be the actress in all of them," I tempted her.

"Maybe," she said dubiously.

"Promise me you'll do it," I insisted. "Promise me at least that you'll go over to The Lion and sign up."

"Maybe," she said.

"Listen, guys, I gotta beat it," Carl said.

Barbara and I both looked up. Carl was standing at the door, his guitar packed away in its case, ready to hit the road. We had both completely forgotten about him.

"Oh, Carl," Barbara said, standing up and going over to him. "Listen, thanks a lot. The tape is terrific." She looked over at me. "It's okay, isn't it, Barre?" she asked.

"It's great," I said. I was glad Carl was taking off. It would give me more of a chance to work on her.

Barbara stepped out in the hall to walk Carl to the elevator, and when she came back in, she closed the door and leaned up against it.

"So?" she said. I didn't say a word, just stared at her. "Why are you looking at me like that?" she asked, getting spooked.

"Come over here," I said. Barbara looked worried and didn't move. "Stop looking so scared," I said. "I'm not going to eat you. Now come right here," I insisted, and patted the place next to me. She slunk across the room and sat like a schoolgirl afraid of being told off.

"Look..." she started.

"I just want to play something for you," I said, continuing to talk while I stood up and sprang over to the LPs, searching for a certain record I had in mind. "You have to go anywhere?" I asked her.

"Nope," she admitted. "I'm all yours."

"You know how bland all the singers sound these days? I mean like Doris Day, Rosemary Clooney, Joni James?"

"I like Joni James!" Barbara protested. I shuddered.

"Yeah, I guess she's all right if you're giving a prom," I said. "But, see, there's this whole tradition of songwriters and singers in Europe. Particularly in France. Cabaret singers, music hall stars, *chanteuses*," I expanded.

"Like who?" Barbara said curiously, then suddenly added, "Listen, you got a matzo or something to nosh on?"

"In the kitchen, on the shelf with the cookies. Above the sink," I said.

She went into the other room, calling back over her shoulder, "Keep talking. I'm listening. I can hear you in here."

"Like who," I repeated. "Like Charles Trenet, Mouloudji, Edith Piaf..." I called out.

"Edith Piaf," Barbara's voice drifted out of the kitchen. "*Her*, I've heard of. Wait a minute, before we go on, you got any buttah?"

"In the fridge," I said, continuing to riffle impatiently through the records.

There were busy noises from the kitchen, drawers sliding, the refrigerator door being opened and closed, and suddenly, like a magician's assistant, Barbara reappeared delicately holding a whole piece of buttered matzo in her hand. She took a big bite and a few flakes fell to the ground. She looked down.

"I'm getting crumbs on your floor," she noted apologetically. "I should've taken a plate."

"I don't care," I said.

"You got a vacuum? A dustpan and brush?" she asked.

"I don't care about the crumbs!" I insisted, raising my voice. At that moment I found the record I was looking for and, buckling the sleeve, removed it carefully by its label and edge and placed it on the turntable.

"You're very careful with your things," she noted.

"Yes," I agreed impatiently. "Now listen," I said. "I'm telling you about some very important stuff here."

"Okay," Barbara said, kicking off her shoes and curling up on the couch where she took another big crunchy bite. I watched the matzo crumbs fall into her lap. She was adorable. She brushed them off, then noticed me looking. "You said you didn't care!" she protested defensively.

"I don't!" I replied.

"Okay, okay," she said. "I believe you."

"So anyway," I pressed on, "these guys write the most wonderful, unusual, captivating songs about things American songwriters would never even dream of touching."

"Oh yeah? Like what?" Barbara said, chewing up a mouthful of matzo.

"Oh, like, uh … there's a song by Trenet about these two deep-sea divers. They fall in love, but when they go to kiss, their air hoses get tangled up and they drown."

Barbara nodded her head patronizingly. "That's different, all right. I don't know any Irving Berlin tunes like that," she admitted.

"Now, this is a song by Piaf," I explained. "The thing about Piaf is, everything she sings is sad, even the happy songs. This is a song about a guy whose wife has left him for a younger man." I started playing the record. It was a wistful waltz, a beautiful song by Michel Emer, all accordions and violins.

As the song went on, Barbara gradually stopped eating and leaned forward, sitting stone still and listening intently.

When the third chorus began, I translated what Piaf was singing. "She's describing all the little things he does as he gets ready to go to sleep: he puts on his pajamas, blows his nose, turns out the light, says his prayers. Then," I said, pausing dramatically, "he turns on the gas and gets into bed."

I shut up so Barbara could hear Piaf eerily whisper-sing the tag, hissing like the open gas jet:

> You were so sure,
> So...sure,
> So...ssssssssssssssss...

The record finished. I lifted the tonearm from the groove. There was an impressive silence.

"Wow," Barbara said softly. "That's really something."

"You could do that," I said. "You could move an audience to tears, or laughter, or make them shiver, or whatever you wanted," I said. "If you decided to sing."

"If, huh?" she said, and stroked her throat. "Hey, Bar, you got anything cold to drink?"

All the rest of that afternoon I played Barbara an enormous selection of wonderful songs by great singers: Ruth Etting's "Ten Cents a Dance"; Lee Wiley's "Baby's Awake Now"; Billie Holiday's "Strange Fruit"; and comedy vocals by Bea Lillie, Helen Kane, and Mae Barnes. After a few hours we took a little walk to get some fresh air and cigarettes, then went right back to the phonograph. Record after record, number after number: Helen Morgan, Ethel Waters, Marion Harris, Libby Holman. I don't think Barbara had ever really heard old records like these before, but she sat there mesmerized and transfixed, as if I were leading her by the hand into an enchanted and potentially dangerous wild forest.

Suddenly it was ten o'clock in the evening and there were tons of things I still wanted to play for her. Barbara stood up.

"This has really been fabulous, Barre. I love that stuff you played me. But I really should be going home now," she said. "I gotta get something to eat."

"You want to stay here?" I asked. "I could make you an omelette or something."

"The boy cooks, too," she said, coming over to me and putting her arms around my neck. "Thanks, anyway," she said. "I gotta get up in the morning, early."

We kissed and then she slowly gathered up her things. I walked her over to the door and opened it. Barbara stepped out into the hall and we strolled along together to the elevator.

"Listen," I said, "I'm going to change my name."

Barbara looked at me quizzically. "Change your name? What the hell for?"

"Oh, I went to an audition yesterday. They told me they didn't know if B-A-R-R-E, *accent aigu*, was a boy or a girl! I'm fed up with it."

"I think of you as a 'Barre.' What are you changing it to?"

"Barry," I said. "B-A-R-R-Y."

"That's not so bad," she said. "At least I don't have to re-member a whole new name."

"Don't forget about The Lion," I reminded her.

"The Lion," she repeated, looking a little uneasy. "The talent contest. Yeah. Let me think about it, okay?"

She smiled, waved a little goodbye and then she was gone.

All that evening I was in a tremendous state of agitation, pac-ing up and down, puffing on cigarettes and thinking about Bar-bara. I started to pull out some records into a Barbara stack, things I wanted to play for her, songs I could hear her singing in my head, then put them all back. I wondered: would she really go down to The Lion and sign up? I needed that little bit of commitment from her, that minimum physical act of involvement, before I was willing to do anything more myself.

79

Much later, I learned that that night, when Barbara went back to her own apartment, her roommate, Marilyn, was home.

"Hi, Barbara," Marilyn said. "Your mother called. She wanted to know where you were."

"What did you tell her?" Barbara asked, moving to the kitchen and opening the fridge.

"The truth," Marilyn said. "That I didn't know."

"I've been down in the Village, at my friend Barry's. You remember, I told you about him."

"Sure," Marilyn said. "From that insect play."

"Yeah. He's a bright guy," Barbara said.

"Uh-huh," Marilyn said, sticking her head inside the kitchen door. "And...," she added.

"And...he wants me to sing," Barbara said nonchalantly, producing a celery stick and taking a bite.

"Sing," Marilyn repeated. "What do you mean, sing?"

"He thinks I should do a nightclub act," Barbara persisted. "He says he'll work with me on it."

"Oh, really?" Marilyn replied. "Well, that's a new kind of come-on, isn't it?"

"Do me a favor, Marilyn?" Barbara asked.

"Sure, honey. What?"

"Let me sing a song for you and you can tell me if I'm any good," Barbara said bravely.

"Sure," Marilyn said, going to take a chair.

"No, no, you can't look at me. I won't be able to do it," Barbara said nervously. "Stand up against the wall, and don't peek. I'll sing to your back."

Marilyn shook her head and smiled. "Sure, Barbara," she said ruefully, and added, "The things I do for you." She went over to the wall and stood facing it.

"Now don't laugh, even if it's terrible," Barbara implored.

"I won't laugh," Marilyn said. "Okay, I'm facing the wall. It could use a paint job. Sing."

So Barbara screwed up her courage, took a big breath and sang a ballad she knew from a Broadway musical, *a cappella*. When the last notes died away Marilyn didn't budge, she just stayed facing the wall. Barbara became uneasy.

"What's the matter?" she said, worried. "You're not laughing, are you? Was it terrible? Tell me if it was terrible."

Marilyn turned around slowly, tears trickling down her face.

"No, honey," she said. "It was beautiful. Absolutely beautiful."

The next day went by and I didn't hear from Barbara. I assumed she'd taken an acting class or had gone out to see her mother. That usually put her in a bad mood and nobody heard from her for a while.

Late the following morning my phone rang. I surfaced from a sound sleep and groped bleary-eyed around the coffee table, locating the receiver and knocking it off the cradle. I snatched it up.

"Hello," I said, croaking gravel.

"Hello, Barry, this is Barbara."

"Hi," I said.

"Hi," she replied.

"What's up?" I asked her.

I sat up on the side of the bed listening for what seemed like an eternity, my head still foggy with sleep, while I hunted vainly for my cigarettes among the piles of books, papers, and detritus on the coffee table. Finally I located my Parliaments and wiggled my finger around inside the frustratingly empty pack.

"You still there?" I asked.

"Yeah, sure," she said. "I'm downstairs."

"What do you mean?" I asked, locating a half-smoked butt in the ashtray and struggling with a sputtering, recalcitrant match. "Where, downstairs?"

"Downstairs, in front of your apartment building. Across the street," Barbara explained.

"What are you doing down there?" I asked, a little confused.

There was a pause.

"You know, The Lion?" she said finally.

"Uh-huh," I said.

"I signed up."

Yes, I thought, yes!

"Hey," I said, looking around for my bathrobe, "why don't you come up here and let's talk about what you're gonna sing."

"You sound like you just woke up," Barbara said.

"I did," I confessed.

"Are you naked?" she asked.

"Kinda," I said.

"I'll be right up."

Like Dorothy, Barbara had taken her first, tentative step on what would become a long, winding, yellow brick road, sprinkled with gold and stardust.

But that's all hindsight. Back then, we were both young and inexperienced, stumbling around in the dark sexually and professionally, not having any real notion of where all this ultimately was going to take us. All I knew was I had to give Barbara the confidence to sing in public.

Barbara was so desperate to make it, so hungry for attention and success, that it had become a kind of living, breathing ache inside her that blotted out everything else. And I was so dazzled by her talent and at the same time falling in love with her that I would have done anything to help her. It seemed like we were the only two people in the whole world, and nothing else mattered.

What neither Barbara nor I could begin to imagine in those early, dawning days was that the key to a fabulous, glittering, unparalleled career lay, literally, right under her nose.

6

The Lion's Mouth

I can only guess what was going through Barbara's head that warm June morning in 1960 when, all alone and probably scared, she stood at the top of the steps leading down to The Lion to sign up for their talent contest.

Many preposterous stories and much folklore have grown up around Barbra Streisand's first exciting appearance before the public in June 1960:

She said her name was Strinberg. She appeared in unwashed lank hair, half dyed navel orange and the other half colored brown. She wore dead-white Dracula's daughter makeup. She pulled her music out of a bulging red plastic school satchel. She wore a tiny rhinestone shoe in her hair and sang "Happy Birthday." She didn't know that The Lion was a gay bar. After several weeks of winning she retired and worked in the bar as a coat-check girl.

Sure.

I was there, and that's not exactly what happened.

Once Barbara had committed to putting her head in The Lion's mouth, I realized we only had a few days to get a couple of numbers together quickly for her tryout. She hadn't actually moved in with me yet, but we met every day to rehearse for a few hours in my apartment. I decided that things would probably go better if Barbara sang material she already knew and was comfortable with, rather than try to learn and work up something brand-new. As every singer and musical actor knows, when presenting brand-new material, the first performances of it are almost completely concerned with struggling to remember the words.

The song that Barbara had sung for her roommate in her kitchenette debut was "A Sleepin' Bee," a haunting, delicate ballad from the Truman Capote-Harold Arlen score, *House of Flowers*, introduced in the show in a revered (by some) but to me somewhat bloodless Broadway belter performance by Diahann Carroll. Despite its aural complexity, vocal range, and difficult tessitura, it's really a very simple song with a verse (which Barbara never used), a two-line chorus, a short middle bit, then the second chorus with an extended and expanded tag, which is musical slang for a coda, or ending. Her second song, "When Sunny Gets Blue," was an even more down piece of material, and though I felt auditioning with two ballads was fraught with danger, we had to go with what we had.

Barbara went through "A Sleepin' Bee" for me, and although she sang it with an impressive sincerity, purity, and sweetness of tone, her conception of the song was almost generic. All the phrasing and subtle gradations of meaning that should shade the different acting beats seemed to be given equal weight.

"That's very pretty," I said to her, "but what does it mean?"

"Whaddya mean, what does it mean?" she exploded. "It means that if you put a bee in your hand and it doesn't sting you to death, then...you're fine. Sort of."

"Why would you want to hold a bee in your hand, anyway?" I put to her.

"Uh...to test yourself," she suggested. "It's a weird sort of love test."

"Okay," I said. "Let's imagine there's this really young girl living on an island somewhere in the Caribbean. She's pretty, right, she's smart and intuitive, but up until now, she's always had fairly uncomplicated feelings."

"Just like you and me, huh?" Barbara said, looking at me teasingly.

"Right," I said, "her life is sun, rain, eat, sleep, canoe, fish, Astaire, Rogers, just like you and me."

"Exactly how old is she?" she asked. I was beginning to notice and love how Barbara chased after and worried about the specifics of things. She never let anything go until she'd pinned down all the loose edges.

"Let's make her eleven or twelve," I said. "Just coming into puberty, her sexual awakening, her first flashes of femininity. Stop looking at me like that," I said. Barbara was busily watching my mouth with a naughty, sexy grin spreading over her lips.

"Fine," she said, and composed her face into that of an intelligent but disinterested listener. "Go on."

"On this island there's no television and no radio...," I began.

"And no phonograph records, no sheet music, no tapes of weird, obscure nightclub performers," Barbara added, laughing.

"No nothing," I agreed. "She just sleeps in this simple hut made of palm leaves and runs around the island all day on her little bare feet," I said.

"Where's her mother?" Barbara asked.

"In Brooklyn," I said.

"Sure," Barbara responded jokingly, then looked at me dubiously as if she were asking herself where all this was leading.

"So one day she's hiding in the sugar cane fields. Maybe she's been playing Hide and Seek with her friends and she's ditched 'em, and all of a sudden she sees this gorgeous-looking guy saunter by on the road, long and lanky, with a beautiful, handsome face."

"Yeah," Barbara exhaled. "It's hot, right? And she's younger than he is. What's his name?"

"Melvin," I said.

"Would you stop?" Barbara laughed.

"Would *you* stop interrupting? Anyway, she looks at him, he looks back at her and all of a sudden, bang! The *coup de foudre*! The lightning clap. She feels something she's never felt before, but she's not sure he feels it too, right?"

"Right," Barbara exclaimed. "Ah, she's fallen in love, but so fast!" she said, raising a finger.

"Ah!" I said, also raising a finger. "Maybe too fast."

"So . . . *nu?*" she asked.

"*Nu?*" I said. "Whaddya mean, *nu?*"

"*Nu,*" Barbara repeated. "You know what '*nu*' means: So? Well? What happens?"

"She goes to the witch woman, the obeah lady or whatever, maybe her old grannie, and she says to her—"

"She says, 'Help, help, what am I gonna do, I'm in love!'" Barbara interrupted.

Barbara and I looked at each other for a moment as the talk dried up. I felt my heart thump in my chest but decided to ignore it.

"She tells her about the man and asks her how she can find out if he feels the same way," I said.

Barbara's eyes were glowing like polished stones. She was loving this.

"Go on, go on!" she said. "What does the witch woman or bubba, or whoever she is, say . . . what *happens?*"

"She says, 'Go find a bee, a bee that's all sleepy from the sun-

86

shine and drinking too much honey, and you enfold it in your hand. And then you think about the man. And if the bee doesn't sting, he loves you back.' "

"Listen, Barry, I know all this already," Barbara complained, mildly annoyed. "It's all in the words of the song."

Despite her infinite capacity for play, I was finding I had to keep a few steps ahead of Barbara if I didn't want her getting impatient with me.

"Sure, but I want to give you some pictures in your head you can call up and look at when you sing it," I explained.

"All right, okay. So, where does she find a bee?" she asked. "The local Bee Emporium on 8th Street?"

"She walks down the road to the avenue of lime trees," I went on, "and at the crossroads, there's an old man who keeps bees in his garden. That's how he lives, he sells these luscious, sweet-dripping combs of lime flower honey," I said.

"Mmmmm..." Barbara savored it. "But still, where does he get all the bees?" Barbara persisted. "Bloomingdales? Mail order?"

"People," I said. "People go for a walk in the woods, and when they come out they say to him, Hey, Mr. Beeman, I just saw a whole big buncha bees up by the old banana grove. And the Beeman goes up there with his net and captures the queen, and all the rest swarm back behind him, following him through the woods like a rippling banner of bees on the breeze."

Barbara shook her head and smiled. She loved wordplay. "You're too much," she said, and put her hand on mine.

"Thank you," I said. "And when he gets home, he puts the queen in a wooden box and the colony does all the rest. They build the hive and spin the wax and gather in the nectar, and choose the wallpaper samples and furnish all the little apartments."

"Where did you learn all this stuff?" she asked me.

"Maurice Maeterlinck, *The Life of the Bee*," I confessed.

"Huh!" Barbara said. "I always thought honey came in a jar from a shelf in the market."

"Very funny," I said, and tried to steer the conversation around back to the song. "Listen, have you ever really thought about what it must feel like to hold a real, live bee inside your hand … wondering if at any moment it's going to sting you?"

Barbara thought for a moment. "Nope," she said honestly. "No, I never really did."

"Well, a bee sting hurts, a lot. My brother stepped on a bee getting out of our swimming pool and his whole foot got swollen. We had to take him to the doctor for a shot," I said.

"Getting out of your swimming pool," Barbara mused. "The problems of the rich."

"Oh, stop that. A bee sting hurts whether you're rich or poor," I said.

"Yeah … I'm sorry," she apologized.

"Never mind," I said.

In those days, Barbara had a sprawling, idiosyncratic collection of all sorts of stuff—sequins, scraps of cloth, buttons, lace, fabric edging, trim, accessories, and costume jewelry—each sorted out and organized in its own paper shopping bag. When we'd set up this rehearsal session, I asked her to bring along her bag o' feathers. She'd looked puzzled, but agreed.

"Listen, did you bring over your bag o' feathers?"

"Yeah, I remembered," she said, and hauled the bag o' feathers over to me so I could rummage through it. "But I can't figure out what you want them for."

"Wait a minute, you'll find out."

"Be careful, my feather fan's in there. It's really old and delicate," Barbara fussed.

"I know, I know," I said, finally finding a small white feather that was fairly stiff, something from a pigeon or a dove, I imagine.

"That's trim for a hat," Barbara said. She always remembered everything she had and pretty much where it was all kept.

"Close your eyes," I said.

Barbara obediently closed them.

"Now cup your hands together, one over the other," I said. "Loose," I added. She brought her hands together and I wiggled my finger in between her palms to make a little cave. Barbara giggled.

"Stop," I said. "We're working."

"Okay," she said compliantly, and concentrated.

"Now I'm going to put a living, buzzing bumblebee in there," and I insinuated the feather between her two hands. "Now," I said softly, "sing the song."

My intention was to slightly, subtly scrape the feather around inside her cupped palms, to give her the sensation of an insect drunkenly crawling around.

"'When a bee lies sleepin''..." Barbara began to sing, then stopped.

"What's the matter?" I asked.

"I can't go on," she said. "It tickles."

"Come on," I coaxed, "imagine that it's a real bee with a big fat stinger in there."

"When a bee..." she began to sing, then broke into hysterical giggles. "I can't, I can't!" she said, falling back on the sofa bed, her arms coming up in front of her face.

Without thinking at all I put my hands on her arms and gently pushed them down and out of the way. Barbara looked up at me so seriously. Then I leaned over and for the first time kissed her right on the mouth, my lips on top of her lips. Suddenly our mouths opened together, over each other. I remember it being all soft and voluptuous, our tongues finding each other, working my hand up under her blouse, my nails tracing a path down her side as I continued to kiss her silky mouth, just like I'd always wanted to. I could feel the electric-eel currents running through both of us, the little shivers, the shocks of sexual discovery. We were both very new at this stuff, both feeling that fresh thrill not only of finally doing it, but of *knowing* that you're doing it: finally kissing and being kissed back, deep and deeper, warm, liquid, lost in it.

We kissed and kissed some more. It was like a song lyric. When we finally came up for air, I said raspily, "I don't think we're gonna get a lot of rehearsing done today, if we keep doing this."

"Maybe not," Barbara said and looked up at me, clearing her throat and smiling with satisfaction.

I looked back down at her. We were both really aroused and wanted to make love. And then I remembered that I didn't have any contraceptives. We could both get into a whole lot of trouble. I immediately lost my erection.

"Barbara," I said as gently as I could, "do you want to … make love with me?"

Barbara looked introspective for a moment, then locked eyes with me. "Yeah," she said. "Yeah, I really do."

"Then we've got to be careful," I said.

"Yeah," she said. "Okay. I guess."

"I tell you what," I said. "Later today, I'll go buy some condoms and maybe you could pick up some baby oil or something," I suggested.

"It's a little … uh … unspontaneous, isn't it?" she said.

"Yeah, I know, it's not very romantic. But you don't want to get pregnant, do you?" I asked.

"No," she said decisively. "Okay," she added with a provocative smile. "Deal."

"Deal." I kissed her on the cheek. We lay next to each other a while without speaking. I stroked her hair, ran my fingers across her forehead, down the bridge of her nose, across her lips. She nibbled at a forefinger, ran her tongue over it. I shivered.

"Listen, I wanna ask you something," she said, turning on her side to face me, her head resting on my upper arm, her voice taking on a totally practical tone. "Do you think I should change my name?"

"Why would you want to do that?" I asked.

"Everyone says it's hard to pronounce."

"Who's everyone?" I said.

"Everyone," Barbara said. "Agents. Casting people. My dentist."

"They'll learn how to pronounce it. Did I ever tell you about Chekhov naming *The Cherry Orchard*?" I asked her.

"No," she said.

"Well, one day in rehearsal, Chekhov runs up to Stanislavsky, laughing his head off, and says, 'I've got it! I finally found a name for the new play. I'm going to call it The *Cherry* Orchard,' and still giggling, he runs away. Later the same day he comes up to Stanislavsky again. 'I've changed the name of the play,' he says. 'Now, I'm going to call it The Cherry *Orchard*,' and he breaks into hysterical laughter and runs away again."

Barbara stared at me as if I'd just sprouted a second head. "What is the point of that story?" she asked.

"I think the point is, changing a name doesn't make any difference, it's still about cherries and orchards. Like Shakespeare said, what's in a name?"

"A lotta letters," Barbara replied.

"Well, maybe the point is, the more you change a name, the more it stays the same."

Barbara stared at me quizzically, slowly shaking her head. I was beginning to feel a little ridiculous.

"Actually, now that I think about it, I'm not sure what the point is. It's just a funny story. Anyway, no, don't change your name," I finished lamely.

*   *   *

Later that day, I was standing in the Bigelow Pharmacy, waiting for the druggist to come over, when the obvious suddenly occurred to me: I was asking Barbara to do something she had no direct experience of. She'd never watched a cabaret singer live, she'd never even been inside a nightclub. It reminded me of the famous theatrical designer Robert Edmund Jones's crack about an English shoe looking as if it had been made by someone who had heard about a shoe but had never actually seen one.

"Can I help you, sir?" the white-coated pharmacist asked, materializing magically in front of me.

Now, this was 1960, and although "marital aids," as they were called then, were widely available, they didn't sit on the counter in brazen, attention-getting Buy Trojan, The Athlete's Choice! display stands. They were literally under-the-counter items, and asking aloud for them in a drugstore still took some grit and boldness.

"Yeah," I said, deliberately holding my voice steady, "I'd like some … uh … rubbers."

"Prophylactics," the druggist intoned, in the kind of piercing, nasal New York accent that carried halfway across the store. I refused to look around to see if people were staring at me. "What kind?" he said.

"Uh … what kind do you have?"

"Natural. Latex. Pre-lubed. A whole selection."

"Why don't you just show me a whole big bunch?" I asked, and he knelt down, opened a drawer, retrieved a small cardboard box and dumped a colorful cascade of condoms on the counter top.

"Take your time," he said and, to my immense relief, walked off to deal with another customer.

That evening I dusted off Dad's Diner's Club card, invited Barbara out, and we both got dressed up and trekked uptown to the

RSVP, near Third Avenue on East 55th Street, to watch and listen to Mabel Mercer, reigning doyenne of New York cabaret chanteuses.

Mabel Mercer was wonderful, a real bright penny of a performer, and I loved her. But to be honest, by this point in her career Mabel's voice was tired, crusty, and wobbling; she jousted gamely with accurate pitch, and like certain ripe cheeses, she was something of an acquired taste.

Mabel scraped her bottom through an opening number and during the polite applause, Barbara turned to me, totally perplexed, and whispered behind her hand, "I don't get it. She can't sing!"

"She's a song stylist," I said. "Her voice isn't important. What's important is the way she phrases and her material," I explained.

"Oh, yeah?" Barbara wondered.

We sat through Mabel's second number, a ballad.

"What kinda *voice* is that?" Barbara hissed behind her glass of Coca-Cola. "Is she...famous, or something?"

"Listen, I know her voice is shot, but watch her," I argued back in an undertone. "You can't take your eyes off her. She keeps you interested because she doesn't *do* anything."

"You got something there," Barbara grumbled.

We listened to Mabel sing an upbeat Bart Howard tune, and as she warbled the penultimate line, "Would you believe it?" she gazed over at us from beneath her half-lidded eyes, then snapped her fingers only once, saucily, and finished with, "I'm a real gone girl!"

"Pretty good!" I said, smiling and applauding exuberantly. "That's the only time I've ever seen Mabel snap her fingers," I enthused. Barbara turned and looked at me as if I'd gone completely out of my mind.

"God," Barbara mumbled, "I could do better than that."

My head snapped around. "What did you just say?" I asked her.

"Nothin'. Nothin'," she mumbled darkly, finishing her drink. "Can I have another Coke?"

I just sat in the dark and squeezed my knees together, put an arm around Barbara's shoulder and pulled her in toward me. Getting there, I thought.

Mabel Mercer had refined the presentation of a song in a form so simple and classic that today, in retrospect, it seems obvious to the point of cliché. Her accompaniment was the bare minimum: in a club, a piano; sometimes on records she added a dual piano or a small group, but except for a couple of overproduced efforts later in her career, that was it. This bare-bones approach afforded her the immense flexibility of singing a song the first time through completely *rubato*, freely, out of tempo, pausing for effect, pulling back on the phrasing, pushing on ahead. Whatever Mabel did, her pianist was right with her and solidly underneath her. Then the second time through Mabel sang the song in rhythm, to demonstrate elegantly to us, like a jeweler laying a diamond on a velvet cloth, its colors and shape. It was an ingeniously simple formula but immensely effective, and I don't know of anyone before Mabel Mercer who conceived of presenting a song in precisely this classy, polished, throw-away style.

And it was exactly the way Barbara and I mounted "A Sleepin' Bee."

The next morning I awoke early. There was a buzzing around my head, a brushing, tickling irritation. Yeah, of course! My eyes flew open and I rushed into the kitchen and grabbed a clean, empty marmalade jar out of the cupboard and banged holes into the lid with a tin can punch.

When Barbara arrived at the apartment I ushered her right in, offered her a drink, and then told her we were going to pick up where we left off yesterday.

"No, please," she begged, "no more feathers. I can't take it."

"No more feathers," I promised her and carefully slid the jam jar from a bookshelf, then moved determinedly toward Barbara, unscrewing the lid slowly and deliberately.

"Whaddya got there?" she asked a little nervously.

"A bee," I said. "A real, live bee."

"Oh, my God," she said, "you're joking."

"No," I said. "I'm not joking. I went to a lot of trouble to get this. Give me your hand."

"No . . . no!" Barbara said. "What are you, nuts?"

"Listen, you want to be an actress?" I said. "Well, I want you to put this real, live bee in your hand," I said, "and sing the song."

"No, Barry," Barbara exclaimed, suddenly sitting on her hands. "No!" she panicked. "It'll sting me."

"Maybe it will and maybe it won't," I said, tipping the insect out of the jar, tapping it down and trapping it inside my own hands. "But whatever, you'll *really* know what it means to sing that song."

"Oh, my God, you're crazy!" she squirmed.

"Come on," I said. "I'm doing it," I said, and held out my hands in front of her. "If I can do it, you can."

Barbara's eyes widened in alarm and disbelief. "Come on," I said, holding my two hands out in front of her face. "I dare ya."

For several excruciating seconds Barbara struggled with her anxiety, then with exquisite unwillingness, looking away and grimacing, she held out her palm. I made a tent of my hands over hers and shook the bug down, held it in place while I gently took her other hand and placed it on top.

"There," I said softly. "How do you feel?"

"This is awful!" she whispered. "I'm terrified. And excited," she admitted unwillingly.

"Sing the song, Barb," I said.

"I can feel it moving! Barry, I can feel it crawling around on my hand!" she said, hardly able to breathe.

"Sing the song," I said.

Very softly, as if afraid that anything loud might alarm the insect into some violent reprisal, Barbara sang the first three or four lines of "A Sleepin' Bee," waves of wonder and anguish and astonishment washing over her face.

"Now," I asked, "how do you feel?"

"I hate you," she said, trembling and perspiring. "I can't believe I let you do this to me."

"Fine," I said. "But do you understand the song now?"

"Yes," Barbara said. "Totally. Now, get it off of me! Barry, please! Get this goddamn, fucking bee out of my hand before it bites me," she pleaded.

I took her wrists in mine and slowly pried open her hands. Barbara looked down, then shot me a look that would have turned ice cubes into water.

"A fly?" she screamed. "A *fly*?!"

"A housefly," I clarified.

With utter contempt and disgust Barbara shook the fly away. It flew around once in a lazy circle and landed with a discontented buzz on the window glass.

"Come on," I said, starting to laugh, "do you honestly think I'd let you get stung?"

"A *FLY*?!" Barbara yelled indignantly, grabbing the pillows from the sofa bed and furiously pummeling me over the head with them. "I can't believe you would do that to me!" she shrieked, whacking me again and again. I let her give it to me, swacking me with the pillows, too weak with glee to protect myself, laughing my head off. She started to laugh, too, in relief and revenge. I tried to crawl away but she tackled me and flipped me over, sat on my chest and tickled me under the arms.

"I hate you!" she said, but I was laughing so hard, and she was laughing, too, I didn't care. "I hate you!" she said, doubling up her fists and pounding me on the chest. I looked up at her and grabbed her wrists.

"No, you don't," I said, and tried to kiss her, but she was having none of it.

"I do!" she said, pulling free and pummeling me some more. "I do, I do!"

"Be careful," I said, laughing and writhing and trying to grab her hands, "you'll break your nails."

"I don't care!" she said, banging her little fists against my chest, "I...don't...care!"

When we finally got through roughhousing and back to rehearsing, I suggested to Barbara that we approach "Sleepin' Bee" like a three-act play. In the first part, Barbara was the young island girl we had talked about, opening up to the joys of love for the first time, and I urged her to use the emotional memory exercise of how she felt when she really thought I'd put the bee in her hand: the thrill, the fear, the growing excitement.

As she moved into the middle of the song, I suggested that Barbara grow into a middle-aged woman, talking to her own child now and remembering her own first love. Maybe she and her man were no longer together, maybe he was dead. But I wanted a deepening feeling to tinge her performance, a wash of regret and melancholy which Barbara hadn't really experienced yet in her own young life. Her final transformation moved into yet another sphere, into dreams, ripe with remembrance. I told Barbara to imagine herself as the grandmother now, telling her own young grandchild the secrets, the passing-on of feminine knowledge, the awareness of life's patterns being lived through again and again.

The first time Barbara sang the song ringing these emotional changes, going deeper and deeper into the character, exploring and reinventing herself, it was electrifying. I knew we were on to something very different and special.

On the day of Barbara's tryout the apartment took on the chaotic frenzy and catastrophic appearance of a war room on

D-Day. Sheet music was spread all over the floor, makeup laid out all over the bathroom and tables, and there were endless last-minute trips to the drugstore. The phone never seemed to stop ringing.

For her audition Terry Leong had chosen a feathered boudoir jacket in shades of violet and orchid, with a dress of lilacs and purples underneath. It was, as Terry exulted, a thrift-shop find, spectacular and unexpected, and serendipitously it proclaimed what Barbara was: a songbird of plumage, a nightingale about to be set free from her cage. The only problem was, the dry cleaners said the jacket wouldn't be ready on time as promised. Piles of clothes were frenetically yanked out of the closet and piled on the bed in a frenzied search for an alternate outfit.

At the last moment, Terry arrived with the feather bed jacket, looking fluffed and fresh, which he held aloft triumphantly on its hanger under its clear plastic bag. We all whooped and cheered. Barbara seemed to take forever doing her makeup but finally the bathroom door flew open and she appeared, looking excited and very pretty.

But just as we were about to walk out the door, Barbara had an attack of soul-wrenching fear and self-doubt. She started to thrash around in a kind of spiritual agony, panicking, ready to bolt, insisting she couldn't go through with it: "I'm an actress, an *ehk-tress* ... I'm *not* a singer, I don't *wanna* be a singer!" In my heart, I guessed she was bone-deep terrified.

I sat her down, took her hands and looked deep inside her, steadying her, holding on. "You can do this," I said. "And you're going to do this. We're going to do it together, and it's going to be just... *great*," I insisted, using every bit of my willpower and trying to drill into her soul with my eyes. "Come on," I said. "Do it...like an *actress*."

Barbara just looked back at me, pulling herself together hesitantly, a little calmer and more composed. But I don't know if she honestly believed me.

"Okay," she said finally, standing up. "Hey, what have I got to lose?"

The Lion was unexpectedly overcrowded that night. It was a weekday, but the place was jumping like it was Saturday night. Excited talk and whoops of laughter, the piano pounding, men packed in against each other. The bar was doing a roaring trade.

Barbara, Terry, and I had to fight through the crowd to get to the back room where there was a little area that acted as a kind of stage, with the piano backed up at one end and the audience sitting at tables all around it. The room was as packed as a jar of artichoke hearts, but a table had been saved for us near the front.

Suddenly Barbara became very cool. She sat up perfectly straight, leaning away from the back of her chair, and looked around the room, interested but slightly withdrawn. "Who are all these guys?" she asked, then, lowering her voice, added, "Do they all, ya know, like men?"

I looked at her, then at Terry and said, "I wouldn't be a bit surprised."

We sat through three other faceless contestants, but the only one I thought might give Barbara any competition was a young jazz singer who was the niece of a famous black musician. Finally it was Barbara's turn: "And now, ladies and gentlemen, our last contestant. Please welcome Miss Barbara Streisand!"

My stomach clenched. Barbara threw me one final look, I nodded, she took one big breath and stood up. I could tell from her body language, standing ramrod straight, head turning aloofly, what she was thinking: now I'm on my own. There was a spattering of automatic applause followed by an uneasy caesura while the audience waited, gossiping fitfully among themselves. Barbara pulled out her sheet music and handed it to the pianist, who unfolded and arranged it on his music stand. She pointed to the beginning of the piece and whispered close to his ear. I guessed she was reminding him that she didn't sing the verse, the first two choruses were ad lib and the final chorus in tempo.

Then Barbara turned forward into the spotlight to face her audience. Her eyes glided over the faces at the horizon level. There were a few scattered coughs, ice clinked against glass as here and there someone took a final sip. The piano moved into her introduction and I held my breath as Barbara stood poised to plunge into the cool water of the opening phrases.

I stared at her hard with all my heart and soul, willing her to be good, to remember what we'd gone over and how we'd planned the song. But whatever nerves or stage fright Barbara had been feeling earlier were completely gone when she opened her mouth to sing. As the first words tumbled out, liquid and languorous, I felt she was remembering the feeling of that insect moving in her hands. She seemed to be inventing the words spontaneously as she moved through the song, her eyes half-lidded, lost in the feeling, the words, the melody of her own voice.

As Barbara swung into the last rhythmic chorus, her eyes closed and her body swayed, her head tilting back slightly as her tone floated miraculously higher and higher above the atmosphere of smoke and ice cubes, only deigning to open her eyes on the last few words, "...when my one...true...love...I has found," when she looked out over the heads of the audience as if she were looking back into the past and forward into the future simultaneously, and taking all of us with her. The thick piano chords clustered up around her final note into a crescendo of sound and then, suddenly, it was all over: utter silence.

There was a breathless pause. The audience was dead still, frozen in time. I looked around the room at their freeze-frame faces. What's the matter with them? I thought. Don't they like her? And then suddenly the whole room crashed into applause, an eruption of yells and whistles, ear-shattering stomping and screaming. They wanted another song!

I looked over at Terry. He was shattered. Tears were streaming down his face. "What's the matter?" I yelled at him over the unbelievable din.

"I've never heard Barbara sing before...I'm devastated!" Terry yelled at me, wiping his tears away with a cocktail napkin.

I shook my head. "Not bad, huh? Are you okay?" I hollered over the clamoring din.

"Sure, but you're squeezing my hand," Terry said.

"What?" I answered and looked down. I was so nervous watching Barbara sing that I was completely unaware I had been crushing Terry's hand, nearly mashing his fingers to a purée.

The audience was quieting down and I realized Barbara was about to start her second number. She had been giggling nervously during the applause, enjoying the acclaim and the power she was exerting over her audience, tremendously flattered and excited. It was her first, heady whiff of the awareness that she could do anything she wanted and get away with it, I guess, because she began the second song as we'd rehearsed it, but then suddenly decided to take matters into her own hands, throw the painstaking work we'd done to the winds—and improvise.

She yanked the microphone from its stand and, to my dismay, floated around the room, walking between the tables, singing into people's faces. The spotlight wasn't equipped to follow her so she was immediately plunged into darkness, still singing and waving her hand in the air as if to say, "I'm over here!" The mike cable snagged under a table leg and Barbara tried to yank it loose, but only succeeded in tipping one patron's chair. The sound system popped and crackled. Barbara retreated to the piano in a somewhat awkward confusion of feathers and mike cords but managed to finish the number with the big ending we'd planned.

It didn't make a bit of difference. This gawky, impromptu dollop of schmaltz from the Ethel Merman School of Entertaining didn't seem to dampen anyone's enthusiasm, and the crowd went wild a second time. The joint was rattling. Barbara was a bona fide wow. She won the talent contest at The Lion that night hands-down, which meant fifty bucks and she could come back again to compete next week. We swept out the front door of The Lion on a tidal wave of excitement and congratulations and landed on the beach at the Pam Pam Coffee Shop.

The rest of the evening, we all flew high. It had been such a remarkable event and we all wanted to go over and over moments in it, moments of indelible triumph. Terry was very moved and tried to tell Barbara how touched and overwhelmed he'd been to hear her sing: "I had no idea" was all he could manage.

I gave Barbara a few notes but I'd wait until we worked again to talk about her floating like a dirigible all over the room and getting her wires snagged in the furniture. This was her triumph, her premiere success. Why ruin it with a lot of carping? We ordered something to eat, some coffees for Terry and me and a Coke for Barb.

While we were waiting for our order, one of the guys who'd been in The Lion that night and who'd also repaired to the Pam Pam with a bunch of his friends came over to our table and, wide-eyed with adoration, asked Barbara for her autograph. Flattered and pleased, she took a napkin and signed it. Fan number one went back to his table, tucking his personally inscribed prize into his shirt pocket.

"My first fan!" Barbara enthused.

"Well, I'll bet he's not your last," Terry said. We both smiled at him.

"Ya know, Bar," Barbara said, "I'm thinking of changing my name."

"Oh, yeah? You mentioned that earlier," I said. "To what?"

"To 'Barbra,' " she said.

I stared at her, perplexed. "To... *Barbara?*" I said, misunderstanding. "That *is* your name."

"No!" she protested, "without the 'A'," and grabbed a napkin and printed it out: B-A-R-B-R-A, then with a flourish, signed her new and forever name: Bar...bra Strei...sand. She pushed it over to me, saying, "Looks nice, doesn't it?"

At that moment the waitress delivered our drinks, looked down at the napkin and said, "I didn't know you could spell 'Barbara' that way."

"Sure," Barbra said, and the waitress shrugged and went away.

I looked at the freshly minted signature. "So now you're 'Barbra?' " I asked.

"Yeah, why not?" she said. "Now I'm Barbra." She picked up her straw and tore off the paper wrapping.

"You look the same to me," I said.

"Well," she replied as she took a sip of her Cherry Coke and looked over at me, "I'm not."

7

The Making of Barbra

$\mathcal{A}$ s the next few simmering weeks of summer heated up, Barbra's and my relationship boiled over, too—living, loving, lust, and life at The Lion became complicatedly overlapping and interwoven. We were both sexually inexperienced; the difference was, I knew Barbra was something of a novice but I don't think she realized that I, too, was in many ways an erotic amateur. To further perplex our overheated hormones, I asked Barbra to move in with me, and she did.

I think I hoped subconsciously that being Barbra's mentor would help throw a drape over an area of my life I preferred not to deal with: my nagging, unsettling libidinous interest in men. Maybe if I ignored it, the theory went, it would all go away. But it didn't. Things only got more confusing. In my brief erogenous history I'd been back and forth over the sexual fence on several occasions, but this time I was well and truly stuck in the middle, and distinctly at risk of snagging my pants on the barbed wire.

And then, too, I'd fallen in love with Barbra. Falling in love with Barbra was easy, as the rest of the world now knows. Professionally I was happy on many levels to plunge into a Svengali-Trilby relationship with her. We each had exactly what the other needed: I, the musical taste; she, the incomparable voice.

And then there was the sex itself. We were both full of trepidation and hesitancy about sleeping with each other, coupled to an overwhelming, desperate desire to get it on. As for Barbra, although she may not have had that much hands-on practical experience with men, she was driven by her unrelenting curiosity, intuitiveness, and hunger to learn about everything, including her own body. And so, bursting with love and anxiety, we moved closer and closer toward each other.

The night after Barbra moved in, we both sat tentatively on the side of the bed, I in pajamas and she in a soft flannel nightshirt. I told Barb I wanted to play something special for her, and as I went around the apartment lighting a few candles, she made a little nest for us of cushions and pillows on the bed.

Barbra and I lived our lives surrounded by music. We were ruled by it, orchestrated by it; we lived as if every conversation were a scene in a movie with Max Steiner underscoring. We felt that music, like sex, was God's gift to us.

This particular late evening I had decided to play some opera for Barbra, probably some of the first she'd ever heard. Back home in Los Angeles several years earlier I had found a thick, heavy 78-rpm album of Richard Wagner duets which I had transferred to tape so that the whole thing played on and on for over an hour. I wanted her to hear the "Love Death" from *Tristan and Isolde*. It was sensuous, rapturous—delirious. I was sure she'd love it.

As we sat there listening, letting the music wash over us, Barbra became more and more worked up, more moved.

"God, this is so *gorgeous*!" she said to me. "Who *is* this guy?"

"You mean the singer or the composer?" I asked her, raising my voice over the soaring music.

"Either. Both. What is she saying? What are they singing about?" she demanded to know.

"Shush. Listen to it. I'll tell you all about it later."

Whatever Barbra was feeling was making her squirm on the bedside. It was as if the music were piercing her, penetrating directly into her heart. She was thrilled in a way I'd never seen her before, overcome by some deep, passionate emotion that had taken even her by surprise.

"God, I just *love* this!" she panted. And putting her arm around me, she murmured, "And I love you, too, Barry."

I leaned over to embrace her. Her mouth was so moist and sweet. She savored each kiss as if experiencing it for the first time, inhaling it whole, offering herself as a young girl would present a bouquet of spring flowers. Going back, visualizing her again in my mind, I realize now it was the inexpressibly beautiful sight of Barbra in love.

Our heartbeats bumped up a notch. I began to slide my hands down the front of her body, exploring. I slid her nightshirt up over her head. She sat there, tremulous, shy, and naked.

We both fell back on the bed. I cupped my palm around her breast and squeezed it gently. It just filled my hand, her perfect aureole framed in the space between my thumb and forefinger. We tasted each other open-mouthed, hungrily, our tongues darting in and out in a little dance, while I ran my thumb around her nipple, over it, all the while licking, biting, sucking her. Teenage sex—it was thrilling.

Barbra pulled away, trying to turn her head aside, but I wouldn't let her. I took her face in my hand, brought it back to mine, and placed my lips on hers.

I moved my hands downward, over her thighs, as we explored deeper and deeper into each other with our tongues.

When I pulled my palm up gently between her legs, Barbra suddenly stiffened. Immediately, I withdrew.

"This is the part that scares me," she whispered softly. The *Liebestod* continued to pour out of the loudspeakers. "I feel like I'm drowning."

"Me, too," I confessed. We were both trembling, and frightened, but incredibly aroused. "Come on," I said, my voice sounding raspy and a little out of control, "let's do it. We're not gonna die."

Her lips parted and so did mine. Barbra never refused a challenge. I could sense how all at sea she was. We were both thrashing around awkwardly, all elbows and knees and gasping for breath, but I knew that eventually I'd have to take care of Barbra, teach her things, show her what my needs were. That could wait. Right now I wanted to give her all my attention.

Once again I caressed her, moving my fingers upward, inward. "Oh, my God," she exclaimed excitedly, "oh, my God! You're touching me! Stop, stop!" Barbra pulled away and begged me. "Oh, God, Barry, please ... let me catch my breath!"

I stopped and looked down at her. Barbra's cheeks were shiny-wet with kisses. She was gasping for air and smiling up at me with love gleaming out of her eyes. And to my surprise, I found that a deep feeling was stirring inside me. It was sex and it was love, and it was also an overwhelming sense that I was responsible for Barbra.

Stinging tears welled up. Oh, Christ, I was crying. A man isn't supposed to cry at a time like this. I scrambled upright and sat on the side of the bed.

"Whatsa matter?" Barbra asked me, suddenly concerned, sitting up beside me. "Barry, what's the *matter*? Did I hurt something?"

"No," I said. "I don't know. I can't explain."

She leaned toward me, moved close to my face, and looked inquiringly into my eyes. "You okay?" she persisted. "You sure?"

"Yeah. Sure. I'm fine," I said.

"Lie down," she commanded, and pushed me over on my back.

"Barbra..." I began.

"Just shut up and stay lying down," she said, smiling. "It's my turn."

She straddled my hips and then, looking down at me, leaned over and caressed my mouth with hers, her hair brushing my shoulders, her eyes brimming with the sweetest affection. I felt overwhelmed, even though my erection had been washed away in the floodtide of emotion. We stared at each other. I started to realize that this was it for the evening. For our first experience, it had been pretty wonderful.

"Listen," she breathed in a soft, low, intimate voice, "did you ever get those things we talked about? Those condoms?"

"Yeah, I went to the drugstore," I said.

"Where are they?"

"In a paper bag on the top of the fridge."

"You want I should go get them?" she smiled down at me naughtily.

My hard-on was long gone. Nipping around the edges of my mind was the debilitating, guilty thought that maybe I was, well, inadequate. Maybe I didn't like girls. Naw, I liked Barbra a lot. I felt totally mixed up.

Barbra ran her hands down the front of my pajamas and fumbled with the drawstring and buttons, then wiggled her way inside. I watched wide-eyed as she fiddled around for a moment, then stopped. Sitting back on her haunches, she stared at me, perplexed.

"My fingers don't feel anything," she mumbled.

"I'm not surprised," I said ruefully, totally exhausted. "Your nails are so goddamn long."

Barbra snorted and smiled. "I'm not cutting them," she said, "not even for you."

"Listen," I said, "I've gone...soft. And I don't think I can do any more tonight. In fact, I know I can't. I feel all...drained," I finished feebly.

We lay down next to each other on the bed, both staring up at the ceiling. I began to stroke her hair softly.

"Barry," Barbra said finally, "are you worried that we...you know, that we haven't *done* anything yet?"

"No," I said, but I wasn't sure I meant it. "Besides, we have 'done' things. We just haven't done 'it' yet. Anyway, we've got plenty of time to work all this stuff out."

"But listen," she said, "this sex stuff, it's getting me all *ferblunget*, all mixed up. I mean, the thing is, I haven't...been with a lot of boys, you know what I mean? I don't really know what I'm doing...exactly..."

"Sex is very confusing," I agreed, as if I'd owned my own harem at one point and this was all old hat to me.

"Yeah, but does everybody go through this kind of tumult?"

"I think so," I said. "In one way or another."

"But we haven't even...you haven't...you know...," Barbra stammered.

"What?" I said. "Say it. I'm not going to get angry with you."

"You know, you haven't...haven't even...penetrated... there's been no penetration!"

"Barbra," I said, sitting up on one elbow and sounding as mock stern as I could. "A nice Jewish girl like you, and in front of my own ears you're using the 'P' word?"

She laughed, then suddenly her face creased. "No, but seriously, Barry, I'm getting all confused."

"Listen, Barb, I have to tell you," I said, "the truth is, I haven't really made love to a whole lot of girls before, either."

I looked around the room at the candles flickering in their soft pools of light, at our shadows dancing on the walls, hoping she'd intuit that although I wanted to be there for her I didn't know the answer to everything, that in many ways I was groping around in the dark, trying to find my way as much as she was.

After a long pause Barbra spoke, her voice sounding small and lost. "No?" she said.

"No, not really," I confessed. "Twice. And both times turned out with what you might call mixed results."

"What happened?" Barbra asked, a note of practicality coming into her voice as she propped her head up on one elbow and stared at me. I sighed, sat up, turned down the volume on the music, then fumbled around on the coffee table for a cigarette and an ashtray.

"Well, I had a girlfriend at Beverly High. Stephanie. We would make out in the car but she wouldn't let me touch her...breasts. She had nice tits," I said, crawling back on the bed and sitting down beside her.

"Why not?" Barbra said. "Why wouldn't she?"

"I dunno. She was a nice girl and nice girls didn't do that, I guess."

"Do I have nice tits?" Barbra asked. I looked over at her. I'd never seen her look so small and insecure, like a little bird on an ice floe. "Yes," I said, "you have beautiful tits."

"Thanks," Barbra smiled. "God, if my mother heard me talking like this, she'd faint."

"If your mother saw us sitting like this, all naughty and naked..." I began.

"...she'd drop down dead," Barbra finished it for me and slipped her nightshirt back over her head. I helped her pull it down. "She thinks I'm rooming with a girlfriend. So," she persisted, her head popping out of the collar, "tell me about all the other girls you slept with."

"You don't give up, do you?" I said.

"Nope."

"Well, I had a boyfriend at Beverly High, an exchange student. Jean-Maurice. He was having sex with his girlfriend, Harriet, our whole senior year. When we graduated and he went back to Belgium, I tried to fool around with her, but—"

"Go on. So what happened?" Barbra said sitting up, suddenly very alert.

"Well, I felt a little guilty about Jean, like I was betraying him," I tried to explain.

"But he was gone, he was back in Europe," Barbra said. Sometimes her practical assessment of the obvious floored me.

"Anyway, Harriet had her own apartment by then. Her roommate was home, in the bedroom, so we lay down on the floor in the living room."

"She didn't have a sofa?" Barbra said.

I had to smile. "It was too narrow."

"Uh-huh, okay," Barbra said, making herself comfortable, tucking in a pillow behind her back and leaning against the wall. I thought, she's really going to make a meal out of this, sitting there cross-legged like a Talmudic Buddha, to listen to my story, consider rationally all the facts, perhaps even to deliver a cosmic judgment on my youthful sexual peccadillos. She looked so completely absorbed, so involved, so totally—edible.

"Oh, I don't know," I sighed. "The floor was cold and the carpet was scratchy. We could hear her roommate wandering around, flushing the toilet. Then Harriet had to stop halfway through to insert her diaphragm. After that, I couldn't get it up. I can't believe I'm telling you all this," I petered out.

"What happened the second time?" Barbra asked.

"Look, I don't want to talk about it. Oh, all right. The second time, it was a one-night stand, here in New York. The night of the Big Blackout. Patty's roommate from school, Christine. Four months later she called and told me she was pregnant."

"You got her *pregnant?*" Barbra asked, amazed.

"It wasn't difficult," I said defensively. "She told me it was her time of the month, she was absolutely safe, blah-blah-blah, *nothing* could happen. And then next thing she knew...," my voice drifted off.

"Did she want you to marry her?"

"I don't think so. Hey, we weren't in love or anything. It was a one-night stand, for Chrissakes. We hardly knew each other. I told her I'd help her in any way I could."

"Whaddya mean? How could you help her?" Barbra pressed.

I shrugged. "Money?" I offered lamely. Barbra stared at me. I felt my cheeks redden. "Listen, I'm not very proud of all this," I said, looking down at the morass of rumpled sheets and bed-clothes.

"Okay, okay. So what happened?" Barbra asked.

"I didn't know what Christine was going to do but I was very worried about her. A few weeks later she called again and told me she'd met a guy who'd fallen in love with her. Bang, like that."

"Are you kidding?" Barbra exclaimed. "What about the baby?"

"He didn't seem to care that it was someone else's baby, he wanted to take care of her. So they got married."

"Wait a minute, what are you telling me?" Barbra said. "You have an illegitimate kid running around somewhere out there?"

The music finished, the tape ran out and flapped around the take-up reel, and the machine came to a halt.

"Yup," I said, "only he's not running around, he's just a few months old."

"Aren't you dying to know what he looks like, or anything?"

"No, I'm staying way away. Listen, I'm not going to be his real father, the man he's going to call 'Dad.' I'm like some weird sperm donor." Barbra watched me drag a last puff off my cigarette and crush it out.

"So, what else?" she asked.

"That's it for now," I said.

"Oh, yeah?" she said. "I heard there was this girl from Brooklyn you were seeing."

"Yes," I admitted, "there's this singer."

"Actress," she said quickly.

"That's right, this actress slash singer that I'm currently seeing. Yes, that's true."

"I hear she's very cute," Barbra said.

"Oh, yes," I agreed. "*Very* cute. And talented."

"Oh, really?" she said. "You two...fooling around, or anything?"

"We're getting there. Bit by bit. Stay tuned for further adventures in the scandalous sexcapades of little baby Barry. Hey, listen. What say we go to sleep?" I said, wandering around the room, turning off the hi-fi and snuffing out the candles.

Barbra began to tidy up the bed, tucking in the sheets, fluffing up the pillows. "Yeah, all right, all right," she said. "But I wanna hear more about all this."

"Mañana. Let's go to sleep now, huh?" I said, climbing into bed next to her.

We pulled up the covers, kissed and settled down. I looked at Barbra in profile in the dark. Her eyes were closed and she looked contented.

Suddenly her face was right next to mine. "It was nice tonight, Barry," she said.

"Yeah," I agreed. "Very nice."

We gave each other a final kiss and Barbra moved back to her pillow as I rolled over and gazed up at the ceiling. Although in those days I was normally quite reticent about discussing my private sexual affairs with anyone, somehow it was fairly easy with Barbra. We were getting so close to each other in so many ways, and besides, to be a liar you've got to have such a good memory. Hell, she and I were trying to love and have sex with each other, as intimate as two people can get, why shouldn't the truth come out?

But how and when could I bring myself to tell Barbra about Freddy, the blond Dane in Los Angeles who kept inviting me up to his apartment two summers ago to give me oral sex in the hot California afternoons? When would I tell her about Marvin, the teaching assistant at UCLA, whom I invited for dinner to my parents' house and who, with my mother cooking in the kitchen next door, grabbed me by the arm when we were alone in the family room and kissed me open-mouthed, to my distress and intense excitement.

Tomorrow, maybe.

The next morning I was wrapped in a towel, shaving, when there was a knock at the bathroom door.

"Who is it?" I said, and opened the door slightly. Barbra's blue eyes flashed at me through the crack.

"Jes' little ol' me," she said in a syrupy Southern drawl. I handed her a bathrobe as she stared dumbfounded at the lather on my face. "What are you doing?" she asked.

"I'm shaving," I said. "It's what men do."

"I know, I know. God, I don't think I've ever seen a man shave before," she said, "except like in a commercial, or something. Can I watch?"

"Sure. Take a seat," I said, indicating the toilet. Of course Barbra had never seen a man shave, I thought to myself, not even her father. He died when she was only fourteen months old.

"You know, there's a famous scene like this in the play *Victoria Regina,* where Helen Hayes comes into Prince Albert's dressing room on the first morning of their marriage and he's shaving and she asks if she can watch."

"Get out!" Barbra exclaimed. "Just like me, huh?"

"Exactly like you, only she's the Queen of England," I said and soaped up my face a second time.

"What are you doing?" Barbra asked. "You just shaved and you're shaving again?"

"Ja!" I said in a heavy German accent, "I am puttink ze soup back on mein face—Prinz Albert vas German, you know—because I haf got a very heavy beard und if I don't shave tvice, I'd scratch the shit out of you when I kissed you."

"Heavy beard, huh?" Barbra said. "That's very masculine, right?"

I wondered why she was talking about my masculinity all of a sudden. It made me a little nervous. "It's incredibly masculine," was all I could think of to say.

"So what happens in the Queen Victoria play?"

"Nothing happens. She watches him shave and she's worried that he's a 'bleeder,' a hemophiliac, but he isn't. Then Albert tells her she won't always be as interested in watching him shave as she is today. She'll get used to it."

"And I bet she tells him she'll always be as fascinated as she is right now, right?"

"That's right, that's what she tells him."

"What do you think?" she asked.

"I think...she'll get used to it," I said.

"Mmmm, well, I can't say as I agree with you," Barbra said in her best Mae West. "Personally, I'm fascinated. I was fascinated before and I'm fascinated now, and I will always be fascinated in the future."

"I hope that's true," I said, and as I leaned over and kissed her on the mouth, a swath of soap transferred from my face to hers. When we separated, Barbra had a white foam moustache. "C'mere," I said, and stood her up and pointed her toward the mirror. Barbra began to giggle. "You look like Santa Claus," I said.

"That's a fine thing to say to a nice Jewish girl," she laughed, and then, in a pretty good pastiche of an upper-class English accent, she went on, "I say, p'raps you'd better sit there, my good fellow, and watch me finish my shaving."

"Certainly, Your Majesty," I said, unscrewing my razor and carefully placing the blade on the rim of the basin. "Here you go," I added, and handed her the empty razor and took a seat on the throne.

Barbra picked up the can of shaving foam and shook it vigorously. "How do you work this?" she said in her own voice.

"Just press the top."

She did, and a large glop of soap flopped into her hand and spritzed up on the mirror. Barbra laughed even harder as she spread the soap on her face and began to "shave."

"I say, jolly nice of you to come in and watch me shave, Barry," Barbra said. "Tell me, do you like to watch?"

"Sometimes I like to watch," I said, "but mostly I like to participate."

"Good show," she said, and scraped the razor up her neck and over her chin with a flourish. "Oh, my God, I've cut myself!" she screamed.

I stood up in alarm. "You haven't, have you?" I said panicking. "I took the blade out!"

Barbra doubled over laughing. "I'm a bleeder, it's bloody awful!" she laughed.

I took her by the shoulders and shook her. "You scared me," I said in dead earnest. "Don't do that."

Barbra sobered up immediately. "I'm sorry," she said.

"It's okay," I softened, and took a washcloth and gently began wiping the soap off her face. She pressed up against my towel and took little nibbling pecks as I wiped her cheeks.

"Stop that," I said, "I can't concentrate."

She wiggled her hand down in between us, lifted a corner of my towel and with Mae West suddenly back in place said, "Well, well, big boy, whaddya got under there?"

"That's my masculinity, Mae," I replied. "You were wondering what it was getting up to."

"Oh, oh, whatsa matter with your animal?" she asked, and sank down below my eyeline.

"Barbra, don't do that," I said after a moment, and lifted her back up.

"What's wrong?" she asked. "Don't you like that? I thought men liked that."

"Have you ever done that before?" I asked.

"No," she said simply. "But it's interesting. All salty, like a pickle."

"Oh, I'm so sorry," I said. "I'll just roll it in powdered sugar and desiccated coconut and pop it in the freezer for five minutes."

"That's disgusting," she said.

"After what you've been getting up to down there, you naughty girl, you're criticizing me?" I said.

"Not really," she said.

"So, you wanna try some of that tonight?" I suggested.

"Sure. Okay," she said, looking upset. She looked at me piercingly for a long while without speaking. Finally she blurted it out: "What's wrong with *now*?"

"Nothing, honey," I said. "Nothing at all. It's just, I've gotta be uptown for an audition very soon and when we fool around I'd like to be able to take some time, ya know what I mean?"

"Sure, Bar. Sure," she said. She paused and looked down at the floor, then finally looked up at me and said, "Tell me something. Honest. Do you think I'm beautiful?"

Oh, God, I hadn't meant to make her feel insecure.

"I think you're incredibly beautiful," I said. "I'm just gonna be late!"

"Okay," she said, and shrugged, and turned and walked out of the room.

That same day, on my way back to the subway after another hopeless audition for an off-Broadway production of *The Lesson*, I ran into Terry Leong in front of Lord and Taylor. I told him I really needed to find a way to make Barbra feel more confident about her looks. Terry and I both concurred that Barbra's looks were not standard beautiful, but singularly, stunningly unique.

"She's very insecure," Terry agreed, nodding his head sagely.

"Terry, help me. What am I gonna do? How am I gonna convince Barbra she's beautiful?" I implored.

Terry nodded his head again.

"Good luck," he said helpfully, patting me on the arm.

But whatever spirit was watching over us in that blessed season must have heard me, for later that day the gods handed me another incredible stroke of luck on a platter.

That evening, over a brandy stinger, I opened the Arts and Entertainment Section of the *New York Times,* and there, on page 2, my eye fell on a photograph of a statuette currently on exhibit in a borough museum. It was a diminutive, simple little thing, but it gave me such a great idea.

The only trouble was, I had to get Barbra back out to Brooklyn.

8

Cleopatra Eyes

"*I* should never have let you talk me into this," Barbra moaned over the clacking wheels of the subway as it clattered along the rails, trying to rattle the teeth out of our heads as it barreled toward Brooklyn.

"It'll be fine," I reassured her. "We're not going to a forced labor camp. I just want to show you something."

"I don't wanna go to Brooklyn," Barbra complained. "It makes me nervous. I got *shpilkes*, like pins and needles," she said, twisting around in her seat like a cranky child.

The hot summer air blasting from the train windows didn't make either of us feel any cooler, and the churning and shaking of the car was relentless.

"You're just hot. We'll soon be there," I said, glancing up at the subway map for confirmation. "It's only a couple of stops."

"God, I feel like I'm traveling through a tunnel inside a hair dryer," Barbra complained, and reached behind her to pull her damp dress away from her body. "Why am I doing this?" she whimpered.

"This is a special trip. I told you. There's something I want you to see," I reiterated.

When Barbra wasn't given all the facts up front she was impossible.

"Yeah, sure," she said, searching in her bag for a handkerchief and blotting her forehead. "A bird's-eye view of the Brooklyn Bridge."

"Nope," I said. "It's much better than that."

"Why won't you tell me what it is?" she pestered. "C'mon. Tell me. Tell me or I'll pretend to faint, right here, a hundred and fifty feet under Pulaski Street," she threatened.

"As long as we're in Brooklyn," I said, changing the subject but also trying to distract her a little, "when am I gonna meet your mother?"

Barbra looked at me stricken, like I'd tried to stab her. "Never," she stated categorically. "That's when. Never." She rummaged around in her bag, produced a small compact, swirled a large brush over the cake of rouge and started to freshen up the blusher on her cheeks. "Whaddya think?" she asked, displaying her cheekbones for my approval. "Too much?"

"Barbra," I wheedled, not to be deterred, "you've been staggering home from your mother's house with bags and bags full of groceries. She sends us enough food to feed a Prussian battalion—chopped liver, potato pancakes, chicken soup, matzo balls. It never stops. We could open a restaurant and still have leftovers," I said. "At least let me call her up, thank her for the soup."

"No," she insisted stubbornly, snapping the rouge compact closed and pitching it back in her purse. "I already thanked her," she declared dourly, the edges of her cute, petulant mouth plunging downward. "Consider her thanked."

I had been struck, early in our friendship, at how tight-mouthed Barbra was about her home life and how far away from it she wanted to keep all her friends. She'd told me the barest of essentials: her real father, the beloved Manny, had died when she was fourteen months old, too young for her to know or remember him. Several years later, her mother had married what sounded like a mega-monster of a stepfather, one Louis Kind, whom Barbra loathed with unabashed fervor. He had screamed at and belittled her mother in a series of blood-curdling, daily arguments. He hated Barbra with a burning passion, and never passed up an opportunity to ridicule her, belittle her, to point out how ugly she was, or how uncomfortable and clumsy she looked in her clothing. It sounded like a living nightmare. No wonder she didn't want to talk about it.

As the train roared into the station in one of those vertiginous, warp-speed 9 decelerations that sent grown men hurtling down the car like Nureyev, Barbra folded her arms and pressed her back against the wall.

"But Barbra, it's rude," I insisted wickedly, not able to stop myself from enjoying the mother angst I was stirring up inside her. I understood about mothers. I had one of my own.

"No. No. It's not possible," Barbra anguished. "She doesn't have a telephone. So that's it," she said, as if the subject were irrevocably closed.

"No telephone?" I said, raising my eyebrows but keeping a straight face. I had a famous poker face; it was really hard to break me up. "What are you saying?" I pressed. "She can't afford a telephone?"

"Yeah, well, sure she had a phone, but she dropped it out of a window," Barbra replied.

The train completed its violent halt and with a noisy flourish, the doors flew open. A couple of people got on and a few got off.

"What are you talking about?" I said. "That's the most improbable thing I ever heard in my life."

"Oh. Yeah. Well," Barbra explained.

"I'm sorry," I said. "I'm having a hard time believing you."

The doors slammed shut, reopened suddenly for no apparent reason, then banged shut once more and the train lurched forward up the track.

Barbra sighed. "She was sitting on the ledge, talking to my brother, Shelly," she explained, "and she got all excited about something and the phone went flying out the window. Smashed to smithereens," she finished with an off-hand insouciance, as if this sort of thing went on every day in her mother's household.

"So?" I said. "Why doesn't she get a new one from the phone company?"

"Oh, she tried!" Barbra hinted darkly, as if the effort involved in getting a new telephone was as emotionally unnerving as having a mystical experience. "They're all out. No more phones until November. She's on a waiting list."

I knew Barbra was hammering yet another nail in the closed door that led to her past, a barrier that would remain firmly shut and locked forever. Of *course* her mother had a telephone. This was America: *everyone* had a telephone.

I harumphed. "You just don't want me to talk to your mother, do you?" I accused her.

There was an enforced pause while the subway car took a sharp corner, rocking us violently from side to side, and the wheels began their awful, excruciating screech, like a massed chorus of dentists' drills. Up the tunnel, I could see the station lights ahead as they swung into view and the train started to slow its hurtling catapult toward the platform.

"That's right, Barry," Barbra informed me in no uncertain terms, pitching her voice above the shrieking metal. "No talking to mothers."

"You know something?" I yelled, "I don't even know your mother's name."

"It's Diana, Diana Kind," Barbra shouted. "She's a kind woman. That's how you can remember her name."

"And was she kind to you?" I asked.

There was a longish pause.

"Kinda," Barbra said. "Come on, kid, this is our station," she added and stood up, waiting impatiently for the doors to open.

As we walked the short distance from the subway stop to the Brooklyn Museum, I asked Barbra if this was near the part of town where she used to live.

"Not really," she said. "I guess it's not far," she added. Her voice was low. She seemed embarrassed, subdued.

"Why don't you take me to your old neighborhood?" I asked suddenly. "Show me around, where you used to live?"

"No. No, I can't," she balked. "It isn't there anymore. It's all torn down."

Barbra put on some speed as we crossed the street. She never looks back, I thought with wonderment. I'm always looking back, over my shoulder, back to the past, but she never does.

Barbra was always rushing forward, as if afraid she'd be late for her life.

As we came through the front door of the Brooklyn Museum into the entrance hall, a cool breeze hit us and I could feel the sticky heat of the afternoon begin to evaporate almost at once. The hollow, underwater echoes of voices and the scuffling of feet ricocheted around the ceilings of the side galleries as we studied a map to find the place I was looking for.

"Hey, look," Barbra said as we passed the museum store, "they got a gift shop."

"Maybe we can pick up some goodies on our way out," I said, shepherding her in the right direction.

We passed a couple of cute young guys in tight jeans and white T-shirts, one dark-haired with a ducktail and the other blond in a crew cut. Could they be lovers? I wondered. I like museums, but I always wind up looking at the people in them rather than at the art.

Barbra and I walked through several rooms of expressionist and modern paintings. In one gallery, a young, good-looking sailor squeezed into his whites and his girlfriend were gazing up at a large cubist nude, possibly a Picasso.

"Looka that," the sailor marveled. "She's got an eye where her tits oughta be," he said, a little too loudly.

"Honey, shut up," the girlfriend protested, embarrassed.

The sailor, showing off, grabbed her around the waist and pulled her in closer, reaching over to feel her up. "C'mere," he said, "you got something in your eye."

"Stop that!" she said, and slapped his hand away as Barbra and I continued through the room and out the far door. God, I thought, it must be wonderful to be so uncomplicated and uninhibited—and so butch.

Finally we found the gallery on which depended the success or failure of my plan.

This part of the museum was cool and quiet, away from the packs of goofing-off school kids being led around in bunches. Even the guards seemed not to bother much with the Egyptian wing. Occasionally one would walk by the portal, peer briefly into the room, then slowly shuffle away. Barbra and I stared into the glass and wooden cases.

In front of us, laid out on velvet, was the Queen of the Nile's jewelry, beautiful beaten-gold foil necklaces studded with blue-green, lapis lazuli scarabs in gold wire cartouches.

"Nice stuff, huh?" Barbra exclaimed softly, stuffing a stick of gum into her mouth.

"Yeah," I agreed.

"These things would look good on me," she sighed.

Top: Barbra's moth costume, in layers of grey chiffon, for *The Insect Comedy* (1960).

Right: This 1900s bodice of jet and gunmetal sequins combined with a black velvet skirt was designed by Terry Leong for Barbra's extended run at The Lion (1960). Sketches ©Terry Leong.

Photo inset: Terry Leong in Paris, ca. 1963.

Our little den of iniquity. ©1996 Barry Dennen.

Left: Barbra faces the New York winter in a heavy wool coat and *sunglasses,* already. ©1996 Barry Dennen.

Below: Me, at the time this book takes place. ©1996 Barry Dennen.

This and next two pages: A chic Sunday at home: we ate brunch, read the papers, played old records, danced, and I took these shots of a beautiful eighteen-year-old Barbra. ©1996 Barry Dennen.

Me, behind the lens, taking a picture of Bob Schulenberg taking a picture of Barbra. ©1996 Barry Dennen.

Above, left: Here's Barbra unadorned: young, fresh-faced, and sweet. *Above, right:* Here's Barbra in her Schulenberg-designed makeup: cool, elegant, divine. ©Robert Schulenberg.

Right: Barbra onstage at the Bon Soir, where all the magic first came together. Anyone who saw her sing there will never forget it. Photos by Craig Simpson.

Below: A table card from Barbra's supper club debut at the Bon Soir. The printer was obviously short on spelling skills. Barbra had already changed her name and "Phyliss" doesn't fare much better. On the back Barbra scribbled out a shopping list and reminded herself to bring a stool for sitting.

Bon Soir
presents
In order of appearance

Jimmie Daniels
Barbara Streisand
Phyliss Diller
Tony and Eddie

Music by
Peter Daniels
The Three Flames

Backstage at the Bon Soir, in their claustrophobically crowded dressing room, Barbra and Phyllis Diller, a protective hand firmly in place. ©Robert Schulenberg.

The cast of
"I Can Get It For You Wholesale" invites

Barré Dennen

to a party in honor of

Barbra Streisand's Twentieth Birthday

tendered by Irene Kuo at the

Lichee Tree Restaurant
65 East 8th Street
New York City

on Thursday, May 10th, at midnight

Admission by invitation only

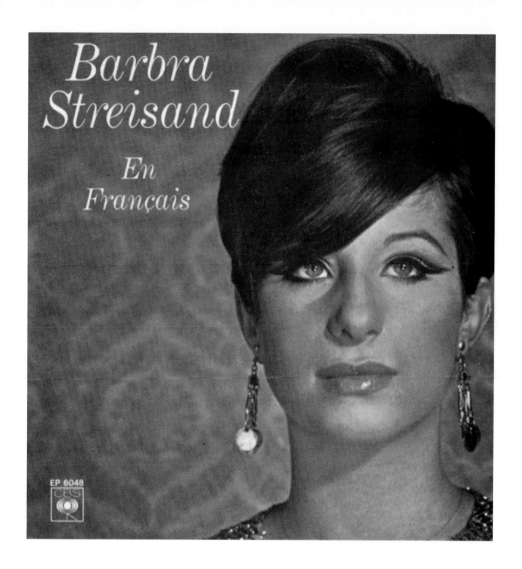

Barbra Streisand

En Français

EP 6048

CBS

Opposite page, top: The invitation to Barbra's celebrity-stuffed twentieth-birthday party.

Opposite page, bottom: Barbra in her new apartment, the day before she went out of town with *Wholesale* (p. 229). ©1996 Barry Dennen.

This page: I was always playing French songs for Barbra, several of which appeared on the LP version of this album. She sent this EP (extended play) to me as a gift and expressed the hope that I'd like it. *Barbra Streisand en français*, EP 6048. ©CBS Records.

Jon and Caleigh Peters
would like to invite you
to join them in celebrating
the child in you
with your children

Come to
Barbra Joan Streisand's
Birthday Party
She's 50 years young!

Saturday, April 25, 1992
3:00 p.m. into the evening
#9 Beverly Park
Beverly Hills

Please R.S.V.P. by April 18th
Alex (310) 246-4859
Casual dress

Another birthday, Barbra's fiftieth, which I may or may not have attended (p. 270).

"They go with your eyes. Maybe I'll buy you one for Christmas."

"You can't afford it," she commented. "It's not in the budget."

"I could steal it for you," I offered.

"Sure. Why not?" she asked and added, "And when you do, don't forget the earrings!"

Then I spied what I was looking for up ahead and deftly steered Barbra down the aisle toward it.

There, in a glass case all her own, lit by one judicious spotlight, was a painted plaster bust of Nefertiti, wearing a tight headdress of gold beads arranged in a classic bob. Somehow it reminded me of the way Louise Brooks, the ravishing silent-film star, wore her hair.

"You ever see *Pandora's Box*?" I asked her.

"*Whose* box?" Barbra asked.

"It's a silent movie about this high-class whore named Lulu. It's good," I added.

Barbra's voice level rose. "Silent movies are boring. I *hate* them. Nobody *talks*!" she complained. She cracked her chewing gum for a moment and thought about things.

"She's beautiful, Nefertiti," I said, turning to look at Barbra's face beside me. "You know," I added, "she looks a lot like you."

Barbra winced, as though she were stabbed by a sudden toothache.

"No. No," she said, shaking her head slightly.

"Sure she does," I said. "Look at her big, liquid eyes. The black eyeliner. If Nefertiti's eyes were blue, that could be a statuette of you."

"I don't think so," Barbra stammered. "I don't like..." her voice trailed off.

"She's got your neck, your eyebrows, your ears," I went on, not letting her off the hook. "You're the Nefertiti of Brooklyn."

Barbra slumped, her hand moved up to her forehead, the fingers curving over like a swan's broken wing.

"What's the matter?" I wanted to know. "You got a headache? You want to go the cafeteria, get some tea?"

"It's her *nose!*" she blurted out, her hand flapping away from her face. "Just get a load of that *schnozz!*" she exclaimed, shaking her head. "If she's got anything, she's got my nose!"

Barbra looked around desperately, as if she were searching for the nearest exit, then stopped and with an enormous effort of willpower, took control of herself. She took a deep breath and put her hand on my chest, intimately. "Listen," she said softly, "you gotta tell me the truth. You think I should change my nose?"

"No," I answered decisively. "Don't even *think* about changing your nose."

"It's such a *beak*," Barbra muttered, then looked at the statuette thoughtfully. "Well, at least no one ever told her to change *her* nose," she finished, giving her gum one last, decisive crack, then added, "They wouldn't dare. She'd cut off their heads, or whatever they did in those days."

"How could she change her nose?" I asked. "There were no plastic surgeons in ancient Egypt."

Barbra considered a moment, thoughtfully chewing her lip.

"She could walk into a wall."

I put my hands on Barbra's arms and drew her in toward me. "Listen," I said. "I really mean this, so listen: don't change your nose. Never. Don't even think about it. It's wonderful and so are you. Besides, it might affect your voice," I said, and gave her a soft smooch on the tip. Barbra giggled shyly, and turned her head away.

"You know something?" I said. Without looking back at me she shook her head. I knew I had her. What I was saying might be hard for her to hear, but she was believing me. "They might not call you pretty," I went on, "but someday they're going to say you're *beautiful*."

Barbra looked back at me, stunned, and suddenly our lips were together and our tongues were darting in and out of each other's mouths.

A sudden delighted burst of childish laughter startled us, and we broke apart and looked. Standing in a little bouquet was a circle of eight-year-olds, giggling with embarrassment and delight in their girlish sopranos. A short, stout teacher, her cheeks mottled with popping red veins, bustled them off in the other direction.

"Right this way, children," she honked, "I think the mummy and his artifacts are over here."

Barbra looked back at me, radiant, unguarded, unthinkingly happy.

"Hey," she said. "Why don't you buy me some postcards?"

The shop was a treasure trove. They offered an opulent selection of cards, art books, posters, bronzes, sculptures, even a wooden case of reproduction jewelry from their collection spanning ancient Greece to art deco.

I left Barbra leaning over the illuminated counter, the light reflecting up into her face and hair like a De La Tour painting, her long fingernail gently tapping on the glass to show the sales assistant the piece she wanted to look at.

I dashed into the men's room, faced off against the urinal and unbuttoned my jeans. I needed to pee so badly I was aching. Finally there was a painful surge of liquid, but a moment later the lavatory door banged opened and the sailor in whites sauntered into the tiled restroom. It was so sudden and alarming I almost froze up. The little butch number looked around. We were the only ones there. Although every urinal was available he sidled up to the fixture right next to mine and began unsnapping the buttons on his fly: pop, pop, pop. Then I sensed him pull out his dick.

I tried not to look over but I couldn't help it. His unexpectedly pale penis cradled in both his hands, the sailor took aim at the white porcelain trough in front of him. With a sigh of relief, he suddenly squirted a forceful yellow stream that splashed up and bubbled around the blue sanitizer cake in the bottom of the bowl. It seemed to go on forever, then dribbled dry, followed by a few short, throbbing squirts.

Then suddenly he turned his head, looked me right in the eye and winked. "Hey," he whispered, tossing his head toward the toilet stalls as a sexy smirk crinkled his cheeks, "ya wanna have a quickie?" In sharp detail, like one of Weegee's flash photographs, I registered his freckles, his pale red eyelashes, his inviting blue eyes. My heart thumped.

He gave his dick one sharp shake, and I saw the last drop fly from its tip, splatter down and spot his pants. Hot with confusion and desire I looked away, rapidly stuffed myself back into my jeans and hurried out of the men's room without even washing my hands.

I almost ran across the expanse of floor back to the museum shop, my sneakers squeaking in protest across the marble squares. What was I doing? What in the world did I think I was doing?

When I came up to the sales counter Barbra wasn't where I left her, so I went around to the other side. There she was, gazing at herself in a mirror on the counter. "Barb," I began, and she spun around to look at me.

On her head Barbra was wearing a reproduction of the Nefertiti headdress. It hung down in a golden, beaded pageboy, framing her face, and I realized my prophesy had come true right in front of my eyes.

For suddenly Barbra looked amazingly beautiful, stylized and sensuous, unapproachable and desirable, all at the same time. She was breathtaking: regal, chic, androgynous, sexy, like reincarnated ancient royalty; magical and divine, like an earth goddess.

A loud bell went off in my head, and I felt my brain circuits were overloading. Between the way Barbra looked, which stopped me cold and sent shivers up my back, and my upsetting men's room adventure, which was throwing all my feelings and reactions into a tumultuous confusion, I was completely disoriented and disturbed.

"So, whaddya think?" she said. "Do I look like a queen?"

That's just the question I was asking myself.

"Whatsa matter, Barry?" Barbra said, looking at me more closely, concerned. "You don't look so good."

"I just feel…a little dizzy, that's all," I managed. "I'm sure," I croaked, "it's the heat."

"Look," she said, sounding worried, "let's sit down for a minute. There's some benches over there."

"I'm okay," I said, "I just felt funny for a moment. Come here, I want to show you something."

"You sure?" Barbra said. "You still look a little pale."

"Come here," I said, taking her by the shoulders and spinning her around to face the mirror on the counter. Barbra looked at her reflection, then at me standing behind her, over her shoulder. "What do you see?" I asked her.

"Uh…I see Barbra Streisand in a funny gold Egyptian hat," she said.

"Look again," I demanded. Barbra turned her head this way and that. The strands of gold beads chinked against each other, fell into place.

"Look," I said. "Look, Barbra. You look beautiful."

"Yeah," she said finally. "It's kinda cute." She pulled the head-dress off and laid it down on the counter. "But," she added, "it's definitely not day wear."

On the subway back home Barbra was reflective and quiet. She stared out the car windows at the tunnel rushing by, her eyes heavy and tired looking.

"What are you thinking about?" I asked her.

Barbra put her arm around mine. "Nothing," she said. "Nothing really."

"I know what you're thinking about," I said.

"What?" she asked.

"Your nose," I said.

Barbra punched me lightly. "Oh, you think you're so smart," she said. "You're not so smart."

"You've got something there," I confessed. "Hey, do you know the story of the Ugly Duckling?"

"Sure," Barbra said. "Hans Christian Andersen. Wasn't he homosexual?" she asked.

My heart stopped. "Uh, yeah, I think he was," I said.

"He was Danish, too," she added.

"That's right," I said. "Well, at the end of the story, you remember after everyone's kicked the Ugly Duckling around and told him to go away, he looks in the water and sees this beautiful swan."

"Yeah," Barbra said and yawned. "And that's him," she finished.

"Reflected in the water, just like Narcissus," I replied. "And Hans Christian Andersen writes, 'It doesn't matter that you're born among ducks if you've been hatched from a swan's egg.' Or something like that."

"That's nice," Barbra said, and leaned her head on my shoulder. "That's a nice story. I'm sleepy," she said drowsily. "Don't let us go past our station."

"I won't," I promised. "I'll wake you up."

9

A Doll's House

*W*hen Barbra finally moved in with me, 69 West 9th Street was still a brand-new building and we were the very first tenants in our apartment. You walked into the lobby, called upstairs on the speakerphone, were whisked to the twelfth floor in a spanking-clean elevator, walked down the spare, carpeted hallway and rang the bell on apartment 12A. But when our door opened, it was something else.

In stark contrast to the uncluttered lines of the building itself, our apartment was ... richly filled. In fact, it was stuffed and crammed in every inch of space with feathers, fans, antiques, candles, books, records, recording equipment, tapes, costumes, lace, clocks, plants, flowers, vases, Mission Oak furniture, paisley, posters, playbills, scripts, dolls, puppets, ventriloquist's dummies, scales, glass fruit, hats, headdresses—in short, *everything*. When Barbra shared a dressing room with Phyllis Diller at the Bon Soir, Phyllis dropped by the apartment one afternoon to have a cup of tea with us. I don't know what she expected—an uncluttered glass-top coffee table and two minimalist chairs, perhaps—but when she first walked in, she was floored. The effect was impressive.

In any case, it was a real pleasure to be finally living in New York in a freshly painted apartment, to be able to walk into the kitchen, flip on the switch and not find a hundred and seventy-seven *cucarachas* caught in the light and scurrying for the exits.

Late one morning I entered the kitchen to find Barbra next to the fridge, a piece of toasted bagel and cream cheese halfway to her mouth. "Hi," she said, and popped it in. She was wearing a crinkly, light summer dress and smart, simple heels.

"Hi," I said. "How come you're all pootzed up?"

"I'm meeting my girlfriend, Marilyn, for lunch," she explained between chomps.

"So why are you eating? It's almost lunchtime. Is this a pre-lunch lunch?"

"Sort of," she answered, licking the cream cheese off her fingers. "I figure if I eat something now, I won't eat so much when I go out. It'll be cheaper," she added, as if it were self-explanatory.

"So at least sit down. Only Jews eat standing up," I told her.

"Since when are you such an expert?" she countered. "You're only half a Jew."

As she smiled slyly, I moved to the sink and began to deal with a stack of dishes piled up there, scraping leftovers into the trash and rinsing off the plates.

"What are you doing?" she asked.

"What does it look like I'm doing? I'm washing the dishes."

"Yeah, but there's no soap," she pointed out.

"First I'm washing the food off the dishes, then I'll use some soap," I said.

Barbra looked puzzled. "So, you're washing the dishes *before* you wash the dishes?" she asked.

134

"That's right," I said. "I try to do everything I really like at least twice."

"Well," she said archly, doing her best Mae West, "I like a man who's good with his hands."

What was she up to, I wondered. She was being so sweetly provocative. Then suddenly a little *ping* went off in my head.

I remembered something that had happened a few days earlier. I had been playing a 10-inch LP of Gertrude Lawrence singing songs from Cole Porter's *Nymph Errant*. Barbra had been listening to these records with half an ear, going through her clothes in the closet, pulling garments out, looking at their hems, their sleeves, then hanging them carefully back in place. When she'd finished, she closed the closet door and came back into the living room, cuddling up next to me on the sofa bed.

"So, what's so special about this Gertrude Lawrence person?" Barbra asked. "She can't sing, she's squeaky, she's flat." She picked up the album cover, flipped it and pored over the photographs. "And," she went on, "she has a *really* big conk. I hope she was better-looking than her pictures," she added, in her arbitress of glamour mode.

"Barbra," I said, "listen to her. Listen *through* the squeaks and the faulty pitch. What do you hear?"

"Uh . . . an English accent?" she offered.

"Yeah, but no. Gertrude Lawrence took a very little talent and a great deal of charm a long, long way. She was the quintessence of *vulnerability*. She was a big, glamorous star, but she made every man in the audience feel like she was singing only to him. They all wanted to wrap her up and take her home with them after every performance. She was probably the most calculating, clear-headed woman in show business, but she made men everywhere feel like they wanted to tuck her up in bed. 'Someone to Watch over Me,' that was her song, she introduced it. What you are hearing, Barb, is the heart of femininity."

Barbra went very still for a moment, looked down at the floor and licked her lip, thinking. Something about it bothered her.

"So what are you saying?" she finally asked me. "She wasn't really feminine but she *pretended* to be feminine?"

"Not exactly," I said softly. "She wasn't really helpless but she made you *think* she was helpless."

"Huh!" Barbra snorted. "Not very truthful, is it?"

"Barbra," I said, "it's called *acting*."

This conversation all came back to me in the kitchen as I stood there washing the dishes. She popped the last bite of bagel into her mouth, then distractedly leaned over to examine what might be a run in her stocking. She moistened a finger, extended her shapely right leg, and dabbed it with a morsel of saliva, cocking her head and looking up at me out of the corner of her eye.

"So, which half of you is a Jew?" she asked provocatively.

I got it. Barbra was learning how to flirt. I stared right back at her, raising an eyebrow.

"The bottom half," I said, and threw my sponge into the sink, then suddenly whirled around toward her. "C'mere," I said, lowering my voice to a dangerous growl and lifting my wet, soapy hands in the air. Then I lurched toward her, wiggling my fingers like a movie monster, dishwater dripping a trail of droplets on the floor. "C'mere, little girlie," I slobbered, tottering jerkily toward her like the Slime Creature, "gimme a kiss."

"No! No!" she shrieked and doubled over in the middle, starting to giggle helplessly as if I were going to grab her and tickle her.

"C'mere, c'mere," I said, lunging for her but allowing her to escape past me, "let me squeeze your firm, young, nubile breasts!"

"Help, somebody, anybody, help!" she called out, laughing hysterically, tip-tapping away on her little high heels, and disappeared into the living room.

We were living together in a kind of daydream, watching Astaire-Rogers, Busby Berkeley, and Shirley Temple films, then playing back the soundtracks of "Isn't This a Lovely Day" or "At the Codfish Ball" and dancing on the beds, table tops, and chairs. To our unbelievable delight, a season of Mae West pictures started to be shown late at night.

We snuggled up together one night in front of the television set and thrilled as Mae sang "My Old Flame" with the Duke Ellington Orchestra.

"Boy," I said, "it would take someone with Mae West's clout to insist on bringing the whole Ellington Orchestra to Hollywood in those days."

"Why? Because they were black?" Barbra asked incredulously.

"Absolutely," I said. "Listen, when Billie Holiday was on the road with Artie Shaw, they made her use the restaurant entrance and the service elevator in the hotels they played."

"Unbelievable," Barbra said.

Mae finished the song with a flourish. "Now watch," I said as the band charged into one final, very marked, big brassy instrumental chorus and Mae West took a long, slow, majestic exit up a long, curved flight of stairs.

"That's incredible," Barbra marveled.

"Yeah, I bet she had a fight royale with the Paramount brass to keep that in."

Another night we watched *I'm No Angel*, and were impressed by the scene in Mae's apartment in which she and Cary Grant sit side by side at a grand piano and skip back and forth between dialogue and singing in the number "I Want You, I Need You."

"Now normally," I explained, "they would have prerecorded the entire vocal, but look, it's pretty clear that there would have been no way to do that with this song. See: first she sings, then she cracks a joke, then he talks, then she sings some more..."

"Shush, I'm listening," Barbra said. I looked over at her profile. Without turning her head away from the TV, she added, "Well, I *am!*"

We were living together, all right, but we really didn't have a clue *how* to live with someone else. We were making it up as we went along and a lot of games got played. I don't mean psychological games, although we had our share of those, too, but real games we invented for each other and played together.

"Dead Movie Star" was a game we played mainly in large department stores, and sometimes restaurants. In the game we were married, only one of us was the eponymous "Movie Star" who had died in a plane crash and only the surviving spouse could see them. It was thrilling to come up Bloomingdales' elevator into the Fashion Electrics Department and find Barbra standing there, dead, and have her whisper things into my ear while I was shopping, words from the Other Side, words only I could hear:

"Don't buy that blender, darling. It's got a short. It's defective. Buy that Osterizer over there."

Another game we played at home was "My Hero." We both lay on the bed, side by side, and the rules were that the edge of the bed was a precipice over a yawning, treacherous mountain gorge. We'd tangle our arms around each other's bodies and then with a violent lurch Barbra would roll off the brink, yelling, "Help! Help! Save me! I'm falling!" I'd struggle and strain to haul Barbra back from the abyss amidst shrieks and shouts from both of us, because if she touched the floor with any part of her body, she was dead. With one final effort I'd eventually haul her up on top of me and Barbra would scream, "*My Hero!*" and kiss me on the mouth.

In Jean Cocteau's book *Les Enfants Terribles*, Paul and Elizabeth are a brother and sister who live a hermetic, encapsulated life in a large apartment with their ill mother. They also play a series of dangerous games with each other, one of which is the shoplift-

138

ing of entirely meaningless, useless objects for the sole purpose of experiencing the thrill and adrenaline rush of possibly getting caught, for the intense pleasure of nearly dying of fear. When I told Barbra about the novel and described this game, her eyes glowed like pearls in the dark.

To leap forward for a moment, shortly after Barbra got her big break at the Bon Soir, she and I wanted to celebrate, so I took my father's trusty charge card and made a reservation at the Brasserie, the wonderful but, for our pocket books, ultra-expensive eatery in the Seagrams Building.

We ordered carefully, because although my dad had told me to use his card whenever I liked, I still felt quite guilty about it and embarrassed I wasn't making enough money myself to be able to afford a night out like this. But what a wonderful evening it was. We ordered our favorite things and toasted Barbra's imminent success at the club.

When my coffee came, it was accompanied by a beautiful little cream pitcher, the kind of hand-painted jug you find manufactured in the French or Italian country potteries, little flowers and fruits in bright, fresh colors decorating its bowl and handle. Barbra wanted it. She held it up, admired it, and after I'd used all the cream, she said out of the side of her mouth, "I wonder if I could get away with pinching this."

"I dare you," I challenged her.

"Whaddya say? You think I can pull it off?" she asked, surreptitiously dropping the pitcher into the napkin in her lap.

"I double dare you," I replied, watching her arms move ever so slightly as under the table her hands wiped the milky residue out of the little jug with her napkin. Then she opened her purse, ostensibly to check her makeup.

"So? What could happen?" she said.

"I'll visit you in jail, I promise," I answered, not believing my eyes as Barbra slyly slid the pitcher inside her purse and snapped it shut with a click of triumph.

The waiter arrived and asked if we wanted anything more, and when I said no, he delivered the check, cleared away the dirty dishes, and exited into the kitchen. Barbra gave me a cocky little wink.

"I can't believe it, sweetheart," I said like Bogie out of the corner of my mouth. "I think we got away with it."

When I opened the little leather folder that contained the check, my eyeballs nearly popped out of my head on springs. It was for eighty-four dollars! Now, remember in those days a loaf of bread was twenty cents, our dinners at Pam Pam averaged a dollar and a half, including tip. For eighty-four dollars I could have bought a whole new *refrigerator* and filled it with food, for God's sake!

My eyes flew down the list of charges: Brandy Stinger, iced tea, Steak Tartare, Caesar salad, coffee, and...oops! There it was, inscribed in the waiter's dainty little hand: "One Cream Pitcher. Sixty dollars. We Accept Diner's Club." Red-faced and chagrined, I called the waiter over and explained it was a celebration for us and we just wanted some little...momento of the evening and didn't realize how, uh...*valuable* that little piece of pottery was, and having received the purloined pitcher under the table from Barbra, I placed it down firmly in front of him. With a knowing smirk, the waiter struck off the exorbitant extra charge, and as if the little cream jug were a naughty, errant child, he pinched it by the handle between his fingers and led it off to the kitchen.

As we reached the door I said, "Come on. Pretend we're the prince and princess, in disguise, and we've gone out into the city for a night on the town and nobody recognizes us, nobody knows we're rich and famous and powerful."

Noses in the air, we sailed out of the Brasserie majestically, but once we hit the sidewalk we looked at each other, snorted, fell into the back seat of a cab and headed downtown, doubled over with laughter and chagrin.

About this time, a friend of mine won a nice sum of money on a television quiz show and came to visit me in New York, bringing a small film canister full of pot as a gift. One night soon after I talked Barbra into smoking some with me. At first she was very suspicious and cautious about the whole thing.

"This isn't gonna make me go crazy, is it? Ya know, ripping off all my clothes and trying to fly off the balcony?" she asked with trepidation.

"No, not at all," I reassured her. "You'll just get a little buzz and relax."

Barbra had smoked cigarettes before, but very warily and hesitantly. She didn't like the flavor or the harshness, and she never let the inhalation enter her lungs. She just liked the effect of the smoke escaping her mouth in a sophisticated ribbon. I'd watch fascinated as Barbra stood in front of a mirror examining her reflection as the gray fumes curled up around her face: heavy-lidded, mysterious, a Dietrich-like sphinx.

I rolled a joint for us in some yellow Bambu papers on the cover of a *New Yorker* magazine.

"You know, Freud was very interested in drugs," I said, "their effect on consciousness and the human psyche. He took cocaine, too, wrote a whole book about it."

"*Freud* took *cocaine?*" Barbra said, outraged, taking the joint from me, looking dubiously at the glowing lit end and taking a cautious puff.

"Yeah, good old Dr. Siggie," I said. "A brave man."

"Brave?" she questioned.

"To be all alone and look inside yourself so deeply? Oh, yes," I said.

"Well, well, Dr. Freud a cocaine sniffer. Who could believe such a thing? That nice old Jewish man. Say, this isn't bad," she commented, passing the joint back to me.

"It's a lot better for you than cigarettes. Watch: take it in with a stream of air," I said, demonstrating, and passed the doobie back to her.

"Hmmm," Barbra said, and executed the maneuver perfectly. "I feel a little light-headed…but fine!"

"Hold it in your lungs for a moment, then let it out through your nose."

The next thing I knew we were both naked and Barbra was behind me, running her nails down my back. Immediately she went into Mae:

"See, my nails are good for somethin'," she said, slowly and sensuously traversing my spine from my shoulder blades down to my rump.

"God, that feels good," I mumbled.

"Oh, uh…you're all tense and nervous, big boy," she commented, peering over my shoulder at my stiffening penis.

"Don't stop," I croaked breathlessly. "That's so nice…"

"Hmmm," she mused. "Whatsa matter with your animal? He looks all stretched and…stiff. You oughta let him out more, take him for walks."

"Don't make me laugh," I murmured in a sensual ecstasy.

"Why not?"

"Sex and humor don't go together," I said, and spun around and kissed her.

Finally, out came the condoms.

10

Getting Her Act Together

*N*ear the end of June, after winning several weeks of talent contests at The Lion, one of the owners told us the exciting news: he was setting up an audition for Barbra at the Bon Soir. Now the Bon Soir was a famous room which opened in September 1949. Ethel Waters, Mae Barnes, Phyllis Diller, Kaye Ballard, and Larry Storch had played there, and Mildred Bailey in her last years. It was described by Mort Sahl in *Esquire*'s guide as "a relaxed, *intime*, rococo, chichi, offbeat club." And for Barbra's and my sakes, he might have added that although it was only around the corner and one small block further downtown, it was a great, big, fat, important step *up* from The Lion.

This was an amazingly fecund time in off-Broadway theater, cabarets, and nightclubs. Revues sprang up like mushrooms after the rain. It seemed like every time you stood up or sat down, someone was putting on a revue, with talents like Charles Nelson Reilly, Ruth Buzzi, Dom DeLuise, Bea Arthur, and Linda Lavin. I can recall Dudley Moore tinkling the lounge bar piano downstairs at the Duplex, where "Mama" Cass Elliott checked coats, long before either of them became famous.

And everyone was getting a nightclub act together. Upstairs at the Duplex, wonderful Jan Wallman would nightly introduce the likes of Woody Allen, Rodney Dangerfield, and Dick Cavett, who were constantly trying out new material. I remember one night when Barbra was doing a guest spot and Woody was standing at the back of the room looking glazed and nervous, waiting to go on next, probably going through his material in his head. As Barbra finished to wild applause, I walked past him and said, "What did you think of the singer?" He shot me a look like a frightened doe and said, "*What* singer?"

We all knew each other, and we were all trying to make it. When Second City opened in the Village, I got a call from a worried Joan Rivers, who had just joined their company on a sort of trial basis. "Please, Barry," she implored me, "I'm on, and it's Saturday night. Come over—and laugh!" Joan was wonderful, as always, but the comic actor who really caught my eye that evening was this really strange but amazingly funny fellow from England—John Cleese.

But of all the Village clubs, the Bon Soir was the tops. Coming in off the street, you clutched the hand rail as you tried not to tumble down a dizzyingly steep flight of stairs, then groped your way into a room painted entirely in black and so dimly lit, you suspected it might be to hide the dirt. The only real light in the room was a small, shaded bulb over the cash register at the bar, which was tacitly gay and rather raucous. When what little light there was in the room dimmed to pitch black and the performers came on, one might encounter a lot of furtive, illicit hanky-panky in the three-deep crowd of men standing there nursing their drinks. The room had an alive, energized atmosphere, friendly to performers, no small credit to The Three Flames, the all-black, good-time house band.*

"Barry," Barbra said to me, panicking, immediately after we heard the news, "what if they don't like me at the Bon Soir?"

"Hey," I said, "they are going to love you, and they're going to want you."

"They're really gonna hire me? Ya think?" Barbra asked, not daring to believe.

"They're going to fall all over you," I assured her, and sent up a silent prayer, just to be safe.

In the first week of July, on Barbra's last evening at The Lion, I caught her act, took notes, pushed through the crowd, and ran back across the street to field a late-night phone call from the airport.

Bob Schulenberg, my friend from UCLA, was arriving in New York. Bob was a short, handsome, talented fellow, an illustrator who at one time had trained to be a concert pianist, and who was coming to New York to work on the very important Celanese account for Ellington & Company, a medium-size advertising agency with a chic midtown address on Fifth Avenue.

Bob is a pack rat; he throws nothing, but nothing, away. Actually, to say that Bob hangs on to things is like saying Jascha Heifitz plays the fiddle: wherever Bob lives is stacked to the ceiling with the collected artifacts of an entire lifetime. There is literally no empty surface anywhere, not even a chair to sit in. Every inch of every room is stuffed with toppling-over stacks of papers, magazines, books, art supplies, pottery, window display dummies, tapes, fabrics, photographs—an absolute orgy of *stuff*.

---

*The Bon Soir is long gone, alas, as are almost all the great vintage New York nightclubs and, as historian and author Jim Gavin observed, they've all been turned into Mexican restaurants or laundromats. The latest incarnation of the Bon Soir, at 40 W. 8th Street, is as a disco dance club called "40 Below."

When Bob finally got to our apartment, he parked his bags, grabbed his big black sketch book, and immediately we descended into the humid, summer night sweatbath that was one of the many highlights of being in the city in July. "New York Is a Summer Festival!" the posters mockingly proclaimed. It was getting late and I wanted to show Bob around the Village a little, then grab a sandwich at the Pam Pam.

As we crossed the street, heading up to the corner of 9th Street and Sixth Avenue, a figure dashed out from under the awning of The Lion and barreled up the street behind us shouting, "Barry! Barry!" Bob and I both spun around.

It was Barbra, and she looked eye-poppingly amazing. She was schlepping four shopping bags, two in each hand. Out of the tops exploded a wellspring of feathers, fans, boas, sequined fabrics, and beads.

Her tiny feet clacked along the pavement in a pair of gorgeous red satin and gold kid 1920s evening pumps. Above them rose her shapely legs in bittersweet chocolate nylons, cut off two inches above the knees by a cerise Ottoman silk skirt. And on top of all of that, she wore a stunning silver-white damask top, shot through with flecks of cherry red, very Toulouse-Lautrec looking, with puffed sleeves that went from the bodice into the back, where the whole thing surplused and plunged. It was very couture, and Terry Leong must have gone blind sewing it.

"Oh, my God, I'm totally out of breath!" she gasped.

"Take it easy," I said, and gave her a kiss on the cheek. "What are you doing here, anyway? I thought you were going to stay late, talk to the manager."

"Naw, I couldn't stand it, I had to get outta there," Barbra said, looking at Bob curiously.

"Barbra," I said, "this is Bob. I told you about Bob, remember? He did all the sets for that play I wrote at UCLA. Bob, this is my friend Barbra."

146

"Bob," she said blankly, then brightened. "Oh, you're 'Bob' Bob. Barry told me you were coming to town, I've just been so *tsmished*, so confused. Sure, sure. Hi, Bob. Welcome to New York."

Bob stared at Barbra, at her clothes, at the sparkles flashing off her Venetian glass necklaces, bracelets and earrings, as though she'd just jumped out of a cake and landed in his lap. "Hi!" he said, smiling brightly, his glazed eyes dropping to the cornucopia of effulgence overflowing the tops of her shopping bags.

"Yeah, hi," she said, holding her arms forward and shrugging, as if she wanted to shake hands but couldn't because she didn't have a hand free.

"Uh...what *is* all that stuff?" Bob asked, looking completely dazzled. "You look like you're carrying a whole photographic studio."

"Oh, *these?*" Barbra said, laughing and holding up her shopping bags. "It's my last night at The Lion. I had to pack up and get all my things out of there," she added, turning to me.

"I know," I said. "I live with you, remember?"

Barbra giggled self-consciously, put the bags down gingerly as if they were children she was afraid were going to run out into the traffic, and put a hand on my arm. "I'm sorry, Bar," she said, "I'm just so tired."

"Barbra's been appearing at The Lion," I explained to Bob. "She closed tonight, you just missed her. But wait till you hear her sing, she's fabulous." I turned to Barbra. "You sure you got everything?"

"If I didn't," Barbra muttered darkly, "I'm going to kill myself. I'm never going back in that place again."

"Didn't you like singing at The Lion?" Bob asked.

"Yeah. It was swell," Barbra said, then added, "but I've been there long enough."

As we all three walked along Sixth Avenue toward the Pam

Pam, Bob began to talk about the culture shock of being in New York. Only this morning he'd been in California and it was all so ...completely different. Once inside the coffee shop and installed in a booth, Barbra bombarded him with a barrage of questions.

"So, tell me, how did you get to the airport in Los Angeles? Did you take the subway, or what?" she asked.

"No, no," Bob said, "my mother drove me to the airport in her car."

"Your mother has a *car*?"

"Sure," said Bob. "Everybody in L.A. has a car. *I* have a car."

"*You* have a *car*?" Barbra asked, astonished. "What kind of a car?"

"An MG sports car," Bob said. "Barry has an MG, too."

Barbra looked at me as though we'd never met before. "You never told me you had a sports car!" she protested.

"Sure," I said. "You've got to have a car in California. Otherwise you can't get around. There's no ...well, almost no, public transportation," I said.

"Wait a minute, wait a minute," Barbra said, tucking into her salad and redirecting her attention to Bob. "Tell me what your life is like out there. Tell me what you did today, step by step. Don't leave anything out," she commanded.

"Well," Bob said, "I woke up this morning in a house in Beverly Glen—"

"Hold on, hold on right there," Barbra interrupted. She was really getting into it, just like she got into everything she was interested in, fully and deeply—for a while. "What's Beverly Glen?"

"It's a canyon," Bob said.

"What, what, what? What's a canyon? You mean, like the Grand Canyon?"

"It's a mountain pass kind of thing, all woodsy, and there's a stream, with houses on both sides. I live in a small wooden house, like a cabin, kind of."

"A mountain pass. So, what are you saying, Bob? You live in the country?"

"No, it's right in the middle of the city."

Barbra's eyebrows shot up and the questions continued to tumble out. Then Bob described the little house I lived in with my brother, in back of my parents' house, separated by a swimming pool. Barbra was fascinated. She continued to ply him with questions, her eyes wide with amazement and interest. Bob opened the sketch book he always carried with him, and as Barbra chattered on, he began to draw her in pencil.

"What are you doing there?" she demanded, gesturing at his book with her fork.

"Bob's drawing you," I explained. "He draws all the time, day and night, everywhere he goes." Barbra hardly turned to look at me.

"Draws *all the time*? You mean, like, every day, all the time? How long have you been doing this?" she asked.

"Oh, God," Bob said. "For years and years."

"Wait a minute, whaddya mean?" Barbra said. "You have a complete record of every day of your life... in drawings?"

"That's right, more or less," Bob said, filling in some cross-hatching.

"Can I move around or do I have to sit still?" she asked with a touch of self-consciousness.

"Sure," Bob said. "You can move. Just not too much. Listen, tell me about your shoes. Where did you get them? I remember a pair just like them in a 1927 *Vogue*."

As I watched them chatter happily on and on, I realized I was feeling odd: isolated and empty. Maybe I was jealous of the attention Barbra was showing Bob, envious of his obvious fascination with her. And then it slowly began to seep into my mind that Barbra had asked *me* almost nothing about *my* past, nor did she seem very interested in my present.

149

Only a week or so earlier, I had landed the entire summer season of Joe Papp's prestigious Shakespeare in the Park Festival. The whole season: three parts in three plays! When I excitedly ran home to tell Barbra about it her response was "Oh, great. That's good, huh?" but she didn't ask me any questions about which plays were being done, who the other actors were, what roles I was playing, whether my parts were any good. Nothing.

And then I realized that I knew almost as little about Barbra as she did about me. Although I'd asked about her past, her answers were generally vague and evasive. She'd told me the bare minimum about her growing up in Brooklyn: her mother who drove her crazy, Erasmus Hall, her hated stepfather, going to the movies every weekend.

Was it that she wasn't interested? No, on some level Barbra was very interested in me, emotionally involved. I knew that, I could feel it. Was it simple selfishness, then? It wasn't that I felt used, exactly; what I gave to Barbra, I gave her gladly. But there was a distance between us, an elusiveness, a disconnectedness I couldn't even begin to identify.

Then I had a sudden flash of Barbra sitting in a movie theater, head tilted up, totally absorbed in the images on the screen. That was closer to it: Barbra lived her life as if it were a movie constantly unspooling inside her head, projected on the silver screen of her consciousness. Supporting players came and went. In some intangible way, Barbra treated me as if I'd been created the day before yesterday, as if I had a reality only as a character in the motion picture that was her existence. Was I alive for her outside her private, solipsistic screening of the film *The Life of Barbra*, I wondered, or did I simply fade to black in her mind when I wasn't physically there, until my subsequent scene in the next reel?

Barbra and I were living together in the perpetual, oblivious present, I thought, existing only in the here and now, as if we'd had no past before our life together, as if she and I were each half of the same person and there wasn't time or even the necessity to ask questions. Oh, the hell with it, I thought. Maybe I was imagining all this. Maybe I was just tired.

With a deep sigh I realized I was feeling sad and sorry for myself, and slowly descending into a dark blue funk. I was missing California and my life there. And I guess I was wondering where the story of Barbra and Barry was headed.

"Hey, Barry!" Barbra's voice penetrated my consciousness and snapped me back. "You never told me California was so great."

"It's fabiola," I said, and a shiver went through me like a dog shaking off water. "In the spring rains, oranges roll down the gutters like balls of solid gold."

Barbra looked at me quizzically, then shrugged. "God, Bar, I really like your friend here," she said, tipping her head toward Bob and grinning. "He's a living doll!"

In the latter part of July or perhaps early August 1960, on a Sunday evening when the club was closed, Barbra, Bob and I descended the vertiginous flight of stairs into the coal mine depths of the Bon Soir. The stage lights were on and the club dim, just like on a weeknight, but the room, usually so packed and smoky, was completely empty and eerily quiet. We were greeted by the club owners, two cheerless, polite gentlemen, both in the kind of somber, dark suits you might wear to a church function or an assassination.

"How are you feeling?" I asked Barb quietly.

"Fine," she said.

"You ready to sing?"

"Sure," she said, "what the heck."

"There's nobody here to sing to."

"Yeah, I know," Barbra said, looking around the room that

looked as though it had been evacuated in a sudden bomb scare. "It's kinda weird, isn't it?"

"Sing for yourself," I said. "No, sing for me."

Barbra smiled, squeezed my arm, and picked up her music. As she made her way to the little stage, I joined Schulenberg at a table halfway back and looked around the room with its pitch-black walls and crazily tilted ivory wall sconces. It was like a funeral parlor with a bar.

Barbra conferred with the pianist briefly and then sang two songs to the wide sea of vacant tables and chairs. And suddenly it didn't matter about the room, about the emptiness, about anything else in the universe. Barbra sounded simply beautiful.

When she finished, we all sat down around a table. The club owners told Barbra they definitely wanted her; she could start the first week in September. They talked money, a standard house fee for beginning acts which Barbra readily agreed to.

"One more thing, though," Barbra said. "You got a kitchen, right? I mean, you serve meals."

The clubowners agreed they did.

"I want a steak and a baked potato," Barbra negotiated. "Every night."

"A steak and a baked potato?" Clubowner Number One repeated carefully.

"That's right," Barbra said. "With sour cream and chives."

Her stiff terms were readily agreed to, and as we all trudged up the steep, treacherous stairway, I complimented Barb on how well she did. I particularly wanted to praise the way she handled singing to a virtually empty house, an unsettling experience for any performer.

"I thought that went very well," I said.

"Yeah, me, too," Barbra agreed. "I was gonna ask for an avocado and shrimp appetizer, but I thought that was pushing it."

Barbra stared down at the pavement as we walked along 8th Street, looking worried.

"Say listen, Barbra," I said in my best Mae West.

"Yeah?" she said, definitely not playing along.

"Whatsa matter with your animal?" I asked.

"I'm just thinking," she said seriously. "I start September 9th. That's real soon. What am I gonna do? What am I gonna sing? I gotta get a whole set of songs together," she said, looking genuinely worried.

"We can do that," I said. "We've got enough time...just. Besides, I called my dad and asked him to send me all the rest of my records and tapes."

"You did?" she said, dumbfounded. "When did you do that?"

"A week or so ago. The crates should be here any day now."

"God, Barry, I don't know what to say," Barbra stammered, looking profoundly moved.

"Forget about it," I said. "When you make your first record, just promise me you'll let me produce it," I said.

"Cross my heart," Barbra said.

"You know," I mused, "you're going to be standing on a stage in a nightclub in New York City, in front of one of the chicest, smartest, most sophisticated audiences in the whole world."

"So?" Barbra said.

"So, you should sing something really unexpected, absolutely outrageous. Something like..." I stopped walking for a moment and searched around in my mind. Barbra looked at me expectantly. Suddenly I knew. "Something like 'Who's Afraid of the Big Bad Wolf?'"

Bob let out a shout. "That's great," he said. "That's a *great* idea."

"Oh, yeah?" Barbra said. "What is it?"

"It's the song from this Walt Disney animated short. You know, *The Three Little Pigs*."

153

"Hmmm…the three little pigs," Barbra repeated. "Never heard of 'em."

So Bob and I took Barbra by each arm and we all skipped up the street, singing "Who's afraid of the big bad wolf, the big bad wolf, the big bad wolf…"

Two days later, when Barbra returned to the apartment from shopping, she was amazed to find the living room filled with wooden crates, excelsior and packing material, and a ton of records and tapes.

"Hey!" I said, prying the wooden lid from one of the boxes with a crowbar I'd borrowed from the super, "look at this! Not one thing broken."

Then we really went into high gear. We taped the sound tracks of movie musicals that were shown throughout the day and night on New York television. We played records far into the wee hours, plundered the thrift shops with Terry, and searched for sheet music in used music stores.

Sometimes we'd call up and pretend to be secretaries to music publishers to get our greedy hands on free sheet music. Once Barbra got on the phone and in a nasal, twangy Brooklynese, said something like, "Hello, Chappell Music? Listen, honey, this is Vaughan Monroe's secretary."

I snorted my milk right up my nose. Of all the drab, bloodless, personality-challenged musical performers one could pick, Vaughan Monroe was probably first choice, with Rudy Vallee running a close second.

"You are going to get caught," I cautioned, searching desperately for a Kleenex. At this point Barbra looked over at me, put her hand on her hip and rolled her eyes like Betty Boop.

"Yeah, hello, are ya there?" Babs from Brooklyn continued. "Listen, honey, Mr. Monroe is looking for some certain pieces of sheet music. Oh, Vaughan? Yeah, yeah, he's swell, he's a sweetheart. So, anyway, honey, he's making an album. Yeah, I know. It's been a *long* time. Anyway, Millie up at ASCAP told me I should try you. Yeah, yeah, thanks. So here are the titles," and she rattled off a whole list of songs we couldn't lay our hands on anywhere else. And amazingly, the next day, by special messenger, the sheet music arrived.

"Ya see?" I said. "I told you your Brooklyn accent would come in handy someday."

We had "Big Bad Wolf" for our closer; now we needed a good strong opening number. Lee Wiley, a great vocalist and radio star from the late thirties and forties, had just been lured back into the recording studios by RCA Victor after a long absence and had recently released a couple of albums reestablishing her cool, steely, but breezy authority with a good song. Wiley, who'd been characterized as "one bitch of a singer" by a jazz critic, was the first person to perform the raucously up-tempo Gershwin standard "I've Got a Crush On You" as a slow, thoughtful ballad in a classic album of Gershwin tunes she recorded in 1939 for the Liberty Music Shop. Ira Gershwin called it "a Wiley change" and noted that, thereafter, no one ever again sang "Crush" as a hot jazz, up-tempo number. It was a trick Barbra would later use to stunning effect on "Happy Days Are Here Again."

"Keepin' Out of Mischief" was a marvelous but little-known song by the wonderful Fats Waller. It was a tune with a swinging beat and a lively bounce into which we could interject a note of sexy, playful naughtiness that I thought would strike just the right note for an opening number for Barbra, and when I played her Lee Wiley's new recording, she did, too.

In the meantime, Bob Schulenberg had begun to talk about redesigning Barbra's makeup: a thicker base, shading in her nose and cheeks, lifting her hair, extending her eye line to make her eyes seem wider, maybe even eventually sprinkling a band of colored glitter dust or gluing sequins onto her eyelids so they flashed when she blinked. Since I'd seen Bob's makeup work when we were at college together, I trusted his visual eye implicitly and gave him my blessing.

Late one evening, after a particularly frantic day of telephoning, running around, and rehearsing, Barbra and I collapsed on the sofa and began to talk quietly about our plans for the future, and how we felt about each other. It was one of those rare, intimate, and touching moments that you think you'll remember on the day you're dying. The lights were low, and the candle in my antique child's nightlight threw flickering filigrees of red, green, and gold diamond shapes on the walls and ceiling.

I had gone downstairs to the Bigelow Pharmacy and ordered a bacon, lettuce, and tomato sandwich from the fountain and brought it upstairs to split with Barbra. She and I each took bites from the same half, passing it back and forth to each other. It was strangely moving and personal to share it that way, rather than each simply eating their own half.

Ralph Vaughan Williams's gorgeous piece for violin and orchestra, *The Lark Ascending*, was playing on the phonograph. Barbra and I loved playing classical music late at night. That's how she first heard Rachmaninoff's *Vocalise*, Villa Lobos's *Bachianas Brasileiras*, and Faure's *Pavane*, some of which she later recorded. She was particularly fond of the heavenly way Claudia Muzio sang Debussy's *Beau Soir* and of Madeleine Grey's interpretations of Cantaloube's *Songs of the Auvergne*.

The mood was suddenly jarred when the intercom from the lobby buzzed. I reluctantly walked over to answer it.

"Hello, Barry, it's Bob. I was just in the neighborhood and thought I'd drop by. Are you two busy?"

"It's Schulenberg," I mouthed to Barbra. She shrugged and

sighed. I think we were both unwilling to let this moment be shattered, but we didn't want to be rude to Bob. I put my hand over the receiver and whispered, "I can tell him it's not convenient," I suggested.

"No, no," Barbra said resignedly. "Tell him to come up."

A few moments later the doorbell rang and Bob, sketchbook in hand, came in, looked around appraisingly, and took a chair.

"Your place looks so pretty!" he said, settling in.

"We were just having a sandwich from downstairs," I said. "Can I get you something?"

"No, thanks, I'm fine. I just had dinner in the Village with some friends," Bob explained.

I picked up the BLT and offered it to Barbra, who, looking up at me, took a bite from it right out of my hands. It was such a sweet, tender, unashamed thing for her to do. It really moved my heart.

"Why is it we can't make a BLT to compare with this one?" I wondered aloud softly. "It's a simple sandwich. We ought to be able to duplicate it, but I've tried and it never comes out the same. What is it that makes it so special, so ... perfect?"

"Some things you just can't repeat," Barbra said quietly. "They're unique."

"Like you," I said.

She leaned over and put her head in my lap, looking up at me with a sweet smile.

"To be a real BLT," Barbra began.

"Hey," I said. " 'To be a real *BLT.*' Pretty good rhymes!"

"Thank you," Barbra said, and turning back to Bob she continued. "To be a real BLT ... hey, ya know something, you're right," she said, turning back to me. "That's not bad. Suddenly I'm a lyricist!"

We all laughed softly.

"Hurry up," I said. "All this talk is making me hungry again."

157

"Anyway, the point is, the toast has to scrape the roof of your mouth like sandpaper and leave it totally raw," Barbra said.

"That can't be the secret," I said.

"Face it," Barbra said. "The short-order cooks at the Bigelow wave a magic wand over it. It's enchantment. There's no other possible explanation."

We stopped talking and let the last few phrases of *The Lark Ascending* fill our ears. The strings had stopped playing. The little lark on the wings of a solo violin soared higher and higher into its musical sky, in exultation, ascending, heavenward...and then silence, which we all listened to for a moment more.

"Hey, Bob," Barbra said in a whisper. "Barry and I are talking about getting married."

During all this, I was appearing at Shakespeare in the Park. I was in good company: Ed Asner, James Earl Jones, and Mariette Hartley were in the casts that summer. In two of the plays I didn't do anything special, but in *Henry V* I played the French Soldier, a hapless fellow who is deserting, running away from the battleline in absolute terror, and who has the bad luck to run into Bardolf, himself a coward. Bardolf can't speak French, the French Soldier has no English, and what follows is a slap-bang comic scene in which Bardolf shows off his mock heroics by terrorizing and picking on the Frenchman. It was high farce, very difficult to play, with a whole lot of physical comedy, gags, and business: Bardolf chased me, clumsily brandishing his sword, I scrambled away, and crawled up and tumbled down the raked stairways that made up the set. I stole the scene, which got a tremendous lot of laughs and applause every night. I even got singled out by Ward Morehouse in the *New York Times*'s review of the play.

Well, of course, I desperately wanted Barbra to see me in my first real moment of triumph on stage in New York, but the only night she and Bob could come was the very last night we played. I reserved two house seats for the both of them, and was in a tremendous state of agitation and excitement that evening as I put on my makeup.

I had checked out the sight lines from my reserved house seats before the show that night. Yeah, they were great. Barbra would be able to see everything I did perfectly. Before the play began, I peeked out through the crack in a curtained doorway to see if Barbra and Bob were there yet. No, the seats were still empty, but a lot of people were late getting to the performances (probably because they were free), and my scene didn't come until later in the play anyway.

"Barry, get away from there," the stage manager hissed at me. "You'll be seen!"

As I made my entrance in the second act, creeping away from the enemy lines, I took a quick gander at my house seats. Yes! They were filled! Barbra must be there, watching me! I played my scene better that night than I'd ever played it, and the applause and laughter at the end went on even longer than usual.

Now, Bob Schulenberg was notorious for turning up for anything and everything incredibly late, with maddening regularity. You could count on it. As a friend wickedly observed, "Never agree to meet Bob on a street corner." And he'd been known to be a little less than thoughtful. Many years later, on a location movie shoot, I once waited the whole evening in my hotel room to go out with Bob while he frolicked downstairs in the hotel bar at an impromptu party with the rest of the cast, where everyone played the piano and sang and told wonderfully funny stories. "It was *so* marvelous," he later explained, "I just couldn't tear myself away to get to a house phone to call you."

But on this occasion, Bob outdid himself. It was hot as hell that night. Even though the theater was next to Belvedere Lake, the blistering heat of the day had stubbornly refused to cool off. As I

159

watched the audience streaming away from the auditorium, I suddenly saw Barbra and Bob walking through the trees in the middle distance, undulating in the muggy evening air like a desert mirage, fighting their way upstream against the exiting crowd as they pushed toward me by the dressing room tents.

I wondered what they were doing there, but I was still high from the performance. Finally the two of them stood in front of me, Bob grinning madly, Barbra dressed all in black and looking a little pallid.

"Well, did you like it?" I asked. "Could you understand the Old French?" I looked back and forth at them. Barbra just stared at me, pale and kind of frightened-looking.

"We just got here," Bob said, smiling fatuously. I was positive this was one of his weird jokes.

"What do you mean?" I said.

"We...were late. And the train didn't come for a long time. And then the theater was much further from the subway station than I remembered," Bob added.

I felt a horrible, sticky-cold, sinking feeling in my stomach. My face started to burn and my throat was dry and strangulated. "You mean...you missed it?" I said.

"Uh...yeah. That's about it. We missed it," Bob smiled apologetically and shrugged his shoulders.

I looked at the both of them, from face to face, shaking my head unbelievingly. Surely they were kidding. "You mean...the *whole thing*?" I asked, hoping I had misunderstood. Neither of them said anything. Bob kept gesturing at Barbra, pointing to her, his grin plastered on as if it had been permanently installed at birth. I didn't understand what I was supposed to be looking at.

"We just got here," Barbra said in a very small voice.

"You mean, *just* now...*after* the curtains calls?" I asked incredulously.

160

"Uh, yuh," Barbra offered apologetically.

"How in God's name could you just *get* here?" I said, my voice rising up, in imminent danger of going out of control. "What were you *doing*, for Chrissakes?"

"We were doing Barbra's *makeup*," Bob said patiently, as if that were the most reasonable explanation in the whole wide world.

Of course. What was the matter with me? Barbra's *makeup*. *Anybody* could understand that.

"Her...makeup?" I said numbly, and they both nodded their heads.

"Well, we just wanted to surprise you, have Barbra show up looking really *glamorous*," Bob said. "We started early, right after work, we really did. And then, you know how it goes, it got later and later and we didn't look at the clock, and...well...we just lost track of the time," he finished airily, as if that made everything all right.

I looked over at Barbra, who stared back at me frailly—ashen makeup, eye shadow, and a hell of a lot of black: black turtleneck, black cardigan, black pants, and black slippers. Okay, she did look nice, a little like Audrey Hepburn in *Funny Face*, one of Schulenberg's icons. But this took six hours?

Suddenly I had a flash of Barbra and Bob together in the apartment. She's gazing into the mirror and—miracles and wonders!—Bob is totally changing the way she looks. Her teenage skin disappears beneath a veil of greasepaint. The sun plunges into the Hudson River. False eyelashes are painstakingly trimmed and glued in place. It's six o'clock, seven o'clock, eight.

"Listen, shouldn't we start getting ready to go to the park?" Barbra asks.

"No, we've got plenty of time. I'm almost finished. Besides, Barry doesn't come on until the second act," Bob says.

And he goes on and on, talking and talking, hour after hour, prettily painting on her face, carefully brushing a band of sky blue

161

on her eyelids. The one thing Barbra couldn't fight, couldn't resist: the seduction of seeing herself being made to look beautiful, and then even more beautiful…ravishing. Her childhood dream come true. Magic. Transformation. Epiphany!

Suddenly I was back in the park. Between the overpowering summer heat and the emotion rising up and strangling me, something exploded violently inside my head—little white squiggles were dancing in front of my eyes. I thought I was going to burst a blood vessel.

"Don't you two understand?" I yelled, my temper shooting totally into the stratosphere. "This is our goddamn closing night! You'll *never* get a chance to see me in this play, ever again. This is *it*! *Finished*! I mean, Jesus Christ, Bob, couldn't you have done her fucking makeup some other time, some other night…like *tomorrow*?" I screamed, in an agony of fury and pain.

"Yeah, but Barry," Bob protested reasonably, wiping away all my objections with a toothy smile and turning proudly toward his creation, who was wincing with guilt and taking a few steps backward, "doesn't Barbra look *great*?"

That evening, Barbra couldn't see how important it was to me that she be in the audience, watching me perform. And I couldn't see how important it was to her that she looked beautiful.

I have rarely in my life been as steamed, as overwhelmed with foaming anger and a feeling of helpless betrayal, as I was that evening. It didn't make things any better that all the way home, on the subway platform and on the train, as I chewed on my fury and glared at the floor, Bob kept whispering *sotto voce* comments to Barbra like, "There's a handsome man staring at you. Over by the gum machine. *She's* staring, too. There's another head turning. Look away. Look bored."

We were young, very young. It was that time of our lives when everything is important, and overwrought, and when your heart gets hurt, it's the big hurt.

"Barry was really pissed," Schulenberg commented years later to one of Barbra's biographers. "But it didn't matter because the point of the evening was made. Everybody was looking at Barbra like, 'Who *is* she?' Barbra *loved* it."

I worked very hard to try to get over it and, in some ways, I did. It was a wise person who said, never wake up with yesterday's anger.

But Barbra's and my relationship had received an internal wound that would continue to bleed slowly and fatally. It was the end of the beginning, and the beginning of the end.

11

Bonjour, Bon Soir

*I*t was my own fault.

I'd been devoting so much time and energy to Barbra I hadn't really noticed that my own career, my own feelings, were taking a back seat. It was easy to get distracted. Barbra's talent, magnetism, and powerful self-directedness created an imperative in which there was always one more thing to do for her, one more piece of sheet music to find, one more outfit to pick up at the dry cleaners.

The last three weeks of August Barbra went to a summer stock theater in Fishkill, New York, to play Hortense the Maid in *The Boy Friend*. I worked with her on the French accent and her character's song ("It's Nicer in Nice"), and together we invented a lot of funny business. At one point in the play, when Hortense is whispering a secret to Mme. Dubonnet and their heads are together, instead of hiding *behind* her fan, I told Barb to open it and shove it up *between* the two of them. It looked hilarious.

When Barbra came back to town, we only had ten days before

165

she opened at the Bon Soir, so we really had to jam to get the rest of the act ready. But there was the question of approach that had to be settled. I had something very specific and unusual in mind for her.

"Listen, Barb," I said, "the thing is, so many of the singers you hear today are so bland and brainless. They sing the same old songs, over and over. Their stuff is so well known the audience could join in. Even Felicia Sanders, everything she sings sounds exactly the same: heavy. Well, I guess Dorothy Loudon stands out, but she's really a comedienne."*

"Yeah, so what are you saying?" Barbra asked impatiently, always in a hurry to get right to the point.

"I'd like to do an act for you that's different. Really different. Wonderful songs, unusual songs, songs that people aren't familiar with, songs they'll pay attention to. Songs that are worthy of your wonderful voice."

"Uh-huh," she said. "So go on."

"So, whaddya think? You wanna go for it?"

It took her all of a nanosecond. "Yeah," she said, "let's go for it."

"Good," I said.

There was a pause, one of those uncomfortable ones that usually precede a statement or a question that's going to land near the knuckle. It usually starts out, "Can I say something?" or "Can I ask you something?" the only appropriate answer to which is "No."

Barbra cleared her throat and said, "Listen, Barry, can I ask you something, I mean, just by the by?"

---

*Felicia Sanders was an overwrought, suffocatingly intense chanteuse who had appeared recently at the Bon Soir, having scored a big success a few years earlier with her recording of "The Song from *Moulin Rouge*." The large tear that welled up and rolled mechanically down her cheek during every torpid ballad annoyed me intensely. Dorothy Loudon charged through a maniacal, peppy, delightfully funny act and was a regular at the Blue Angel. Years later, she'd make her mark on Broadway as the demented villainess Miss Hannigan in the hit musical *Annie*.

"Sure," I said.

"The thing is, how did you get interested in all this stuff? How do you know about it? I mean, I never met a man before who knew about all this stuff."

I have to admit I felt a bit stung; her question struck a deep chord. There was a hint, a whisper of an implication, that as a man there was something twisted, or lacking in me. Was she hinting around, asking me if I was gay? I can honestly say it's one of the few times in my life that I, the sophisticated, knowledgeable, chic young man that I was convinced I was, felt my own face burn.

"When I was a kid, like really young, my folks gave me this phonograph and some records," I said. "I really liked the music. If I'd been a good little boy all week, every Saturday my mom would take me down to Marshall Fields department store in Chicago and I got to buy a record."

"So that's how you started to collect records?" Barbra asked.

"Yeah. I've still got some records I had when I was eight years old. It interests me," I said, "the way some guys are interested in logarithms, or football. Besides, what's the difference? It's just what you need," I added pointedly.

"Yeah, yeah. You got something there," she conceded, but still looked at me appraisingly.

Barbra was sniffing around, daring me, challenging me to speak the truth. Suddenly I decided to take the bull by the balls.

"Listen, Barb," I began, "I don't want to hurt your feelings or anything, but you know my sexual, uh, interests don't lie all in one direction, don't you? I mean, I don't just like girls."

She observed me a moment before she spoke. "Yeah, I figured you were bisexual, or something," she confessed.

"Yeah, well, I don't know if I'd call it that. I don't know what I'd call it. Confused, I think that's what I am."

Barbra smiled, although I suspected what I was saying was

167

puzzling her. I just hoped it wasn't distressing her. "Don't worry," she said. "It'll all work out."

Suddenly I had another bright idea, and besides, I wanted to change the subject. "You know what I'd like to do for you," I asked her.

"What?"

"I'd like to do a set showing the whole life of one woman, you know, just one character progressing from, say, a young girl in love to an old woman in bitter disillusion. Wouldn't that be cool?"

"Yeah," she said. "Yeah, that would be great! Why don't we start working on it right away?"

"Let's get you opened, first," I said. "Then we can start to think about it."

"Oh, come on, Barry," she pleaded.

"Don't worry," I said, "we'll get around to it."

Unfortunately, we never did.

What I figured we were lacking for Barbra's act was a ballad, a comedy number and one wildly exciting, up-tempo tune to whip the audience into a froth and drive the act through to its conclusion.

For the comedy number I started playing for Barbra the records of Helen Kane, that delectable Boop-Boop-a-Doop girl from the twenties who introduced "Button Up Your Overcoat," and "I Wanna Be Loved by You." I reckoned those two particular songs were probably too well known to be surprising and sound anything but camp and precious. On the flip side of one of her records, however, was a song called "I Want to Be Bad," a flapper's pouty lament about her healthy appetite for innocent wickedness:

> If it's naughty to rouge your lips
> Shake your shoulders and swing your hips
> Let a lady confess, I want to be bad!

Once we'd settled on a number, I could break down the lyrics for Barbra, inventing the characters who sang them and what they were feeling: a spoiled princess, a world-weary sex goddess, a wicked vamp, a deserted child. I wanted to invent a whole range of distinctive personae that would highlight the various aspects of Barbra's personality, from the waif to the worldly.

For "I Want to Be Bad," we worked out a whole scenario and character for Barbra to play: after a whole evening of dancing on tables and drinking hooch, a good-time party girl is arrested in a police raid on a speakeasy, thrown into a paddy wagon and hauled off to jail. The next morning she's brought before the judge and, openly flirtatious and seductive, she looks up at His Honor on the bench and explains that she just can't help herself. She wants to be bad!

"I Want to Be Bad," by DeSylva, Brown and Henderson from Helen Kane's Broadway hit, *Follow Through,* was tailor-made for Barbra to sing with sexy, wide-eyed ingenuousness, and it complemented and echoed her twenties flapper outfits perfectly.

But this wasn't all that was going on. As we rehearsed under the impending pressure of her opening night, which was only a few days away, the feeling between Barbra and me flared up in fights and screaming matches.

"*Don't* hold your hands in front of your body like that. It's just a nervous gesture, it doesn't mean anything, it looks really lousy and awkward. Don't do it!" I'd scream at her.

And Barbra would yell back, "*Don't* do this, *don't* do that! All you ever *do* is say '*don't*!' "

In the meantime my closets were overflowing with Barbra's extravagant antique clothing, shoes, and bags. But enough was never quite enough with Barbra. They say less is more; with Barbra, less was…less. She, Terry, and I continued to raid the thrift shops and pick up some fabulous things.

We also made a trip to a costume warehouse that was going

out of business. It was an enormous, spooky barn of a place with literally thousands upon thousands of costumes in aisle after aisle, and the only people in the whole, damp building were Barbra, me, and the old guy who sat at a small, empty wooden desk near the front door. I picked out a brocade and brass-buttoned jacket, just like Prince Charming's, and Barbra swooped down on some interesting shoes.

"Those shoes are new, you know," I cautioned her.

"Newish," she said.

"Rhymes with..." I said.

"All right, enough already," said Barbra, annoyed at having her concentration put off.

I couldn't resist distracting her. "Are you actually going to wear shoes that aren't forty years old?" I asked incredulously.

Barbra looked at me and shrugged one of her "whatever" shrugs. "If the *new* shoe fits," she said smiling, "wear it!"

Barbra loved her clothes and took beautiful care of them, interleaving them with tissue paper when she had to pack, constantly examining them closely for any little rips, snags, or spots. I'll never forget her sending a beautiful butterfly negligee out to be dry cleaned and when it came back, some enterprising soul at the cleaners had sewn a clunky, sequined clasp on the front, tearing the fabric where they stitched it on.

"Maybe they thought they were doing you a favor. It's from the same era," I offered as tepid consolation.

Barbra stared at me with a look of total upset and distress, as if the dry cleaners had murdered one of her children.

"I don't care if it's from the Metropolitan Museum!" she almost cried. "I didn't *ask* them to sew anything on it!"

We spent hours under a bright light with a magnifying glass, painstakingly picking the stitches out. Then I called the cleaners and blistered their ears.

*　　*　　*

Stories have been told over the years that have gained a certain aura of veracity (if only because they've been repeated so often that they *must* be true, mustn't they?) about Barbra's alleged grubby personal habits. I remember once reading an interview with a musician who was supposed to have worked on one of Barbra's Columbia albums, talking about a recording session on a very hot afternoon. He complained that Barbra didn't bathe, and although the studio had electric fans strategically placed, no one wanted to sit downwind of her.

Or take, for example, this ripe passage from Randall Riese's Streisand biography describing Barbra's appearance the morning she auditioned for *I Can Get It for You Wholesale*: "She entered the theater and trudged onto the stage, wearing a coat of many colors. Made of tattered fur, it resembled the hide of a neglected horse, splotched with browns, yellows, and whites. She wore a pair of dirty tennis shoes... her hair, a studied disaster." The whole impression Riese paints is one of tacky slovenliness.

In fact, Barbra spent the night before, Thanksgiving eve 1961, at Bob Schulenberg's, having come to his Gramercy Park apartment directly from her performance at the Blue Angel. She was in the chic black evening dress she wore on the nightclub stage, with black nylons and matching shoes. Barbra spent the night at Bob's, eating a beautiful turkey dinner, staying up late and talking and, later, sleeping on the couch.

When she woke up in the morning to go to her *Wholesale* audition, Barbra realized she was still dressed for a nightclub. When she "trudged onto the stage" she *couldn't* take off her coat because there was an evening dress underneath, not at all the right outfit for a Jewish garment district musical. The "tattered fur coat" was, in fact, the famous, stunning caracul coat which Barbra would have copied in leopard and mink for the film *Funny Girl*. Standing wrapped in it in her pale makeup, she looked like a Richard Avedon photograph from the pages of *Vogue* come to life. It was a silhouette Julie Christie would bring into high fashion five years later, a style which became one of *the* iconic looks of the 1960s.

I would like to categorically state, once and for all, that these are unprincipled calumnies. Despite the malicious gossip, Barbra never, *ever* appeared in public with unwashed hair or in tatty or dirty clothing. She was always compulsively neat and immaculate about her appearance and dress, and all the scandalmongers who say the opposite are simply trying to puff up their own importance, to appear to be "in-the-know" insiders. But all they are is outright liars.

Barbra could be credited with creating the "grunge" look and changing the face of fashion forever; she was certainly the first to talk about how she enjoyed finding and wearing second-hand clothing on television on the Jack Paar show. But she was never "grungy."

If Barbra went over the top in any direction, perhaps it was in converting window-decorating fabrics into clothing of extravagant design, then *ferpotching* it, that is, overdressing it with earrings, necklaces, bracelets, and rings. Her clothes were guilty merely of being flashy, and perhaps her reputation for kookiness came from that flamboyance.

These were the days where, when a young singer in a club wanted to stand out, she'd wear gold lamé, or a red satin dress with sequins and feathers. Schulenberg taught Barbra to simplify her clothing, to take an antique sequined Victorian top and wear it with a simple dress, and perhaps only one piece of jewelry. (Simplicity wasn't the only concern with this problematic garment. If Barbra wasn't careful about her onstage gestures, when she leaned back, the whalebone stiffening would make the bottom of it flip up like the prow of a ship!) Bob taught Barbra restraint; he designed a look for her, and edited what she wore.

Schulenberg later described one evening in 1960, when I had gone home for Christmas (about which, more later). Barbra was getting ready to go to the club and asked him to help her with the zipper on the back of a beautifully simple, long, dark wool, one-piece dress. The zipper was meant to go all the way to the top, creating a turtleneck. But Bob stopped zipping at Barbra's shoulder blades, exposing her beautiful bare back.

"You know, Barbra," Bob said, "it looks very nice like this."

"Oh, yeah?" said Barbra, taking a look over her shoulder in the mirror.

"Yeah," Bob enthused. "Let's leave it unzipped down to your shoulders and tuck in the front, like a boat neck, so it's high in front and low-cut in back. Like Marilyn Monroe, only in reverse."

Barbra tucked in the front and took another look. "I really like this," she said. "It looks great."

"Yeah, it's timeless. Why don't you wear it in the club tonight?" Bob asked.

"Bob, it's wool. They think I'm crazy already. Now I'm gonna wear *wool* at *night?*"

"Yeah, but you look classic. It's got the line of an evening dress; it's kind of great that it's wool. I tell you what, let's pick out a pair of really elegant evening shoes to wear with it, just so it looks like we know what we're doing," Bob said.

"I think I've got a pair that would be perfect," Barbra said.

"And then let's find two rings that match, and maybe wear one on each hand," he suggested.

Barbra pulled out her boxes of accessories and like two kids at Christmas, she and Bob went through them.

"Barbra, you've got beautiful stuff here," Bob enthused. "Nice jewelry, beautiful garnets…"

"I found them all in thrift stores," Barbra said.

When they'd finished, Barbra was very pleased with the result.

"See, there's nothing to focus on except your face," Bob explained. "It all says, 'Look at this face!' And your face is enough, because it's such an extraordinary face."

Barbra smiled a satisfied smile and gave herself a last once-over in the mirror.

"Pretty neat," she said. "And not a bit *ferpotched*!"

"Barbra had a good eye for finding things that were very simple and architectural, but she dressed them up too much," Schulenberg said later. "Maybe it was insecurity. I told her: Women of fashion say you look at what you're wearing, and then you take off what you don't need, and then you find one more thing to get rid of."

I had to smile, imagining Barbra listening to this advice, stripping herself down to the bare minimum, and then taking off one more thing—a shoe—and limping away down the street.

Barbra always had a flair for fashion. At one point she bought a rhinestone-punching machine and was decorating men's dress shirts with colored rhinestones—still not a bad idea. It's no surprise that today one of her best friends is the famous clothes designer Donna Karan.

But back to the music: "Lover Come Back to Me" was a Sigmund Romberg ballad from his popular operetta *New Moon*. Mildred Bailey, one of the all-time great jazz singers, had made a recording of it that really swung, but in a very laid-back way. We decided to take this approach even further and accent the beat, swing, and bounce. When we finally got "Lover" up to speed, Barbra drove the song like a freight train.

I taught her that if she didn't know how to sing a phrase, say it, and then she'd know how to sing it. When she was rehearsing "Lover," her tongue kept tripping over the line "When I remember every little thing you used to do…" She started to get a psychological block about it, so instead of worrying about the words, I told her to think about my socks hanging out to dry in the bathroom. That was one of the "little things I used to do" that drove her crazy. She latched right on to the idea and, with that image in her mind and a sardonic smile twisting her lips, forever after the phrase flew out like a bullet.

What I always tried to do with Barbra was to draw things out of her own experience, to pull on the events of her life to project a song, so she would never get hung up on just making a beautiful sound. That way, it didn't seem so much like singing as acting for her, and besides, Barbra's tone was so gorgeous, it was unearthly. The less attention she paid to it, and the less self-conscious she was about producing it, the better.

As we worked on "When Sunny Gets Blue," I asked Barb if she'd never had a friend who got depressed, whose life just never seemed to work out. With the amazing ability to make connections, to directly link herself and her history to the work she was doing, Barbra said, "Yeah! I had a girlfriend like that at Erasmus High. I was always making goofy faces at her, to cheer her up, ya know?"

"Well, think about her when you sing this song. In the first part, you describe her, how sad she gets, what she looks like. Then in the second part, let all your hopes and wishes for her to have a happy life come through," I said.

"Too late," Barbra said.

"What do you mean?"

"She died." She stared at me poker-faced, then burst into helpless laughter and collapsed in my lap. "Just kidding," came her muffled apology.

When she saw what it did for her, Barbra fell under the spell of makeup and spent all her money on it. When I wasn't hammering at her, Schulenberg would take over. He'd make up one side of her face, then Barbra would say, "Hey, let me try," and she'd go into the bathroom. While Bob watched television or drew, Barbra tried to match what Bob had done by applying the makeup herself on the other side of her face.

What Bob was doing for Barbra was teaching her classic nineteen-thirties glamour makeup technique, the kind Dietrich and Garbo wore in the movies. He combed Barbra's bangs off her forehead, and used the "prune Danish" hairpiece *under* her own hair to lift and give it height. Bob felt that her nose was *there*, so he'd just work around it. He used a no-color lip gloss on her beautiful mouth, and disguised the slight, youthful roundness in her cheeks by contouring them with dark blusher, which enforced the underlying structure.

And then came the eyes.

With a tiny, triple-zero watercolor brush, Bob extended the shape of the eye outward with a long line of thinned-down, black cake mascara. Then, painstakingly, hair by hair, he trimmed down a pair of false eyelashes, which were cut to a shorter length than Barbra's real lashes. (Bob had noticed that real lashes were tapered at the ends, whereas cut hair was blunt. Bob's fake eyelashes supplied the fullness; Barbra's real, tapered lashes finished off the look.)

Today, you can buy false eyelashes in a supermarket, but back in 1960, they could only be bought from a theatrical supplier. Bob remembers taking Barbra to the Garden Pharmacy, right next to the Winter Garden Theater, where row after row of "stage" and "screen" eyelashes were on display, and how excited they both got looking at them. The movie lashes were thinner in width; the stage ones had three times as much hair, to be visible to the audience from a distance. Dancers/singers, those fabled "gypsies" from Broadway shows, jostled with theater ticket buyers and people dropping in for a quick egg cream at the fountain before the matinee in this tiny, hole-in-the-wall drugstore. It was all incredibly thrilling.

Once the eyelashes were carefully glued in place, Bob drew a tiny, thin, subtle white highlight above that. He explained to Barbra that, where the lashes grow out from the lid, there is a little ridge that catches the light. If you want the makeup to look less artificial, he taught her, you draw, like, a 64th-of-an-inch-wide white line to replicate that highlight. (This is a makeup technique which Barbra still uses today.)

Now normally, the false eyelash would have cast a shadow on Barbra's face which would have disguised the long, painted line. You wouldn't have been able to see it at all. Barbra's eyes would simply look big, and when Schulenberg did her makeup, that's what happened. But Barbra simply couldn't get the false eyelashes in place herself.

Over and over she would slave at the bathroom mirror, painstakingly trying to position the false eyelashes in place without smearing the sticky adhesive all over her own lids and fingers. Then she'd wander disgustedly into the living room, one eye glued closed, hold up her gummy hands and lament, "Help, somebody! I got my fingers all stuck together and I'm going blind!"

"If she'd been able to do the eyelashes," Schulenberg later commented, "nobody would have been aware that she was wearing as theatrical a makeup as she was. It would just have been a more almond-shaped eye. But because Barbra couldn't glue the eyelashes in place successfully herself, the line became visible, apparent, a statement. A mistake turned into a stylistic signature."

Hour after hour Barbra would work carefully at the coloring-in of her eye shadow, the flow of the mascara and length of the eyeliner, the careful shaping and filling in of the lipstick line, the exact placement of the blush on her cheeks. Then she'd come once again into the living room and stand in front of Bob for inspection, like a foot soldier being reviewed by a general.

"Well? How's this? How did I do?"

And Schulenberg would critique her job, saying things like, "You got the eye a little too heavy...make it a *little* less...."

Barbra would absorb it all, then she'd disappear into the bathroom and vigorously scour one side of her face with Pears soap and warm water.

"Why don't you use makeup remover or cream, honey?" I'd ask her. "Something that would be a little easier on your skin."

"I can't, because if I use cream to take it off, the next time I put the makeup on, it's all greasy, it doesn't stick. Naw, I gotta scrub," she explained dutifully. "But by the time I'm finished, I'll have the cleanest pores on 9th Street!"

And she'd begin all over again. And again and again and again.

We had almost all the music now, except for one ballad yet to be found, but nothing perfect came to hand immediately. Barbra and I switched from listening to records and tapes to sifting through thousands and thousands of titles in used sheet music shops. Finally, in a Rodgers and Hart songbook, I stumbled across "Nobody's Heart." Larry Hart was a lyricist whose work touched me particularly. He seemed such a talented misfit and loathed himself so deeply for a thinly hidden homosexuality he could do nothing about and tried so desperately to drown in drink. "Nobody's Heart" was a moving, world-weary ballad that I felt came directly from Hart's own feeling that he himself was "Nobody's Hart," that he would never find anybody in the entire world to love him—so the hell with it.

> Nobody's heart belongs to me
> Heigh ho, who cares?
> Nobody writes his songs to me
> No one belongs to me
> That's the least of my cares....*

---

*Richard Rogers and Lorenz Hart, "Nobody's Heart" (New York: Chappell and Co., Inc., 1942). Courtesy Dorothy Hart.

"Who's Afraid of the Big Bad Wolf ?" is such a rag bag of camp sensibility that it was hard to find a way to anchor it for Barbra; basically hers was a comedy performance full of *shticks*. The idea I had was "The Singer's Nightmare": stuck with singing this bizarre little piece, Barbra is alarmed to find that aspects of her performance keep going way out of control: The Three Flames, Barbra's accompanists at the Bon Soir, join in the chorus manically, scaring the wits out of her. Her own voice unexpectedly keeps trying to get away from her in semi-operatic swoops and shrieks. To her surprise, Barbra assumes her Mae West persona when she sings about the third pig, saying, "Nix on tricks, I will build my house of bricks." And finally she's horrified to find herself warbling gleefully about the wolf getting fried in the fire.

Though Barbra tries throughout to keep a tenuous hold on reality, the whole thing has driven her mad. So for the tag, during the manic play-off, I told her about Jean Anouilh's play *The Flies*, in which the hero gets attacked unmercifully everywhere he goes by a swarm of flies and that she should flee the stage laughing crazily, as if being chased by the Furies. It worked. The Bon Soir audiences went nuts.

The last piece had fallen into place. We had Barbra's Bon Soir lineup:

> "Keepin' Out of Mischief Now"
> "A Sleepin' Bee"
> "I Want to Be Bad"
> "When Sunny Gets Blue"
> "Lover, Come Back to Me"
> "Nobody's Heart"
> "Who's Afraid of the Big Bad Wolf?"

On September 9, 1960, Barbra began a two-week booking at the Bon Soir, and anybody who knows anything about Barbra

179

Streisand knows what happened next: she was an absolute wow. Six days later, Dorothy Kilgallen, an influential gossip columnist with an acerbic wit, wrote a rave about Barbra in her syndicated column. Barbra's engagement got extended to eleven weeks.

Every night I could I dragged the Ampex to the club and back home again. We taped and retaped her act, listened to it between shows, critiqued, and rehearsed some more. We erased most of these recordings because they were "work tapes": their quality wasn't very good, they were, at best, referential. Perhaps in retrospect this seems shortsighted, but at the time I didn't know, I didn't begin to realize what Barbra was going to become. I just had to serve that wonderful voice, right there and then.

"Don't listen to the tapes, they're inferior," I used to say. "Wait till you see Barbra in person!"

The nights we didn't tape, I showed up at the Bon Soir, took notes, and gave them to Barbra all night long, and sometimes late into the following morning.

"You were looking at the audience again tonight, in 'A Sleepin' Bee,' " I read off the list. "Don't do it."

"Yeah, I know," she said, "but sometimes I feel like I *wanna* connect with them, make eye contact. Ya know what I mean?"

"Of course I know what you mean, Barbra," I shot back, "but don't *do* it. I've thought about this a lot, whether you should look at the audience or keep your distance. Don't look. It...it dissipates the mystery."

"But look, Barry..." Barbra began.

"Please," I cut her off. "Trust me, I've been watching you carefully, I know what it looks like. You're there in the same room with them, but also you're not. I don't know how to explain it. If you feel you *have* to look at the audience, look at them in the middle distance, out-of-focus. Don't really nail them with direct eye con-

tact. It's unsettling, distracting. You're different from them, you're
… apart. Rarefied. Special," I explained.

"Special," she mused. "I like that."

I ran a red pencil through the note and moved down to the
next one.

Barbra continued to schlepp shopping bags full of food home
to the apartment from her mother's, but I had learned to stop
asking questions. She kept on slaving away at her makeup. Schulenberg tried gluing sequins and silver paper on her eyelids to
make them shine and sparkle iridescently. The first night they did
this, Barbra walked into the room and batted her metallic eye
shadow at me. It was startling and somewhat alarming, a bit like
the female robot in Fritz Lang's *Metropolis*.

"Bob," I said, a little unnerved, "Barbra's got aluminum eyelids."

"Yeah," Bob agreed. "It's a look."

Another experiment evolved when Barbra noticed the phos-
phorescent glow on herring skin and wondered if a band of it
could be laid in a patina on her eyes. Like medieval alchemists
fussing around with glass jars and potions, the two of them soaked
the herring skins in Chanel to get rid of the smell, but it also bled
the pattern out of the fish. I confess I was secretly relieved.

But that was later. Going back in my mind to the very night
Barbra opened at the Bon Soir, I remember watching her pace the
apartment floor like a caged puma, taking little puffs on a cigarette
like a young, maddened Bette Davis.

"You okay?" I asked her. Barbra exhaled a long, soulful sigh
and crushed out her smoke.

"Something's happening inside of me," she said. "I feel…
ferblunget, all mixed up. I don't know what it is."

"Think about it. Talk about it. How do you feel?" I asked her.

"I'm scared," she said. "I'm excited. I guess I'm ready. I'm fine.
I'm a wreck. Oh, I don't know.…"

"Come here," I said. "Sit on my lap."

Barbra came over to me dutifully and sat on my knees, looking me in the eyes. "Why am I doing this?" she asked plaintively.

I thought a moment. "Because you want to," I said.

"What am I going to do?" she said.

"What do you mean?"

"Everything's...going to change," Barbra said. "What am I going to *do*?" she said, laying her head on my shoulder.

I made my answer as steady, real, and sincere as I could: "You're going to deal with it."

A therapist once proposed to me the interesting idea that there were only a few feelings, only a handful, really, and that most complicated human situations evoked a rich admixture of what were, in effect, simple emotional coordinates. Ambivalence was the confused child of this coupling (Lodged in my mind right next to this idea was my own observation that a really good actor was distinguished by his ability to show several feelings simultaneously.)

In Barbra's case, however, complex compounds of emotions flowed through her about *everything*. She was profoundly affected by sensory experiences, she thrived in a state of flux. Everything she felt, she felt deeply and dichotomously. And that was just the simple things. You can imagine how distraught she was by this very important, pivotal turning point in her life.

The curtain was about to go up.

These were the beginnings of her glory days, when Barbra first began to grapple with the dilemma of being Barbra Streisand.

12

A Day Out

After the stunning triumph of her opening night we might have expected that the second night would turn out a disappointment, and it was. In the theater, after the excitement and buzz and adrenaline rush of the opening night, "second night letdown" is virtually a tradition, and Barbra came tumbling down with a crash.

I walked her home from the club that evening. The weather was turning cold; winter was just ahead. It was that particular kind of New York evening that makes everything seem clear and sharply in focus. Barbra's heels stabbed at the sidewalk as she stared stonily downward and charged forward, slightly ahead of me. I took a couple of big steps and grabbed her by the arm.

"Okay, what's the matter?" I said.

"They're talking," she said.

"Who's talking?"

"The customers! The nightclub audience! They're talking through my ballad!" she wailed.

She had lost control of her audience. Now, Barbra out of control was not a pretty sight on a good day; perhaps it was a lessening of energy or a relaxing of purpose after the mad grab for the golden ring a night earlier. But by the time she got to "A Sleepin' Bee" that second night, the audience was *talking*. Talking through her ballad!

"Oh, Barb, nightclub audiences have always talked through a singer's set."

"Not through mine, they don't!" she insisted. "Listen, Barry, I don't get it. Why would anyone pay all that money and go to all that trouble to come see me and then *talk* through my set?"

"I don't know," I said, shaking my head. "Maybe it's one-upmanship, you know, I'm so rich or I'm so chic or I'm so bored that I don't have to shut up for this. I've got much more important things to talk about, like what the kids did at school today or how I can't find my laundry ticket."

"Yeah, well," Barbra said, and came to a halt and faced me. "What am I gonna do about it?" she demanded.

I took her arm and we started to walk along again, a little slower. "I'm not sure," I said. "Let me think. You know, I bet it's television. Watching television has given everyone the illusion that they're at home, wherever they are, in a nightclub or a movie, or whatever. The minute the show begins is a signal to start talking and commenting."

"I don't *care* what the reason is," Barbra insisted. "I just want them to *shut up!*"

"Yeah," I said. "Of course. Here's what you do: Just...stop. Wait. If they're talking, don't start the number. *Will* them to shut up, in your mind."

"You mean, just...*stand* there?" Barbra said.

"Yeah. Just stand there. Stare them down. *Make* them be quiet."

The next night the audience was very jazzed and garrulous

and when Barbra got to the start of her ballad, they were buzzing. And Barbra…just stood there. Her wonderful pianist, Peter Daniels, played her intro, then played it again. And Barbra just stared the crowd down and waited. Finally a few soft "shushes" flitted around the room, the audience miraculously, obediently became utterly still and attentive, and Barbra began the song. It was totally amazing.

Our life together was becoming a series of manic ups and crashing downs. We veered violently from hysterical fits of uncontrollable laughter to the black pit of unassuageable upsets and misunderstandings, with arguments and screaming thrown in the middle for good measure. Maybe it was the hothouse atmosphere we lived in, the circumscribed universe, the bubble in which nothing else existed except what we were doing together: the creation of "Barbra." We were living inside a myth, Pygmalion and Galatea, God creating Eve out of Adam's rib in the Garden, except we weren't naked. We had clothes, lots and *lots* of clothes. Perhaps ours was a good mind-set for working out a fairy tale, but was it good for a relationship between two flesh-and-blood human beings?

One crisp October afternoon I flew into the apartment excitedly. In the elevator, I'd overheard another tenant in the building, the comedienne Kaye Ballard, talking nervously about meeting producer Ray Stark and how desperately she wanted to play Fanny Brice in his new musical.

"Fanny *Who?*" Barbra asked me.

It was hard to believe that Barbra had never heard of the most famous Jewish comedienne ever to light up Broadway, but she hadn't. I suppose secretly, in the supercilious part of my heart, I was a little bewildered that Barbra knew almost nothing about the history of the theater, that she wanted so desperately to be a part of something she knew so little about. Nevertheless, she was voracious to learn and I was flattered to teach.

I told her about Fanny Brice, about her singing these outra-geous comedy numbers in the Ziegfeld Follies, her marriage to Nicky Arnstein, a forger and con man who wound up in Sing Sing. I played Barbra almost all the original Brice recordings, including "Second Hand Rose." I also played her the rare, alternate take of "My Man," in which Fanny breaks down in the last chorus and can't go on singing . . . you can hear her heartbroken sobs quite clearly on the record. It's a very moving performance, and Barbra was impressed with it.

"That's . . . pretty good," she said, nodding her head and smiling in admiration.

"*You'd* be great playing Fanny Brice," I told her.

"Oh, yeah?" she asked.

"Yeah," I said.

"Say, sure, why not? Hey, *I'm* ready to play the lead in a Broadway show." She snatched up the telephone. "Hello, this is *Barbra*," she yelled into the receiver to the dial tone. "That's right, *Barbra Streisand*! Someone told me you're looking for an *ehktress* to play Fanny Brice. So, here I am, already. Cast me! Cast me!"

The record of Fanny singing "I'd Rather Be Blue" was still playing on the phonograph. Barbra slammed down the phone and gesticulated at the hi-fi speakers. "*Listen* to her!" Barbra exclaimed. "How can she get *away* with that? Singing in a Yiddish accent!" She got up, wandered over to the window, looked down at the cool autumnal cityscape and muttered, "Hey, I guess when you're a star, you can get away with anything."

It confounded me completely when, during *Funny Girl*, Barbra gave interviews in which she insisted she'd never heard a Fanny Brice record. I know that the perception of truth is molded by one's own reality; and perhaps Barbra really didn't remember or didn't want to remember, but whatever the reason, it simply wasn't true. She'd heard all of them, right in our apartment.

186

I also played her Kaye Ballard's album that had recently been released, "The Fanny Brice Story," in which Kaye makes a pretty good meal of the songs associated with the legendary performer. And that afternoon Barbra also heard Kaye's recording of "Lazy Afternoon" from the original cast recording of that marvelous musical *The Golden Apple.* Now Barbra and I had ridden up and down in the elevator with Ballard a couple of times, and it's fair to say that Kaye was a noticeably large, full-figured woman. When Barbra heard her sing, her comment was, "Brother, she's got a really wide...(and here she held her hands two feet apart measuring the distance)...vibrato."

One Sunday morning I read an ad in the paper for a shop that rented all kinds of bicycles, even tandem bikes. That sounded like a lark. So I peeked over the top of my *Times* at Barbra, sipping a cup of tea and nibbling at a piece of toast at the breakfast table, and said, "Hey, kid, how would you like to ride down to Wall Street with me on a bicycle-built-for-two?"

"What, are you kidding?" Barbra said.

"No, I'm not kidding. We never get out of the house, you and I. Let's get some fresh air, some exercise. It'd be just like a June Allyson-Van Johnson movie."

"I think maybe I'm not *goyish* enough to play June Allyson," Barbra said.

"Maybe we could stop in Chinatown on the way back for some Dim Sum," I tempted her.

It took most of the morning and part of the afternoon before we were finally ready to extract ourselves from the warm cocoon of our apartment and brave the outdoors, but the October sun was still trying to warm the streets of New York when finally we descended into the subway and headed downtown. We found the bike rental place, a tiny hole in the wall in Little Italy; paid a deposit on a shiny, modern tandem bike, and after a lot of "how do we work this" and "you get on first" and "no *you* get on first," I got up on the back seat and Barbra swung her leg over the front. Finally, with a lot of swaying, balancing, and pawing the ground, we began to wobble in a forward direction.

I felt so good and Barbra seemed so happy we were actually doing something besides working on a nightclub act, I started to sing at the top of my lungs:

> Barbra, Barbra, give me your answer true,
> Lost my star bra, all for the love of you...

"Wait a minute, wait a minute... 'star bra'? What kind of a rhyme is that?" Barbra said.

"A very dumb rhyme," I answered, "but it's the only one I can think of."

"What's a 'star bra,' anyway? There is no such thing."

"Sure there is. It's a brassiere made exclusively for motion picture stars. By Fredericks of Hollywood. The studios would call them up and say, hey, we need a black bra for Joan Crawford, we need a red bra for Joan Blondell. They had busts in their workroom for every major star in Hollywood."

"You made that up," Barbra said.

"Didn't."

"Did."

"You're not pedaling," I said.

"Sorry," she replied.

"Now, if I was singing in French, I could find some terrific rhymes," I said and sang:

> Rapelle-toi, Barbara,
> Il pleuvait sans cesse sur Brest ce jour-là
> Et tu marchais souriante

188

Épanouie ravie ruisselante
Sous la pluie…*

"That's pretty," she said. "What does it mean?" But before I could answer, we hung a left and found ourselves careening down Wall Street.

Every newsstand, every restaurant, every shop was closed. The streets were eerily empty, as if they'd been suddenly evacuated in an air raid warning. There was no noise, either; no traffic jangle, street shouts, no music blaring out of store fronts. Just the wind whistling, the bicycle chain whirring, and the sound of our own breathing. The only other person we saw was a Chinese gentleman in a top coat as he scuttled across a street in the far distance, about seven blocks away. He was gone like the click of a camera shutter, so fast it might have been a ghost.

"This is Wall Street. This is where they keep all the money," I told her, pumping the pedals harder.

"It's not very busy," she snorted. "I guess there's nothin' doin' on a Sunday."

"You can't make money on Wall Street on a Sunday. It's a holy law. You can't even print money on a Sunday. It's the Lord's Day."

"You made that up, just like that star bra business," she protested, turning back to look at me.

"Yes, I did," I admitted. "Why don't you help me pedal instead of asking so many questions."

"Okay," she said. Then immediately: "So, why do they call it Wall Street?"

"Because there used to be a big wall here."

---

*"Do you remember, Barbara / The ceaseless way it rained on Brest that day / And you walked away, smiling / Beaming, gleaming, streaming / In the rain."

Jacques Prevert and Joseph Kosma, "Barbara," *D'Autres Chansons* (Paris: Enoch & Cie, Éditeurs). Reprinted by permission. Translated by Barry Dennen.

"What for? To keep the people from Brooklyn out, I bet."

"No, to keep all the money *in*. To keep it from falling out all over the sidewalk." I looked up at the late afternoon sky. Already it was beginning to get dark. "New York was founded by the Dutch, you know," I said.

"Oh, yeah?" Barbra said, snapping her gum.

"You're not pumping," I noticed.

"Okay, okay."

She pushed the pedals for a short while, then coasted while I did most of the work.

"There were a whole series of canals down here. Just like in Holland. That's why it's called Canal Street," I told her.

"Wait a minute, wait a minute," Barbra interjected. "You mean, you went up and down the street in a *boat*?"

"Yeah," I said. "In a boat. That's right. Like Venice."

"Venice, Italy, or Venice, California?"

"Both."

"So, what happened to all the canals?"

"They filled them all in."

Barbra went glum for a moment, then popped her gum decisively. "Everything good gets covered over or taken away," she said.

"You are such a *forbissner*!" I protested.

"*Forbissner*!" she snorted. "I don't even know what that means."

"Don't give me that," I argued. "You know perfectly well what the definition of *forbissner* is: you. You're such a *sourpuss*! All you can think about is the gloomy side of everything."

"Yeah, yeah," she added darkly. "You watch. God sees that you're happy, he moves in, boom! It all gets taken away."

"Barbra," I cautioned, "bite your tongue. Count your blessings."

"I guess it was just the way I was brought up. Whenever anything good happened, my mother would dry-spit through her fingers," Barbra admitted, in a rare moment of biography.

I wondered why Barbra was so silent about her upbringing, particularly her relationship with her mother, whom she almost never talked about and seemed to hold off at arm's length. Once, in an unguarded moment, she'd let drop that whenever she got any praise from Mrs. Kind, which wasn't very often, there was always some stinging criticism or put-down thrown in for good measure, just in case Barbra was tempted to get "big-headed." Big-headed, I scoffed to myself. Barbra was very shy, insecure, and starved for approval.

"The problem with you," I said, moving close to her ear, "is that you won't let yourself enjoy anything."

It was true, or I felt it was. Barbra seemed constitutionally incapable of allowing herself any experience of joy. Even her great success at the Bon Soir was suspiciously dismissed. We'd had several arguments about it. She was always searching for the dark underpinnings, the trip wire, the pimple on God's ass.

I watched the back of her head, bobbing with the effort of propelling the bike, then peering up at the impressive buildings, the architecture, the whole style of the district, so much more like London, so different from any other part of New York City. Her little hands in knit wool gloves, grasping the handlebars. The soft hairs on the back of her neck. She'd gone quiet.

"Hey," I whispered in her ear. "You okay?"

"I'm out of breath," she admitted, as we pulled up to South Ferry and tried to get off the bike without falling over.

"Hey, why don't we take the ferry to Staten Island?" I suggested. "It'd be just like Fred and Ginger in *Shall We Dance.* Whaddya think?"

"Okay," she said, "but what do we do when we get to the other side?"

"We run around and come back again," I said.

"Sure," she said. "Why not?"

191

Barbra and I had watched *Shall We Dance* only a few weeks earlier on TV and tape-recorded the soundtrack. In the picture, Astaire and Rogers find themselves on the Staten Island ferry in a gleaming, swank two-seater Packard convertible. The mist rolls in, foghorns moan, and in the background the Manhattan skyline glows like a burnished necklace above the water. He buys her a gardenia from a flower lady and then, in one of moviedom's most romantic screen moments ever, Fred sings the Gershwins' beautiful love song "They Can't Take That Away from Me" to Ginger, tears shimmering in her eyes as she stands there in her full-length sable coat.

The minute we lurched away from the pier I knew we had made a mistake. The sun had sunk below the horizon so quickly I hadn't even noticed. It was dark now but there was no glimmering New York City to dance prettily on the shore, just the unfriendly, steely darkness, the stretch of water like black oil, and a freezing, penetrating wind that turned our noses red and made us shiver.

As the ferry, a long, flat slab of ugly, dirty metal, charged grimly, unrelentingly forward across the lower end of the East River, its deafening motors made the deck vibrate unpleasantly with a monotonous, ear-splitting "*JUG*-JUG-*JUG*-JUG-*JUG*-JUG-*JUG*!" There wasn't the slightest indication that it was a vessel traveling on water; it didn't seem to float or bob or do anything like a boat. We might as well have been in a grimy, noisy tank going into battle, or on a bleak, filthy cattle car headed straight for the stockyards.

I pointed desperately to the inside passenger room and yelled, "Let's go sit down!"

Barbra nodded and I dragged the bike into the room, which was empty and mercifully heated, and we slammed down on the unpadded wooden benches. Barbra was oddly quiet and thoughtful. She stared at the floor as if it knew the answer to what was troubling her. Finally, she looked up at me ruefully and said, "God, this is depressing."

"Totally," I said. I think I was feeling as crushed and let-down inside as she.

"It's not like in the movies, is it?" Barbra said.

"Nope," I said. "The movies are all illusion, honey. Magic. That's what we're looking to give them in the theater. The real magic."

"That's where I'd like to live my life," Barbra said wistfully.

"Where, in the theater?" I asked.

"In the magic of the movies."

"Really?"

"Well, it beats this!" she said, gesturing at the uncompromisingly repulsive reality surrounding us.

"Amen," I said.

"Listen, can I ask you something without you getting sore and all?" Barbra said.

"Well, I can't promise. But I'll try," I said.

Barbra took a breath, a big, big breath. "So... what are we gonna do about sex?"

That stopped me cold. I knew, however, what she was talking about. Barbra and I hadn't touched each other erotically since the disaster at Shakespeare in the Park. I guess honestly I hadn't been able to get over it.

"What do you mean, what are we gonna do about sex?" I managed to get out.

"Sex," said Barbra. "We ain't having any."

"I know. I'm aware of it. Hey, look, we're really busy with your act and I'm really... tired. Let's just get you nice and solid at the club and then we'll see what happens," I said.

"We coulda stayed home today and fooled around, instead of this *fercockter,* stupid ferry boat," she said.

"You didn't say anything," I said.

"Neither did you."

We looked at each other for a long moment. It seemed so sad. She crumpled into my chest and I put my arms around her.

"I feel like I've lost something," her voice rose up from my chest, "but I don't know what it is."

"It'll be all right," I said. "Everything will work itself out."

"Who knows," she said. "Maybe."

"Come on, Barb," I said, "don't spit in God's eye."

The ferry pulled into the docking jetty at Staten Island and we had to run all the way around the station, argue with the man in the booth to buy tokens without having the correct change, struggle the bicycle through the turnstile, and dash back onto the grim boat just as the gate was about to come down for its departure.

On the subway ride home, we both stared at the tunnel walls rushing by the windows. Neither one of us spoke.

13

Sharpening Our Claws in the Catskills

One night in November, between shows at the Bon Soir, Barbra telephoned me from backstage.

"Hello, Bar?" she breathed into the phone. "Listen, you gotta come over here right away. There's this guy who just came backstage. He says he wants to manage me." In the background, I could hear all the sauce pots and frying pans being banged around in the chaotic kitchen, and the waiters calling out orders.

"You gotta speak up, Barb, I can hardly hear you," I screamed.

"Come over now, will ya?" she pleaded. "I'm on a break. I just want you to meet him and tell me what you think. He says he really *loves* the way I sing!" Barbra enthused.

"Well, that's very impressive," I said. "Please don't get married to him or anything, until I get there."

"He's blond!" she blurted. "Legally blond. I never *saw* anybody so blond."

"Uh-oh. Sounds dangerous. I'll be right over," I said, slamming down the phone, and in ten seconds I had thrown on my winter coat and was out the door. It was only a four-minute walk around the corner from our apartment to the club, so before you could say three-year contract, I was sitting at a table with Barbra and Ted.

Ted Rozar was the whitest white man I had ever met. He *was* blond, indeed, he was breathtakingly blond, and his long hair was combed straight back and didn't move, like it was frozen.

Ted flashed me a blazingly white smile that made me want to shield my eyes. I've always been suspicious of men with finger-crushing handshakes. Not to disappoint, Ted tried to pulverize my fingers with a steely firmness that may have been intended to convey honesty, strength, and a misplaced kind of machismo, but it gave me a certain assholey undertaste.

"Why don't we all duck out of here for half an hour and grab a cup of coffee?" he asked, with another blinding flash of teeth.

I looked at Barbra and she looked back at me wide-eyed. We were both dumbfounded, I think, by his overwhelming, all-pervading, distilled Eau D' Wasp. Neither of us had ever experienced anything quite like him before.

As we trudged over to the Pam Pam, Barbra and I stared straight ahead, occasionally shooting looks at each other out of the corners of our eyes, trying not to break into nervous laughter.

Once inside the coffee shop, with its uncompromisingly unkind lighting, I could cop a better look at Ted. He slid into one side of the booth and we sat on the other. He was a big guy, with a football player's build. He seemed to reek of old money. And he was handsome, in an exquisitely bland, lusterless kind of way.

As he sat there, never taking his frosty blue eyes off Barbra, Ted outlined what he was going to do for her: get her club dates, TV spots, records, movies. She would have it all: money, fame, stardom. Ted believed in Barbra and would make sure that she got everything she deserved.

But we had run out of time and we had to get back to the Bon

Soir for Barbra's second set. Before we got up, Ted handed Barbra his card.

"Call me," he pleaded. "Please, please, call me. I really, really want to work for you. I think we can make great music together," he said, looking deeply and sincerely into Barbra's eyes like an actor on a soap opera. "What's your number?" he murmured, twisting his gold Cross ballpoint pen and poising it to scribble on the back of a second card.

Barbra hesitated, and turned to look at me. I shrugged okay and she blurted, "Gramercy 7-7345. Don't call before ten-thirty in the morning."

We thanked Ted for the coffee and left him standing at the corner. After we'd walked halfway down the block, I turned and looked back. He was still there, watching us, and he waved. Even at that distance, I swear I could see his teeth gleaming in the dark.

As we traipsed back to the club, I moved in. "So, what do you think of him?"

Barbra schlepped along, not answering, the corners of her mouth turned firmly down.

"I dunno," she said finally. "He's our age, but he talks like my father. If I had a father."

"Well, look on the bright side," I offered. "He doesn't want to change your name and he doesn't want to change your nose. That's a big plus."

"Yeah, that's good for a start, I guess," she mused. "It's just that he's so...so..."

"I'm waiting," I smiled.

"He's such a *goy*!" she exclaimed.

We both burst into hysterical laughter, clutching each other and rushing along the sidewalk. When we got to the club, still giggling, we nearly tumbled down the steep stairs, until the stern stare of the maitresse d' shushed us into submission.

197

During the next few days Ted called morning, noon and night, begging and cajoling Barbra to sign with him. About a week later, scared, nervous, and worn down by attrition, she did. A few days after that, Ted phoned with great excitement to say he had landed Barbra a job in the Catskills. No, not at the famous Grossinger's, but at a smaller, nicer, more "family" kind of hotel, much more suitable for her. Barbra would love them and they would love her. Furthermore, Ted would drive us up in his car.

Barbra put down the phone and said, "He's got a car!"

We looked at each other. "Ah!" we said in unison, raising a forefinger, "he's got a *car*!"

And so, early in the morning on her next day off, Barbra and I were flabbergasted when Ted pulled up in his seven-year-old, somewhat rusted and shabby clunker. One fender had been badly crumpled, but it had never been hammered out and repainted, and now it was corroded and sorely in need of paint.

"That's his car?" Barbra said, sniffing disaster, as Ted maneuvered his junkmobile into the loading zone in front of our building. "This person's gonna make me successful and rich and famous, and *that's* his *car*?"

"C'mon," I said grimly, "it'll be nice to spend a day in the country, have a free meal, and make a little money."

"I'm not convinced," she said.

Ted hopped out on the driver's side. "Hi!" he grinned, another of his patented, eye-dazzling smiles pasted across his face. He pointed at the crushed fender. "Someone hit me in a parking lot," he explained, which left the condition of the rest of the vehicle open for speculation.

He unlocked the trunk with a flourish, pushing a lot of cardboard cups and take-out containers behind the spare tire. We arranged Barbra's many shopping bags inside and climbed into the back seat.

Ted's wife sat in the front, a pleasant but unmemorable cipher of a woman. We all chatted amiably for a while, until Ted started recounting his difficulties in trying to sell Barbra to an agent. As he talked, I could feel Barbra's spirit draining down into her 1927 pumps.

As we drove further upstate, the city gradually blended into the suburbs and finally the buildings melted away as we plunged deeper and deeper into the countryside. Barbra and I sat talking quietly in the back seat, and to cheer her up I started to play one of our favorite games, decorating our glamorous, expensive new penthouse apartment on Central Park South.

"I've been thinking about the second bathroom," I said, "and I'd really like to do it in black and white. White walls, black trim, maybe a checkerboard floor."

"Black and white is so aggressive," Barbra complained.

"It's masculine," I countered. "And anyway, it's my bathroom, why can't I have it the way I want it?"

"Go ahead and have it," she sniffed. "Just don't expect me to *do* anything in there. Now, listen Barry, about the master bedroom. I'm gonna go with the dusty rose silk wallpaper," she concluded.

"You're having our bedroom walls lined in *silk?*" I protested. "Do you know how much silk costs a yard?"

"So what?" she said, tilting up her head imperiously. "It's only money."

By the time we'd rigged out the private, parquet-floored rehearsal room entirely in mirrors and spotlights, we had reached a little town near the Seven Lakes, where we stopped at a small gas station to fill up. The place looked like it had stepped off the cover of a 1940s *Redbook* magazine, with its old-fashioned glass jar gas pumps and dusty, ancient tin signs advertising motor oil and Coca-Cola in the office window.

The young gas jockey was a towheaded kid with light blue

eyes and an easy smile. He wore a denim work shirt with the name "Scott" embroidered on the chest.

"You like pumping gas?" I asked him.

"Oh, yeah," Scott replied. "I pick up a little pocket change over the weekends and help my dad out. He works the night shift."

When we finally reached the hotel and pulled into its circular gravel driveway, it was immediately apparent that this was not the Ritz-Carlton. A certain shabby gentility had crept into what was originally no more than a modest, second-rate establishment. Everything about the place felt a little old, and cold, and damp.

Inside the fusty lobby, the faint trace of lunchtime's chicken soup still perfuming the air, Mr. Schleigl, the hotel owner, proudly introduced us all to Tina, Rozelle, and Maude.

There, standing in front of me in a cozy little semicircle, were three men dressed in Major High Drag: wigs and dresses and nails and heels and full evening makeup. A nosegay of grinning, garish, dressed-to-the-teeth Grade Z Drag Queens.

I was confused enough about my own sexuality. The last thing I expected to find in a nice little Jewish family hotel was this tacky, transgendered trio.

"These," said Mr. Schleigl, "are the girls. Say hello, girls. They performed here last night. Everybody went crazy, they were pissing themselves, they were so good."

There were hellos all around and then Tina, a pugnacious blonde with big hair, suddenly sidled up to Ted, smiling seductively as she fondled his lapel. "So, Mr. Rozar," she said, in a breathy, Marilyn Monroe kind of whisper, "Mr. Schleigl here tells me you're a great...big...manager."

Ted took a jerk-reflex step backward, grinning awkwardly, and suddenly he had to show Barbra the Entertainment Room right that minute. Mr. Schleigl excused himself to go look after his wife, who, he explained, had shingles, and I was left to chat with Tina,

Rozelle, and Maude. Trying desperately to control my rising panic, I decided this was a good moment to get the scoop.

"So tell me," I said, "what kind of stuff do you do?"

Tina, who seemed be the group's designated diva, piped up: "Well, ya know, I do Bette and Tallulah, and Maude here does Kate," she explained in a suddenly deep, foghorn sort of voice.

"The calla lilies are in bloom again, such a strange flower," Maude interjected, in what was perhaps the world-class worst imitation of Katharine Hepburn I'd ever heard.

"*Stage Door*," I quoted the title of the movie, at a loss for anything better to say. Maude shook her brunette curls at me and batted her eyes as if I'd complimented her extravagantly.

"And Rozelle does Mae West," Tina continued in her basso profundo.

"Oh, Beulah," the alarmingly red-headed Rozelle said, "peel me a grape."

"Yeah," I added, "Barb and I were watching *I'm No Angel* just the other night and—"

"And we all do a musical finale," Tina butted in. "We lip-synch to the Chordette's hit record, 'Mr. Sandman.' Sorry you weren't here to catch us last night," she said, her eyes dropping down first to my crotch, and then spearing me with an appraising, challenging stare. I felt a patch of sweat forming above my upper lip.

"Listen, guys, tell me," I jumped in, "what are the audiences like here? They any good?"

"They're not the brightest, honey," Maude commiserated. "*I* think *they* think we're women."

"Not to be unkind," Rozelle said in her Jersey twang, "they're, how do I put it? Let's say, they're unfocused."

"And noisy," Maude added.

"Basically, they stink," Tina said, planting her fists on her thighs as all three broke into an unnervingly shrill cackle.

"Well, I'd better go see what's happening with Barbra," I said, figuring this was a polite moment to duck out. "See ya later," I added, turning in the direction that Barbra and Ted had gone and trying not to run. Behind me I heard Tina stage-whisper to the others, "So what's *her* story?"

I ducked into the Entertainment Room where Barbra was struggling through "A Sleepin' Bee" with an inept accompanist who was playing all the wrong chords. As I came closer, she looked up at me with the panicky eyes of a drowning person. The piano player turned around and stared at me through Coke-bottle glasses.

"Hi, I'm Murray, the pianist," he said.

I introduced myself, then said, "Listen, I think that was supposed to be a major chord there, Murray."

"I'll get it, I'll get it," Murray muttered as he turned back again to the weather-worn keyboard. Barbra looked at me helplessly, literally wringing her hands in agony as Murray tortured the chord sequences. As she plowed on, I looked around at the medium-sized room: bare walls, folding utility chairs in uneven rows, a tiny, rickety platform of a stage.

Brother, this is grim, I thought.

As we continued to rehearse the set that Barbra would sing that evening, Murray's playing got slightly better but it was still hopelessly inadequate. "Let me take these with me," he said, piling up Barbra's music in a little stack. "I'll look them over. By tonight, everything'll be fine," he finished, and scurried away.

"C'mon," I said to Barbra. "Let's go get something to eat."

Barbra didn't look up at me, she just stood very still next to the piano, looking down at it, slightly biting her bottom lip.

"Barb?" I said. "Are you okay?"

When something bothered Barbra, she usually got upset and flew off the handle right away, exploding in a cascade of verbal invective or outrage. And even when she was boiling over with

202

indignation, she managed to inject a note of humor or word-play that made her vocal explosions vastly entertaining.

But when she was deeply distressed, Barbra went profoundly, chillingly quiet. I'd seen her like this only one time before, over an extremely serious misunderstanding between us. And now she stood, staring into the piano in deathly silence, seeming not even to breathe.

"Barb?" I said softly.

Barbra took a deep breath and looked up at me as if she hadn't realized I was there. A look of deep despair was in her eyes.

"I think coming here was the worst mistake of my life…" she trailed off.

I moved over to her and put my arms around her, holding her tight. She just stood there at first, then gradually I felt some of the tense stiffness leave her body, and she wrapped her arms around my back and allowed herself to melt against me. I gave her a soft kiss on the neck.

"Come on," I said. "It'll be all right."

"No, Barry," she said in my ear. "It won't."

There was a new note of absolute certainty in her voice that caught my attention. I broke from her and looked into her eyes. There was something new there, the desire to face reality head-on, to deal with things as they are, however painful.

"Well, at least it'll be over quickly," I said.

"Sure," she said. "Quick like eternity."

In the dining room, we sat down to a meal they had specially prepared for us: warm, wilted salad and a sandwich of chicken *à la* cardboard. And for dessert, a cup of tapioca with a sad little maraschino cherry bleeding on top.

Barbra just sat, staring down at the table, thinking.

"Eat," I said.

"You sound like my mother," she replied.

"Eat anyway," I insisted.

"I'm not really hungry," she said.

My eyebrows shot up. Barbra not hungry?

"I've made a terrible mistake, not bringing my own pianist," she said regretfully.

"Barb, it would've cost more to pay him than you're making," I reminded her.

She looked at me squarely. "It would have been worth it," she said simply.

After our late afternoon feast, Barbra and I wandered around the grounds. A cold wind had blown up. Autumn was turning into winter, and the leaves had already changed color and blown off the trees. I didn't know how to tell Barbra what I had to bring up.

"Barb, I'm sorry to have to tell you this, but I have some bad news," I blurted out.

Her shoulders slumped. "More?"

"The girls tell me that the audiences here are terrible. They talk right through your act."

"Oh," Barbra said, rapidly pulling herself together and suddenly sounding very practical and professional. "Well, I'll do five numbers and then, off. I've learned how to handle talkative crowds at the Bon Soir. How bad can this bunch be?"

When Barbra got up that night to sing her opening number, "Keepin' Out of Mischief," the audience was shocking, like a crowd at a prize fight. Even though she had a microphone, her voice poked through the raucous din only now and then. The Catskillers shouted across the aisles to each other, boisterously discussing last night's pinochle game, arguing at the top of their lungs the merits of what they had for dinner:

"You had the roast beef? You shoulda had the chicken."

"Ech, I had the chicken last night! It was hard like a rock and stone cold."

"Oh, Harvey, you're going for a pee-pee? Bring your mother back a Pepsi!"

Barbra looked at me in desperation halfway through the song and started to giggle out of nervousness at the nightmarishness of it all. I made my way to the primitive amplifier on a shelf in the wings and brought up the volume. Well, Barbra got louder, but the audience got louder, too. When she finished singing, the audience didn't even know it. Seated in the third row, Ted started to applaud. The people sitting around him looked at him, mystified. Why was this *meshugeneh goy*, this crazy gentile, applauding?

When Murray the pianist started the intro for "A Sleepin' Bee," which is a very delicate song with a poetic lyric, I thought, no, enough of this. I walked right out on stage and Barbra shot me a look like she was afraid I'd gone crazy. I took the mike.

"Excuse me," I said to the crowd, "excuse me! Stop talking for a minute!" The audience continued to yell at and argue with each other. "Hey," I said, raising my voice, "all of you out there, stop talking, d'ya hear me?"

Three or four people stopped shouting at each other and looked up at me curiously. But I'd had enough of this rudeness. Finally I yelled at the top of my lungs, "OH, SHUT!...UP!"

Suddenly an eerie hush fell over the hall. Every face in the audience was gazing up at me quizzically, like rows of little owls on telephone wires.

"Now listen," I said, lowering my quivering voice slightly, "this is one of the greatest singers you are ever going to hear. Ever. Her name is Bar-bra Strei-sand. Years from now, you'll be able to tell everyone you were privileged enough to hear Barbra Streisand sing when she first started out. So be quiet...and listen!"

The audience continued to stare at me silently, not moving, as if struck dumb. I had a sudden pang of remorse, looking at this foolish bunch of *alta cockers* (for the Yiddish-challenged, "old caca makers") who, because they were too busy arguing about whether or not the chickens at dinner were tough, would miss one of the greatest moments of their lives. It was something they could have dined out on forever or told their grandchildren: "I *saw* her, I heard Barbra Streisand sing before she was *anyone*! She was standing *right there* in front of me! And I turned to your grandmother and I said, *that* goil's gonna be a *star!*" And their grandchildren would look at each other meaningfully and nod: Grandpa's off again.

Years later, when I saw the film *Cocoon*, the memory of this hideous evening came back to me in a rush. At the end of that movie, all the old folks were going off in the spaceship with the extraterrestrials to their planet far away in the solar system, as a breathless Maureen Stapleton explained, "To be teachers!" What, I asked myself, are they going to teach aliens from outer space? Canasta?

I turned to look at Barbra standing next to me. She looked embarrassed, grateful, and relieved. "Come on, Barb," I coaxed her, "sing for the people," and I retreated to the side of the stage.

There was a hushed, expectant moment as Murray the pianist softly played her introduction and once again Barbra opened her mouth to sing.

Immediately every person in the audience turned to his neighbor and started jabbering, shouting, and laughing at top volume, louder than before, as if nothing had ever happened. I shook my head. It was unbelievable.

Barbra bravely continued to sing her beautiful, tender, haunting ballad in front of this loud mob. And in the middle of the second chorus, without missing a note, she turned to me in the wings, shrugged her shoulders, and crossed her eyes.

After she'd struggled through her five numbers, one of which she sang in an entirely different key from Murray's, although nobody could have heard it to tell the difference, Barbra ran off-stage into a little room on the side. I entered right behind her and found her standing next to a table, supporting herself with her arms, hunched forward, her body heaving up and down.

"It's over now, honey, it's over," I said, putting my arms around her.

Barbra wheeled around to face me. Tears of laughter were streaming down her face.

"Did you see their *faces* when you told them off?" she erupted.

Happy and relieved Barbra was okay, I started to laugh, too. "Did you hear when Murray couldn't find the key you were in, and kept modulating up and down?" I said, giggling uncontrollably through my clenched teeth.

Barbra pressed her head into my chest, convulsed and shaking, and we both sank to the floor in hysterical laughing and howling.

There was a knock on the door and we both looked up, surprised. Behind his fishbowl glasses, Murray the pianist's wrinkled face loomed in the doorway.

"Hey, c'mon," he said. "They want an encore."

Huddled in the lobby after this fiasco of an evening, Barbra and I were more than ready to head back to New York. Ted, who was busy talking to Irwin, the hotel's talent booker, wandered over to me as we were about to walk out to the parking lot. "Barry," he said, "Irwin and I have some business to discuss, so I'll be taking him in my car with Barbra. The...uh...girls will give you a lift back to town."

At that moment, to my horror, I saw Tina, Rozelle, and Maude heading straight for me across the lobby. They were still in their drag costumes, wigs and makeup, with a half day's growth of beard pushing up through the orange pancake foundation.

"Well, Barry," Tina wheezed in a nicotine-laced exhalation, pinching my cheek, "looks like you're gonna be our little hitch-hiker pickup for tonight."

Oh please, God, I prayed, get me through this.

Barbra, Ted, Ted's wife, and Irwin were almost out the front door.

"I guess I'll see you back at the apartment," Barbra shouted at me, gesticulating helplessly.

I went very quiet as I got in the back of the car, pressing myself into the corner and pretending to fall asleep. The girls' shrill gossip, their campy wisecracks about what they called the size of the waiters' noodles, and their endless chains of cigarettes seemed gaudily out of place among the moonlit, frosted landscapes of forests and farmers' fields we were driving through.

My mind reeled back to my grammar school in Chicago where a small gang of dumb, mean, beefy bullies used to torment me in the playground at recess and after school, holding my head in a hammerlock until they made me cry, spitting on my bike and kicking my shins. One particularly sadistic cretin delighted in coming up behind me in the library, pinching my windpipe closed with his strong thumb and forefinger while I thrashed around like a hooked fish, struggling for breath.

And then they would all chase me, jeering and laughing, until one caught up with me and jumped on my back, knocking me over, pushing me down to the ground to grind my face in the gravel while the rest mocked me in a sing-song, girlish-voiced chant: "Barre is a fairy! Bar-re-Is-A-Fai-ry!"

I came out of my memories with a jolt. The car had stopped and Tina and Maude were opening the doors and getting out.

Tina's face loomed over the top of the driver's seat, staring at Rozelle and me. "What have you two been doing back there?" she whispered huskily, her breath smelling of stale cigarettes.

"Nothing," I snapped.

"Come on, girls, everybody out!" she continued, unfazed. "Time for a tinkle." I glared at Tina as I got out of the back seat.

To my surprise we were in the same quaint old-fashioned gas station Barbra and I had stopped at on the way up, only this time the station attendant was a nice-looking guy in his middle thirties. Somehow he looked oddly familiar. The blue eyes, the tousled hair. Then in a flash it hit me: Scott, the young gas jockey from this afternoon—this man was his *father*. After we had paid him, to my complete mortification Tina suddenly whirled around and slinked over to the guy.

"Say, what's back there?" Tina asked, pointing at the darkened repair shop with its hydraulic lift and long work bench.

"It's j-just the shop," the guy said, backing away glassy-eyed and nervous.

"I'll bet there are *lots* of *big* things back there, aren't there?" she asked, steering him toward the yawning doorway. "Is that where you keep all your tools? Why don'cha take me in there and *show* it to me?"

The gas station attendant stared at Tina in a confusion of fear and lust as a band of perspiration popped out on his forehead and he began to tremble slightly. I doubt that he knew she was a man.

"Why don'cha, huh?" Tina repeated, licking her lips, as she laid her hand with the chipped fingernail polish on his uniform jacket and grabbed it, pushing him back into the dark recesses of the garage.

I crawled into the back seat of the car and curled up in the corner.

Men masquerading as women, giving furtive blow jobs to scared, horny, married guys on a workbench in a garage, in the middle of the countryside, in the middle of nowhere.

I felt a hideous churning in my gut, and sadness, and despair. I closed my eyes and in the dark, one terrible question overwhelmed me: Is this what it's really like to be a faggot? Is this it?

14

Gay Street

*T*he winter of 1960 in New York was a kind of frozen hell. Black plastic garbage bags piled up into barricades on the sidewalks. The traffic, always slow, ground to an utter standstill. And it was freezing.

One arctic morning Barbra and I waited at the bus stop so we could ride uptown together, she to an acting class, I to an audition. We were shivering so convulsively we both started to laugh.

"Let's jump in front of a taxi and get hit," I said.

"For what?" Barbra asked, her teeth chattering, shifting her weight from foot to foot.

"It's warm in the hospital," I explained.

Everything about that winter was oppressive, except the snow. When the snow fell, the air was so cold the flakes swirled down out of the sky in soft, exquisite, crystalline rounds, and when they landed on your clothing, you could see with your naked eye each perfect, geometric pattern.

One winter evening after the club, and another late-night note

211

session at the Pam Pam, Barbra and I walked Bob Schulenberg home. Bob lived just around the block on Gay Street, in an apartment in a row of picturesque Greek Revival houses dating from 1803.

A block long with a bend at one end, Gay Street is a tiny lane that cuts through from Christopher Street to Waverly Place. It's reputed to be the shortest street in the Village and, in fact, in all of New York City.

This particular night the snow was falling thickly and perfectly. The drifts mounded up prettily at the foot of each lamp post as we walked through the circles of light on the snow-covered sidewalk. As we chatted softly our breath described tiny puffs of vapor in the air. The trees still had a few leaves on them here and there, and where the snow heaped up on them, they looked like fat, round cotton balls.

"Look at the leaves," I said. "They look like frozen pigeons."

"You know," said Schulenberg, "this snow is falling so beautifully, it looks fake. As a matter of fact, it *is* fake. We're on a movie set. Look, you can see the wrinkles in the cyc," Bob said, pointing upward at the sky.

"A cyc is a big piece of cloth that—" I started, but Barbra interrupted.

"I know what a cyc is," she said. "It's short for cyclorama. It's a big curtain that goes around the back of the whole set," she finished, sounding a little defensive.

Barbra had been asserting herself a lot more lately, since her success at the Bon Soir. It was great for her.

"Yeah," I added, "if you look up there, you can see two men shaking a big sheet with holes in it and it's full of Ivory Flakes coming down on us. Amazing, isn't it? It looks so real."

"And up there," Bob said, indicating the bend in Gay Street, "right around that corner, is a big table with trays of Danishes and snacks and fruit, and urns of coffee and tea."

"Oh, yeah?" Barbra said. "They *feed* you on a movie set?"

"Absolutely," Bob said, as we all stopped at the steps leading up to his building and looked around at the quaint street which, through some magical alchemy, really was beginning to take on the unreal feeling of a film set, it all looked so romantic and flawless.

"Those houses," Barbra said. "Just a façade. You can tell there's nothing behind them."

"Boy," Bob said, "they've sure got the air conditioning up high. I can see my breath!"

"Actually," I added, "the only thing we need is a spotlight. From the top of one of those buildings," I gestured up, "a big spotlight should be pointed down at us. That's the only thing that's missing."

At that moment, in one of those magical epiphanies that happens rarely in a lifetime, the French doors opened inward on the top floor of the building next door, and a theatrical spotlight on a metal stand was pushed out onto the little balcony, its wheels softly squeaking. A pair of hands tilted it downward and suddenly a bright, focused beam of light ran across the snow and illuminated the three of us.

We all stood agape, caught in the circle of brilliant light, looking up at the window and wondering what in the hell was going on.

Bob whispered, "There are two puppeteers who live up there. They have a little theater and everything. They must have overheard us."

Suddenly Barbra went crazy with joy. She ran up and down the street, laughing, executing little ballerina turns, kicking at the piles of snow, then lifting handfuls of it and tossing them at Bob and me, and all the while the intense beam of light followed her every move. As I watched this brilliant Brooklyn butterfly waltzing down the sidewalk, my eye suddenly caught Schulenberg gazing at her, too. I imagine my face had the same look of amused wonderment on it that his did, and I was curious if he was thinking the same thing I was: would this enchanting girl realize her dreams, get everything she really wanted? What did the future hold in store for Barbra Streisand, where would she wind up? It was anybody's guess, and I shrugged it off.

Finally Barbra turned, looked up into the light, blew a kiss, and collapsed into an enormous full court curtsy, like a swan expiring in a snowdrift. The spot went out, to the accompaniment of soft chuckles, as the two men upstairs pulled the light back inside.

Barbra looked up in the dark, suddenly lost. I gave her my hand, helped her to her feet and she brushed the snow off her coat.

"Thank you!" she shouted up.

"Yes, thanks, it was incredible," Schulenberg laughed.

Barbra looked up at the closing French doors. "Good night!" she said softly.

And as the doors swung shut, from inside we heard the two puppeteers say, "Good night" and "Sweet dreams."

"Sweet dreams," Barbra mused. "I think I just had one."

Flash forward twenty-three years, to the winter of 1983. I was back in New York, working as an actor in a movie. We were on location, it was already after midnight and getting cold.

I drew two coffees from the stainless steel urn on the Crafts service table, then walked around the bend and headed up the street. Set decorators bustled about competing for space with grips wrestling lights and reflectors into place. Wardrobe people rushed back and forth with costume changes as the crew fussed around the camera.

Bob Schulenberg, who coincidentally was production designer on the picture, stood waiting at the far end. I handed him a cup, then we both turned and looked back down Gay Street.

We were both silent for a while, softly sipping our drinks.

"Bob...," I started, turning to look at him, then stopped short. His eyes were cloudy and misted up.

"Look, Bar," he said, pointing up at the sky where the first flurries of snow were starting to whirl down, "you can see the wrinkles in the cyc."

15

The End of the Beginning

$\mathscr{B}$arbra was safely ensconced at the Bon Soir, her engagement having been extended from two weeks to eleven, sharing the stage with Phyllis Diller. The first time I became aware of Phyllis was a goofy photo of her in the back pages of a magazine. It was an ad for her first appearance at the Bon Soir, I think, and she was making an outrageously funny, grotesque face, crossing her eyes and twisting her mouth like a big wad of soft taffy.* I tried to keep away from the Bon Soir kitchen and backstage area because it was so busy and claustrophobic. The few times I did go back there to give Barbra some quick notes or deliver something she'd left behind in the apartment, I'd find Phyllis and her sitting

---

*At home, Phyllis is nothing like her madcap onstage persona. Thoughtful, poised, and articulately intelligent, she's a highly accomplished musician. She invited James, my life partner, and me to dinner and gave us a tour through her twenty-two-room Brentwood home. In every important room there was a beautiful keyboard instrument. The sight of Phyllis Diller pounding out a Bach partita on a harpsichord is something to behold.

soberly side by side in their cramped little dressing room, which was really like a glorified closet.

I gathered that Phyllis had a flock of kids and was rescuing herself from a disastrous marriage. Even though the Bon Soir was her own first big break, Phyllis did everything she could to help Barbra; in fact, she was amazingly generous. She bought her some dresses and was very helpful getting her on a couple of TV shows. When Phyllis's first album was recorded live at the Bon Soir, she made sure the engineers left the tape running to record Barbra's act.

I had planned a trip home to California for the holidays. My father wasn't feeling well and I really wanted to see him. With Phyllis clucking around Barbra like a mother hen with a bad hair day and Bob to help on the domestic end of things, I felt perfectly safe in making the trip.

Little did I know.

"Bob," I said, "I have a feeling when I'm not around, Barbra only eats frozen chicken dinners and coffee ice cream. Keep an eye on what she eats and watch out for her, will ya?"

"I will, Barry," Bob said. "I promise."

Barbra and I were both very discreet about living together. In those days, young men and women simply didn't cohabit unless they were very bohemian or very married. I didn't want Barbra to be the victim of stares, innuendo, or the unwelcome gift of opprobrium, so we simply told our neighbors and the doorman that she was my cousin. If Barbra's mother had known we were living in the same apartment, "without benefit of ring," as the Scots say, she would have shown up at the front door and physically removed her daughter.

In her youth my mother, Rose, was a tearaway whose idea of a good time was dancing the Charleston all night long on a table top, swigging bootleg gin from a hip flask tucked in her rolled-down stockings, and speeding in fast roadsters with the top down.

When the Depression hit and the party was suddenly over, I'm sure she felt personally affronted. My father, Ernie, was a quiet man from an Orthodox Jewish family, and after they married and her children were born, my mother converted, both into a paragon of proper behavior and to Judaism.

I had been very careful not to tell my parents that Barbra and I were living together in our illicit den of sin. They would have been shocked and outraged to be financially underwriting such an unorthodox and, to them, socially unacceptable arrangement; after all, they were picking up the rent. So Barbra's and my separation was going to be difficult because we weren't going to be able to talk to each other on the phone. We just couldn't risk it. I didn't want Barbra calling me at my folks and getting an earload of my mother's suspicious questions and grilling. Conversely, I didn't want to be hauled on the carpet about who I was calling, when my New York apartment's telephone number popped up on my parents' bill.

Before I left we both made the trip to Rockefeller Plaza to see the Christmas tree and for me to say goodbye to my favorite book, which lived in the Librairie Française in the arcade that leads up to the skating rink. This book was so wildly expensive I couldn't even begin to contemplate buying it. But every time I was in the neighborhood of Fifth Avenue, I'd visit my book and hope that someone hadn't bought it away from me yet. It was a French art book of *commedia* characters engraved by Jacques Callot in the early seventeenth century. God, I wanted it.

Just before I left for the airport, Barbra slipped a little package into my bag.

"What's that?" I asked.

"A little something for you to read on the plane," she said. "Don't open it till you're thirty thousand feet in the air. Promise?"

Thirty thousand feet later, with a gin and tonic firmly in my paw, I opened the package. It was my book, and on the dedication page Barbra had written my name at the top and her name at the bottom. Tucked inside the frontispiece was a slip of paper warning me not to riffle through the pages like a movie "flip book" just in order to jump ahead to her next note. She said that one day she would get around to filling in the middle of the dedication page, but today, thirty-seven years later, it is still achingly blank.

Browsing my way through Callot's fabulous monsters and enchanting Columbines and Pierrots, I came across another piece of paper every ten or fifteen pages. One wished me her best for a safe landing and told me she wished she were with me. The next asked me to look at the person seated next to me and tell her what I saw. The correct answer, of course, would be Barbra's own sweet face. And another little slip asked me, if my ears were popping, to open my mouth. Then, it bullied me, shut it, quick.

A further note expressed hopeful wishes about my father's health and, if I could find a way, to say hello to my mother, Rose. And the following told me that she knew it was tough living with her, but when I got back (and here I had to flip the slip over on its backside), a wild scribble informed me, it would be even worse!

And finally, there was one last touching piece of paper telling me that, as I might have expected, Barbra came with me to California after all, in the book, and it was signed from a small bundle of love.

I think this was one of the sweetest, most endearing gifts I've ever received from anyone. It was the final, end-of-spring flowering of the affection between us.

I stayed a week in California and it was wonderful, so warm in the polished Beverly Hills sunshine. I swam in the pool, drove my car, there was scarcely enough time to see all my friends. My dad begged me to stay an extra week; we hadn't seen each other for so long and there was nothing going on for me in New York anyway, was there?

It would be easy to say that then my father's emphysema took a turn for the worse, or a friend got arrested by the police in a raid on a gay bar and I had to stay on and help him out, or any other invented, dramatic excuse; but the truth is, I stayed on another week at home, without calling or telling Barbra, because I wanted to. It wasn't hard to seduce me into staying; the weather was warm and wonderful. And I think that also I must have intended unconsciously to punish Barbra: she couldn't be bothered to show up to see me in *Henry V*, so why should I be in such a damn hurry to get back to freezing-cold New York, just to see her? It wasn't very nice of me, but there it was.

Back in the apartment, at the end of the first week, to celebrate the night of my homecoming, Barbra bought out the delicatessen; she spent a lot of money on a whole tableful of my favorite foods: lox and bagels, cream cheese, olives, and smoked fish. She spread out a pretty cloth with two place settings, candles, and flowers. Apparently it looked beautiful.

When she came back to the apartment that evening with Schulenberg, they opened the door to a dark, empty room. Barbra said, "Oh, he's not here yet. You don't think there's been an accident, do you?" She called the airport and was told the flight had already landed. Then Barbra got very concerned and worried; where was I? They ate what Barbra feared would go bad first, the smoked salmon and the bagels; she froze the leftovers.

The next night the table was laid out all over again, but still no Barry and no phone call. Barbra got really upset, screaming, "He's not coming back! He's *never* coming back!"

Bob replied, "Barbra, he's *got* to come back. This is his apartment."

That second evening the two of them ate up the smoked fish. And as night followed night, Barbra and Bob ate through all the

221

food in the fridge. The flowers wilted and were thrown out. The tablecloth got sent to the laundry. The candles were put away in a drawer. Slowly, over the course of a week, mouthful by mouthful, Barbra ate her way through our relationship and out the other side.

Barbra was on the phone, sitting on a small piece of furniture we called "the throne," an antique, carved wooden seat with ornate, gold-leaf angel heads for arms. She didn't even look up at me when I came in and put down my bags. I sat down and grinned at her. I was so glad to see her. I didn't really realize until that moment how much I'd missed her. But Barbra just stayed on the phone, talking and talking about nothing to her friend Susan out in Brooklyn. By the time she deigned to hang up, about a half an hour later, I was really annoyed.

Barbra was as cold as salted ice. "Hi, how are ya, how's your father?" she asked airily, went into the bathroom and closed the door.

It was all gone, the flowers, the food, and our future. Barbra never told me the trouble she'd gone to, the deli she'd bought, the anxiety she'd gone through. It was like it all had never happened. The bridge between us had collapsed and we stood on opposite sides of a gorge, staring sullenly at each other.

From that moment on, we began to argue violently, explosions of vitriol and sarcastic criticism that flew back and forth, followed by hours of icy silence, elaborate pretenses of ignoring and walking past each other without speaking. It was all young passion, bent out of shape. But we were beginning to do and say things to each other that were genuinely wounding, and it was upsetting me. I felt it couldn't go on. I sat Barbra down and told her I thought perhaps she ought to move out before things got any worse between us. She felt the same.

"The only thing is, I'm worried about where you're going to stay. Have you got a place to go to?" I said.

Without a word, Barbra walked over to the closet, yanked the door open, pulled out a shopping bag and started to rummage through it, finally producing a large ring of keys to several friends' apartments around Manhattan where she could crash. I hadn't seen that ring of keys since the day she moved in.

"Don't worry about me," she mumbled finally. "There's a lot of places I can go."

So, in the first week of February 1961, Barbra moved out of the apartment by mutual consent; we both agreed it was the best thing to do. The place was all torn apart with paper boxes and packing material and moving.

I felt so rock-bottom bad about what had happened that I phoned Barbra the same day she moved out and invited her to have dinner with me that night. Sitting at the table in a romantic restaurant, she looked absolutely radiant that evening, with her hair down and falling softly around her face. I think we were both very unhappy that we'd split up, that things had worked out so badly. We hardly touched our food. It was such a sad, unresolved ending to everything we'd gone through together.

Our affectional relationship may have ended, but Barbra continued to consult me about her work. Between February and April she played the Caucus Club in Detroit, the Jack Paar TV show, and the Crystal Palace in St. Louis. She wrote me from Detroit's Hotel Wolverine to say that she was so busy she couldn't even begin to tell me about it all. Her opening night, she reported derisively, was for an audience of eleven, who talked and clinked their glasses noisily throughout her set. She was trying out some new material and attempting to cope with the jabbering customers. "Lover Come Back to Me," the dependable, powerhouse rabble-rouser we had worked up as a very strong closer, was going over great and if I had a moment, she implored, could I try to come up with something similar to use in that spot?

Ten days later she wrote again, complaining that her pianist was awful. He was too overpowering, he played the wrong chords, he refused to follow her charts, by which she meant her arrangements. Then she told me she'd sung "A Taste of Honey" but it didn't sound as good as our version. How, she wondered, could she find a diplomatic way of letting her clunky pianist know?

A week later, a postcard arrived asking me to write out the guitar chords I'd created for "A Taste of Honey" because it just wasn't working with piano accompaniment. She'd met Leon Bibb, who was a popular, well-known folk singer in those days, but Barbra lamented that even his guitarist couldn't come up with chords as good as mine. (I had taught myself to play a serviceable but not stunning guitar during the folk music craze that swept America in the early 1950s. The "changes" [which is musician's slang for the chord sequences] which I had worked out for "A Taste of Honey," however, were indeed very pretty.)

Then, in the beginning of April, another card dropped through the mail slot, informing me she was returning to the Bon Soir on May 9, and would I be interested in playing the guitar for her on a recording session of "A Taste of Honey"? Oh yes, indeed I would have, but unfortunately nothing ever came of it.

Barbra had met Marty Erlichman, her lifetime manager-to-be, before she left New York. The first time he heard her sing, Marty was knocked out. He desperately wanted to handle her career, even offering to work for her without commission for a whole year, to prove his commitment and belief in her talent. I wasn't there, but her biographies say that Barbra decided to dump Ted Rozar during this Detroit stint, and she called Marty in San Francisco to tell him he had a new client.

Barbra came back to New York with tapes of her Detroit radio shows which she brought straight to my apartment. We played them together, stopping in between each song to discuss and criticize.

224

"What is this song, 'Moanin'?" I asked her. "It's *terrible*. Where did you dig that up?"

"The pianist at the club. He taught it to me," she said imperiously, as if she'd been coached by Rachmaninoff himself.

"Well, I think it stinks. It so jaggedy and clunky. It doesn't do a thing for your voice. You really ought to dump it."

"Maybe," she said, with an "I'll-think-about-it" air. Then she looked at the expression on my face. I loved Barbra's voice and didn't want her singing anything that wasn't worthy of it. "Oh, stop," she said. "I'm just torturing you. I don't like it either; of course I'm going to dump it."

"I love 'Soon It's Gonna Rain,'" I admitted. "That's a really good song for you. I played it for you," I said.

"You did not!" Barbra said. "I knew those songs. I auditioned for *The Fantasticks*."

"Barbra, I *did*. We played the *Fantasticks* original cast album all the time. We *talked* about your singing 'Much More' and 'Soon It's Gonna Rain,' remember? Right here in this apartment."

"No, not really," she said.

"Come on, come on," I insisted. "Lee Wiley singing 'Down with Love,' and 'Any Place I Hang My Hat' from *St. Louis Woman*, and 'Too Long at the Fair' from that revue... all the stuff you're currently singing. I played you all that, and more."

"I guess," she said. "Yeah, yeah, you're right. Listen, let's cut all the crap. What about my voice? How do I sound?"

"Barbra, you always sound good," I said. "You could sing 'The Star Spangled Banner' hanging upside down with a mouth full of carpet tacks and it would sound great."

"That's all I wanted to hear," she said with a big smile, standing up. "So, how's about it? You wanna make a tape of 'Taste of Honey'?"

When Barbra wanted something, she could be as persistent

and charming as hell. I looked at her irresistible smile, then went
to get the microphones and my guitar.

When I first returned to New York from California that winter
back in 1960, I never really understood exactly why Barbra was so
cold and distant to me. After all, it had only been one extra week
I'd stayed away. But nothing I could do or say made any difference.
She was through with me, finished with our relationship, and that
was that. And eventually I began to retaliate and treat her with
equal, frosty indifference.

About fifteen years later the first unauthorized biography of
Barbra was published. I was living in London at the time and its
author, Rene Jordan, sent me a complimentary copy. As I read
about Barbra's and my early days together, a rush of nostalgic
feelings and memories flooded over me.

Then I got to the part about the surprise party that Barbra had
planned for me, the welcome home that never was. I remember I
sat staring at the page, shaking my head, hardly able to believe
what I was reading. Suddenly my eyes were burning with tears and
the book slipped out of my hands and fell to the floor. It was the
first I had ever heard about it.

The next time I saw Bob Schulenberg I immediately brought
it up. Had Barbra really bought all that food, gone to all that
trouble?

"Oh, sure," Bob said, then looked at me quizzically. "You
mean, she never *told* you?"

16

Kiss the Boys Goodbye

$\mathcal{T}$he minute Barbra moved out, suddenly the whole world exploded for her and everything started to move very, very fast.

As for me, with Barbra gone the apartment felt incredibly empty; I felt empty inside as well. Then something inside me cracked. I'd taken enough of my dad's money and lived on his largesse too long. I got a job as slave-wage bookseller at Double-day Book Shops on Fifth Avenue and moved to a cheap, terrible, five-floor walk-up on Prince Street in Little Italy.

The first night I moved in there was the horrible sound of shat-tering glass and a woman's terrified shrieks of panic. I looked out the back to see the sharp, silhouetted shadow of a woman thrown on the opposite brick wall, framed in a smashed-out window.

"Somebody help me!" she screamed. "He's got a knife!"

Oh, Lord, I thought, carry me back to 9th Street!

Barbra made her first appearance on Mike Wallace's "PM East" (on which I also appeared as a performer a couple of times), got a gig in Winnipeg, went back to St. Louis, and then in October 1961, she landed in an off-Broadway revue, *Another Evening with Harry Stoones*. In this show, Barbra's role was more kooky comedy misfit than glamour puss. Her sketch performances were great: underplayed yet terrifically funny. She was wonderful singing "Value," and there was a demented ode to New Jersey which Barbra sang next to a half-packed suitcase, agonizing about "her man," lost in the wilds of New Jersey, and how she had to make the dangerous trip "out there" to find him or die in the attempt.

There was also one of the most hilarious numbers I've ever seen on the stage in this show, "I'm Gonna Build a Dream House," in which the cast, some in workman's overalls with saws and hammers, tried to put together a honeymoon cottage for two but halfway through the number someone bumped into someone else, banging into the set and setting off a chain reaction, the house started to fall apart. As the set began collapsing and picket fences and ladders fell over, crashing to the ground, everyone tried to scramble for safety. Barbra was simply a scream as the cross-eyed bride being carried across the threshold.

But even Barbra Streisand couldn't save *Harry Stoones*. I was invited to a preview and gave Barbra notes afterward; however, despite a distinctive quirkiness and some truly wonderful material, the show played only one night.

Then Barbra opened at the Blue Angel and she auditioned for and got *I Can Get It for You Wholesale*, a new musical about the rag trade by Harold Rome, who had written the very successful 1937 revue *Pins and Needles*, and the Borscht Belt musical *Wish You Were Here*, distinguished mainly by its hit title tune and the use of a real swimming pool onstage. The first-time director of *Wholesale* was Arthur Laurents, famous for having written the books for the smash hit musicals *Gypsy* and *West Side Story*.

Probably in the beginning of February 1962, on the virtual

threshold of her stardom, Schulenberg and I visited Barbra in her new apartment on Third Avenue, over the fish restaurant, to take photographs of her. (The picture of Barbra with her hair down that appears in this book was shot that evening.) It was hard to tell what her apartment was really like because it was in such disarray—Barbra was packing to leave New York the next morning for *Wholesale*'s out-of-town tryouts, and everything was in a jumble everywhere. I remember a window or two at the rear, but long ago another building had been built right up against Barbra's; consequently her back windows had a unique view of a brick wall. There were windows on the front that led to a fire escape, and a beautiful, very large mirror in a gilt frame leaned up against the wall.

"Listen, Barry," she said, "I got this one solo number in *Wholesale* and the director is driving me nuts."

"How? What's he saying?" I asked.

"Well, he wants me to do the number standing up, and I want to do it sitting down."

"What's the number about?" I asked.

"You want I should do it for you?" she asked.

"Do it for me," I said.

And without accompaniment, Barbra performed "Miss Marmelstein" for me.

"It's very funny," I said. "You're going to stop the show."

"Thanks," she said, "but what about this sitting-down, standing-up business?"

"Your instincts are right," I said. "Any director on Broadway would stage this song with you standing up. It's a comedy number and that's the way you stage a comedy number: standing up. But sitting down! It's so *unexpected*. No one will be able to take his eyes off you! You must do it sitting down. Just…insist."

"I have," she sighed, "but he gets fed up and tells me off in front of the whole company."

"You want to get all the reviews, don't you?" I asked.

"Sure," she said.

"Then do it sitting down. And I'll tell you something else. The chair, you said, is on casters? It's like an office chair?"

"Yeah, it, ya know, slides," she explained.

"Okay, make your entrance sitting down, and *slide* in from the wings," I suggested.

"How can I do that?" she said.

"I don't care how you do it! Get some chorus boy or stagehand in the wings to push your chair in from offstage. Pay him if you have to, whatever you have to do."

"All right, already, I'll do it," she said.

"And then," I said, "stop the chair with your feet, crumple over, like Pinocchio, your head down, and hold it, hold it, and finally, slowly raise your face to the audience. *Then* start the number," I explained. "Now *that's* an entrance!"

Barbra shook her head ruefully, but I knew she was going to take the challenge.

"Oy!" she said. "Arthur Laurents is gonna *kill* me."

"Do you really care?" I said.

"No," Barbra replied.

When I attended the Friends and Family preview of *I Can Get It for You Wholesale*, just before it opened in mid-March, I watched Barbra carefully as she worked through Act One with the other actors. She didn't try to steal scenes but she caught your attention … well, maybe I was prejudiced.

But in the second act, for her magnum opus, Barbra *slid* in from the wings on her secretary's chair, brought it to a screeching halt, and crumpled over in a heap. The audience was hushed, hypnotized! Then she raised her head, started to sing … and stepped into show business history.

After the show I waited backstage, outside her dressing room, and told her dresser to please tell Barbra that Barry Dennen was here to see her. (Her dresser? I thought to myself. She has seventh billing, wears only one costume and she has a *dresser?*) Through the door, which had been left open a crack, I heard the dresser muttering to Barbra. Then I heard Barbra's voice, loud and clear, say, "Barry Dennen? Barry Dennen? Do I know a Barry Dennen?" I left the theater without waiting to say hello.

It was in *Wholesale,* I found out later, that Barbra met Elliott Gould, the star of the show, a tall, strapping sweetheart of a man who fell under Barbra's spell almost at once and whom she would marry in September 1963. Apparently their love affair seemed to have been punctuated by a kind of high-energy, manic childishness: there were public food fights, arguments, tears, and overwrought reconciliations. In James Spada's Streisand biography, he cites a dancer in the show who had the room next to Barbra and Elliott during out–out–town tryouts in Philadelphia. She alleges that during a screaming match in their hotel room, Elliott pushed a naked, shrieking Barbra into the hallway and locked the door. That kind of stuff. They divorced seven years later.

It was in April 1964, about seven months into Barbra and Elliott's marriage, that I first saw the famous shot in *Time* magazine of the two of them in the Beverly Hills Hotel swimming pool. A cold shiver ran through me. Barbra is sitting on Elliott's shoulder, both of them staring straight into the camera lens, deadpan, her hand completely plastered over and obscuring his face.

I knew instantly what had happened. They had both thought what a great gag picture it would be. But it wasn't funny, it was spooky: an unconscious photographic portrait of their entire marriage yet-to-come.

Staring at that picture, I realized for the first time something I'd never been aware of when we were together: the true depth of Barbra's ambition, the relentless, driving force inside her to succeed at any cost, to make any sacrifice. It was something she had that I lacked. I wanted to get ahead in the business, too, but not at the expense of literally blotting out my private life. After Barbra and I split up, I'd wondered many times what it would have been like if we'd gotten married. Now I knew.

I didn't hear from Barbra again until she telephoned a few weeks later, in the beginning of April.

"Barry? Barbra. I'm sorry I missed you backstage at the Shubert. Didja like the show?" Barbra asked.

"Yeah, you were great," I said. "What's up?"

"Well, the thing is, Harold Rome, you know, the guy who wrote *Wholesale*? He's doing this, I dunno, retrospective album kind of thing, of a show he did in the thirties. It's a revue, about garment workers," she said.

"*Pins and Needles*," I said.

"Yeah, that's it. Anyway, he wants me to be on the album, and I just wondered if you could go over the songs with me, you know, like at Sardi's for lunch, maybe? I'm buying!" she said.

"Sardi's?" I said. "You're moving up."

"Yeah, well, it's convenient, it's right near the theater. So, will you?"

"Sure, Barb," I said. "Always happy to oblige."

I made a tape of Millie Weitz's original cast recording of "Nobody Makes a Pass at Me" to give to Barbra when we met at Sardi's for my free lunch. I considered it the best number in the show and the one I suspected they would be giving Barbra as a comedy solo.

We met late in the afternoon and the restaurant was virtually empty. I wondered about that. Maybe Barbra didn't want any of the Broadway community to catch her working on songs with me—or with anybody, for that matter. She was already seated at the table, in front of her a big stack of handwritten charts.

"You know," I said, slipping into the booth, "there's no such thing as a free lunch."

"Free enough," Barbra said and snagged a passing waiter with "Can we have some menus, please?"

We ordered, and while we were waiting for the food to arrive, I asked her, "So how are you, kid? How's tricks?"

"Fine. I'm fine," she said. "I'm just really annoyed about the *Wholesale* original cast album."

"What's wrong with it?" I said. "I bought it. It's a really good album. Except some of the songs aren't as strong as they should be. That's the thing about Harold Rome, he's inconsistent. You're the best thing on it."

"Unh!" she *kvetched*. "The thing is, it's not the way I sing it *now*! I've changed it, it's all different. It's a different song, the way I sing it *now*."

"Uh, what are you trying to tell me?" I said.

"It's not the same!" she repeated.

"Well, of course you sing it differently now. You're more comfortable with the material, your interpretation is growing..."

"Yeah, but it's not *now*. People come to the show, they listen to me sing the song, then they go out and buy the album and it doesn't *match* the way they saw me *do* it on the *stage*...you know what I mean?"

"Okay, sure, but it's a *record* of the way you sang it *then*, at that moment. At the moment that the show opened, that's how you sang it. It's historical."

"*Historical?* It's *hysterical!*" she screamed. "It's terrible! If I could, I'd make them let me go back into the studio right now and do the whole thing over again."

"Look," I said, "I've got an idea for you. Why don't you just send all your fans a monthly tape of the way you're singing it *now*. An *update*. That way, they could keep track of how you're singing it at any given moment in time, and keep up with you, ya know... like a refresher course."

233

"The thing is," she said, pondering and grinning at me slyly, "I know you're kidding...but that's not a bad idea!"

After lunch, we went over her songs one by one. In general they were good numbers and they'd show off Barbra's talent, but there was one awful ballad, "What Good Is Love?"

I said, "This is hopeless. It's just not a good tune, there's nothing you can do to save it. Just sing it and get through it."

"Right," Barbra agreed.

We went through "It's Not Cricket to Picket," and we worked through the comedy phrasing and developed a character for her. Then I gave Barbra some ad libs for the end of the song, during the playoff. I said, "Pretend you're being hauled off the picket line by a policeman. Complain, holler: 'Let go of me, you're bending my mink!'"

"Yeah, but what if they don't like it?" she said.

"Just *do* it, on the first take, without telling anybody what you've got in mind. They'll like it," I said.

"You're the boss," Barbra said, and I just didn't know how to reply.

Barbra's twentieth birthday party was hosted by Irene Kuo at the Lichee Tree Restaurant on 8th Street at midnight, May 10, 1962. I picked up Bob Schulenberg at his apartment, where he was busy putting the finishing touches on wrapping an original drawing he'd done of Barbra which she'd used in lieu of a head shot when she was at the Bon Soir. Bob had had it beautifully framed. We whizzed up 8th Street to the elegant eatery, which was jam-packed with close to four hundred people, a lot of them photographers. They served a full, elaborate Cantonese dinner, featuring lobster, meatballs, and all the side dishes. But there were so many guests they ran out of chairs at the tables.

When Bob and I finally squeezed our way over to the gift table to put down his drawing, we were astonished to find it piled high with presents and accompanying cards that numbed the mind: "Happy Birthday, Barbra, from Richard Rodgers." "Many more, sweetheart! Mike Nichols." *I Can Get It for You Wholesale* had only been open two months but Barbra seemed to have formed intimate friendships with every talented, famous, or powerful person in New York. The gift table was like a *Who's Who of People Worth Knowing.*

"Look, Bob, here's Lennie Bernstein," I exclaimed.

"Here's Ethel Merman," Bob said, turning over a card on a box, then added, "What do you think the pope sent?"

"Matzo balls?" I suggested.

"I need a drink," Bob said in a cracking voice.

I pushed my way through the crush of the crowd, recognizing lots of faces from various Broadway shows, many of them cast members of *Wholesale*. At the bar, waiting to get the barman's attention, I turned to one of the actresses from the show and said, "This is really very nice of Barbra, don't you think, to throw this party to say thank you to all her friends."

The actress snorted, took a hard draw on her cigarette, and downed another mouthful of white wine, leaving a rubber-stamp-like impression of red lipstick on the rim of the glass. "Barbra didn't pay for this, not one red cent," she sneered.

"Really?" I said.

"That's right," she said, smearing her filter tip with lipstick as she took another suck on her cigarette. "The restaurant is paying for the whole damn thing. They think they're going to get free publicity!" she said, and a snort of wheezing laughter and smoke erupted from her nose.

I didn't realize until that moment what a true genius for fun-nelling publicity her own way Barbra was.

"You sound like you don't like Barbra very much," I said.

"She's a talented kid," she said begrudgingly, "but she behaves so badly backstage. She's always late, everybody gets nervous about whether she's going to show up or not, and she's so un-friendly, so . . . rude. But, hey, I suppose when you're that good, you don't have to be nice."

"So what are you doing here if you don't like her so much?" I asked with an aggressiveness that surprised even me. "Did you just drop in for the free food?"

The actress looked at me contemptuously. "We were *ordered* to come," she smirked bitterly.

Finally the barman arrived and I ordered two gin and tonics.

"Sorry," he said. "There's a short delay. We just ran out of glasses."

I finally located two empty glasses, brought them to the bar, and for a buck, the barman washed and dried them, handed me a couple of drinks and I squeezed my way back to Bob Schulenberg. "Listen," I said in a loud voice, trying to be heard over the din, "I think we'd better get something to eat before the food runs out."

"I've just been talking to Barbra's public relations man," Bob said.

"Barbra has a public relations man?" I asked, very impressed.

"Yes!" Bob replied. "He said there's *plenty* of food."

"Well, that's something," I said.

"But they've just run out of forks!" he shouted.

"Then, you know, Bob," I said, raising my voice to be heard, "I guess we'll just have to fork ourselves."

I couldn't get anywhere near Barbra. It wasn't just the crowd, Marty Erlichman actually blocked my way, stood between Barbra and me and held me prisoner in captive conversation. I remember wondering why Marty was suddenly so interested in me, why he kept asking me questions and laying a hand on my shoulder when I tried to split from him.

Then, suddenly, I had a dreadful psychic hunch: before the

party, had Barbra asked Marty to run interference, to keep me away from her? I felt stung and hurt by my own suspicion. I could see her across the room, chatting amiably with someone, and if she registered me out of the corner of her eye, she never looked over.

I had the sensation of standing on the end of a long quayside and Barbra was on the stern of a ship sailing rapidly away from me, becoming smaller and smaller until finally she appeared only as a small round white dot on the horizon. I felt heartbroken. It was, as Schulenberg later described it, the big kissoff.

But I wasn't the only old friend Barbra dropped.

Barbra did *Wholesale* just as Terry Leong, Barbra's first wardrobe designer, and Marilyn Fried, Barbra's former roommate, left on a tour of Europe together, and by the time they returned to New York in 1964, Barbra had already made her big smash in *Funny Girl*.

"When we got back," Terry said, "it was very different. Barbra was very, very busy. She was assaulted by thousands of people who wanted to be near her, do things for her, design costumes and give her clothes to wear."

Terry went backstage after *Funny Girl* and said he "got the message that she was way too busy to be friendly, there was no time to be friendly. She was in a totally different stratosphere. She was talking to Harold Arlen about writing songs, meeting this director and that famous author."

Terry felt hurt, but he understood. He said, "Barbra didn't need me anymore. She had top designers to do clothes for her now. When I say she didn't need me, I don't mean it as a criticism. It was just a statement of fact, the way things were. She didn't."

It isn't uncommon for those who make it big to turn their backs on the people who have helped them on the way up, and not just in show business. Stories about wives who slave to put their husbands through college, only to have their spouses dump them when they finally start making big money in their profession, are legion.

I'm sure Barbra doesn't like feeling beholden, needy, or dependent on anyone; and she doesn't want to admit that at any point she needed a helping hand. After all, she is a star, created like the universe in one big bang, an autonomous, self-contained entity, born all in one piece, like Venus rising from the ocean on the cusp of a seashell.

In his *Intimate Nights,** a colorful history of the New York cabaret scene, James Gavin writes that Barbra was famous for burning her bridges in her early years. He goes on to cite a close friend from those days who says, "I don't think it's so much a question of burning bridges as it is of cutting out of her life people who were not directly relevant to her success. I don't think Barbra wants to acknowledge that in her early years she had a lot of people to be grateful to."

"I was astonished," the "close friend" continues, "when somebody told me years later that Barbra's published position was that she listened to her 'voices,' and her voices told her what to do. It had nothing to do with that; she had *people* with voices telling her what to do. People who were helping her with her hair, her makeup, her shoes, her dresses, the material, and her direction. I think it makes her feel guilty and uncomfortable that she's never been able to find it inside herself to repay this in any way. And that's between her and her conscience."

Since I'm laying all my cards on the table, that "close friend" (in the deprecatory quotes) was me.

The last time I saw Barbra during this period was in the winter, after I had moved into a nice apartment on West 89th Street, just off the park. One day I was standing at a bus stop on

---

*James Gavin, *Intimate Nights* (New York: Grove Weidenfeld, 1991).

Central Park West, waiting for a bus which seemed like it was never going to come. It was bitterly cold and I was hopping around, trying to get my circulation going, when suddenly an enormous, shiny black limousine cruised majestically up the street, pulled up to the light and stopped. I peered inside and there, in the chic, pearl-grey interior, sat Miss Barbra Streisand, a fluffy white poodle with black button eyes sitting on her lap.

Barbra stared out, and when she recognized me, she gave a little gasp to her dog, like, "Oh, look who it is!" I thought, surely she's going to lower the window, say hello, maybe even offer me a lift? After all, it's *freezing* out here! She held the poodle up, waved its little paw at me, and immediately the limo charged away from the curb, churning a small wave of dirty slush water up onto the sidewalk.

Well, fella, I thought, I guess the Gravy Train only leaves once. Hey, you could have married her. But what would I have been, some kind of hanger-on husband, fetching cups of tea and rubbing her back, while the others around her whispered gossipy dirt behind their hands and traded innuendos in the rehearsal halls and recording rooms? It would have been awful for both of us.

And as I watched the back of Barbra's elegant head receding down Central Park West toward the theater district in her luxurious Rolls Royce, all I could think of to say out loud was, "Hey, lady, whatsa matter with your animal...."

17

Fanny, Isn't It?

*I*n August 1964, Bob Schulenberg came back from a long stay in France and immediately went backstage to see Barbra. The first question she asked him was whether Barry had seen *Funny Girl.* Bob said he didn't know, but he'd find out.

I was living in a loft on Canal Street with Tomie de Paola, a now-famous children's book illustrator. The phone rang.

"Hello, Barry? It's me, Barbra," said the Voice.

"Barbra *Who?*" I asked.

After we had caught up on each other's news and sundry little niceties, Barbra finally blurted out bluntly, "So, listen, why haven't you come to see me in my show?"

"Well, look Barb, honestly, I just can't afford it."

Seats to *Funny Girl* were $9.90 and little as that seems today, it was a new high in ticket pricing for a Broadway musical. There were even dire predictions in several newspaper articles that at that stiff tariff, people would refuse to go see it. Little did they know that, after it opened, the public would be yanking off their

241

diamond necklaces and *throwing* them at the box office staff, just to wangle a pair of seats.

It was true enough: I couldn't afford the price of the seats; but what I didn't say to Barbra was that part of me felt that perhaps she should have invited me to opening night. But at the time I was too proud to call and ask her, even if I'd happened to have her phone number.

"Look, I really want you to come," she said. I noticed how suave and polished her speech sounded. It was attractive. "Let me buy you a house seat. Do you want to bring a friend, or will it be just you? When can you make it?"

And so it came to pass that on February 18, 1965, I found myself in the eighth row, center, for the evening performance of *Funny Girl.* When Barbra sang "I'm the Greatest Star," my jaw dropped to my chest. *Chutzpah* on a stick! When the hoofer character and her mother in the show sang "Who Taught Her Everything She Knows?" my jaw dropped into my lap.

By the time the curtain came down at the end of *Funny Girl* I sat stunned and almost unable to move from my seat. That was my little Barbra up there, carrying the whole weight of a big, hit Broadway show on her tiny shoulders, singing incredibly, being brilliant and funny and touching, and bringing a stunned New York audience to its feet for curtain call after curtain call.

As I walked around the block to the rear of the Winter Garden I was so proud of Barbra and what she'd accomplished, and my own part in her story.

Before me loomed an enormous black limousine parked at the curb, the chauffeur inside, patiently waiting. And in a turbulent mass in front of the stage door was a huge crowd of Barbra's excited fans, jamming the sidewalk and spilling over into the street. I hadn't seen anything like it since the Beatles came to New York.

How was I going to get inside? I wondered. Taking a deep

breath, I insinuated my way through the crowd, to their extreme annoyance. "Hey, wait a minute!" somebody yelled, as I pulled open the door and stepped inside. A wizened stage doorman crammed inside a little office peered at me through a small glass window. "What can I do for you?" he asked.

"Barbra's expecting me," I explained. "She told me to come back afterward."

"Oh, really?" he muttered suspiciously. "What's your name?"

I told him and he checked down the list on a clipboard. "Sorry. You ain't here," he informed me. "You'll have to wait outside."

"Look," I tried to explain, "Miss Streisand asked me to come here tonight. Honestly, she did. She paid for my ticket and every-thing." I fished in my pocket and produced the ticket stub with "COMP" stamped across it and held it up to the glass. I told him my name again, enunciating it carefully. "Why don't you go tell Mr. Gould I'm here?" I suggested.

This was so typical, I thought, shaking my head with amused exasperation. When I was in love with Barbra I might have found all this endearing. But it was five years later. It was February, it was a few days before my birthday, and it was bone-cold out on the sidewalk.

"Wait outside, please," the stage doorman insisted. "I'll go find out what's going on."

I stepped back onto the pavement, back into the throng of fans crowded around the backstage entrance. A couple of them smirked at me, as if I'd been trying to fake my way inside and gotten chucked out. I took a good look around me—these were the hard-core fans, the fanatic Barbra-ites. As she had done five years earlier, they all shopped in thrift stores and schlock shops, but on them, these second-hand clothes didn't look chic and orig-inal, they looked tacky and strange.

A good fifteen or twenty minutes went by as I stood, shifting from foot to foot on the glassy sidewalk, watching the plumes of white breath coming from the mouths of Barbra's disciples as they gossiped about her.

"Marleen saw her going into Columbia Records last Friday."

"Outta sight!"

"Yeah, she was wearing a wool coat and a knit cap and underneath, her hair was all wrapped up in *toilet* paper."

"That is so cool."

What in the hell was going on here? Barbra had made such a fuss over the phone about my seeing her in the show. Could she have forgotten this was the night I was coming?

I remembered my friend Carl, who had played guitar for Barbra the first time I taped her at my apartment. A few weeks earlier I had run into him on West 56th and he asked if I'd seen *Funny Girl*. No, I'd told him, I hadn't gotten around to it yet. Then he described how, on the night he went, he'd sent a note backstage that he was in the audience that evening and would like to drop by afterward and say hello.

Apparently, Carl hung around for over an endless hour. It was so quiet in the corridor outside Barbra's dressing room that he began to wonder if she and Elliott had skipped out of the theater by some other exit.

But as he moved closer to her closed dressing room door, Carl was certain he heard the two of them murmuring softly behind it. He held his breath and listened intently, only to hear Barbra's faint whisper: "Hey, Ell, do you think he's gone away yet?"

Please, God, I thought, don't let me be another Carl.

After a numbing eternity, the stage doorman finally stuck his head out, spotted me and grudgingly grumbled, "They say it's okay. You can come in."

"Well, who does he think he is?" I heard one fan complain bitterly as the door slammed behind me and the warmth of the theater started to defrost my frigid feet.

I was led past the little vestibule, past the rabbit warren of corridors full of bustling stagehands, costume people, dressers, actors in and out of makeup, down the hallway to Barbra's dressing room, and instructed to wait outside her door until someone came for me.

After a show, performers are generally friendly, loud, boisterous, laughing, looking for praise, familial. But the atmosphere backstage at *Funny Girl* was oddly different: cautious, subdued, with a kind of damp fear hanging in the air, so thick you could touch it. Looks from the scurrying cast and stage crew seemed to ask, "Who are you? Who do you know? Do I have to be nice to you? Could you get me fired?"

There was no place to sit so I stood against the wall and pulled on a cigarette, staring at the large, gold star hanging on Barbra's black lacquer door.

As I waited, impatient with Barbra and annoyed with myself, I remembered an archetypal show business story that recently had been making the rounds at auditions and in rehearsal rooms and cocktail parties. It concerned this talented young girl from Iowa with a big voice, freshly arrived in New York with a burning ambition to make it big on Broadway. *Funny Girl* was looking for an understudy for Streisand, the story went, and on an off-chance, an agent had sent her up to try out.

At the audition, our corn-fed neophyte sang and read very well and, to her own and everyone else's surprise, was offered the job. In a euphoric haze, she stumbled home to her recently rented, furnished one-room apartment west of Eighth Avenue.

But that night she had a dream. In it, Barbra had fallen ill and the newcomer was going to appear in the Fanny Brice role for the first time. As she stood nervously in the wings waiting, she listened hard for the cue for her first entrance. But when she took a step forward to go on stage, she suddenly felt a sharp, icy stab in her shoulder and, with a anguished shriek, collapsed to the floor in searing pain.

Then she looked up.

Rising above her loomed Barbra, dressed in her first act costume, having just plunged a knife into her understudy's back. As the poor stabbed girl lay there begging someone to help her, she dreamed that without even looking down, Streisand stepped right over her body and, with a big smile, glided triumphantly out onto the stage.

The next morning our young hopeful turned down the job, packed, and got on the next plane back home.

I shivered. This couldn't be true, it couldn't be. It was just some envious, bitchy actor's imagination running on high octane.

Another twenty minutes had ticked by. By now the hallway was empty, the stage doused in darkness. Everyone had got out of there so quickly, the theater felt abandoned, ghostly.

Suddenly Barbra's dressing room door flew open and Elliott Gould smiled at me and welcomed me inside.

"Hey, Barry, how *are* ya?" he asked with his most charming smile.

"I'm fine, Elliott, how are you?" I replied, coming into the dressing room. I took a chair. Suddenly I noticed Bob Schulenberg sitting there.

"Bob!" I said, surprised and puzzled. "Did you see the show tonight? How did you get backstage?"

"Oh, uh…hi!" Bob said. "See the show? No! I just came in through the front of house, afterward. We were wondering what happened to you," he added semidistractedly, talking to me but drawing in his sketch book at the same time.

I looked over to Barbra, who was sitting at her makeup table. She looked back at me in the mirror and without turning around said, "Hi."

"Hi," I said to her reflection. There was an uncomfortable silence.

"How are ya?" she said.

"I'm thawing out," I said, adding, "It's very cold out tonight."

"So, why didn't you come inside?" she asked.

"Because my name wasn't on the list and that troll who lives under the bridge at the stage door wouldn't let me," I said, trying to make a joke out of it.

"Oh, yeah, Sam," Elliott offered. "He's very protective."

"Elliott," Barbra said to him in the mirror, "I told you to put Barry's name on the list."

"No, you didn't," Elliott protested. "You said *you* were going to put it on the list."

"No, I didn't," she raised her voice. "I told you I had an interview and asked you to do it," Barbra answered, dusting her nose with a large brushful of powder.

There was a knock at the door and the stage manager stuck his head in. "Everything all right tonight, Barbra?" he asked her. Barbra threw down the brush impatiently and wheeled around to confront him.

"No, everything is *not* all right," she complained. "I wanna see that jerk that calls himself a conductor *right now!*" she said.

"Uh, he's already left the theater, I think," said the stage manager, somewhat embarrassed.

Schulenberg leaned over to me and whispered nervously, looking around Barbra's dressing room, "So, what does this remind you of? The paisley walls, the Tiffany lamps, the potted plants?"

"I don't know, Bob," I said.

"It's just like your apartment on 9th Street!" Bob said, with the giddy enthusiasm of revelation. Suddenly Barbra's voice crashed in again on us both.

"Jesus Christ! The tempo on 'People' is still too fucking fast. Why can't he just *follow* me? Listen, tell him I want to see him tomorrow at half-hour, prompt," she finished.

"He'll be there," said the stage manager.

"He better be, 'cause if he conducts it tomorrow like he did tonight, I'm walking off the stage!" she yelled after him as he scurried out the door. "So," she said, turning to me with a radiant smile, "how was I?"

It took me a moment to switch gears. "You were wonderful. Just wonderful," I told her sincerely. "I'm very proud of you."

"You got any notes?" she demanded.

"No," I said. "No notes."

"No notes at *all*?" she pressed.

I turned to Elliott. "The biggest star on Broadway is asking me for notes," I smiled. Elliott smiled back.

There was another awkward pause.

"You have a good seat?" she asked.

"Perfect," I told her. "Eighth row, center. Thanks very much," I added.

"Sure," she shrugged. "So, listen," she said, leaning forward and looking at me right in the eyes. "Those tapes you made of me at the Bon Soir. You still got them?" she asked ingenuously.

"Of course I've got them," I replied. "My God. Did you think I would throw them away?"

"Well, ya see, the thing is..." she said, crossing her legs and looking at me with a sudden steely resolve that I had never seen in her before, "...the thing is, I want them. I want those tapes," she blurted out.

"What do you mean?" I asked, taken aback.

"I want you to give them back to me," she said simply. "They're mine. They're my voice, my songs, my performance. That's what's on those tapes. And they belong to me," she added. "You don't have any legal right to them."

"Wait a minute, Barbra," I said, somewhat dumbfounded. "What are you talking about? Those aren't your tapes. Those are

248

my tapes. I own them. I recorded them. All the material on them I chose for you, I coached you…they…they belong to me."

"Wait a minute, Barry, Barbra just means…" Elliott interjected.

"Elliott, please," I asked him. "I don't mean to be rude to you in any way, but this is really between Barbra and me."

"Look, Barry," she said, her voice getting slightly shriller, "I'm not trying be difficult or anything but, ya know, I could take you to court and *make* you give me those tapes." I stared at her. "That's what the lawyer said," she added.

I stood up. My throat was tight, as if a hand were squeezing it.

"Barbra," I said, and I felt a rising panic and confusion in my gut, "let me explain. I would be very happy to play those tapes for you, any time you like, as often as you like. But I don't feel obliged, legally or morally, to hand them over to you. They're all I have left of our collaboration, of our work together," I emphasized.

"Oh, yeah?" she slung back at me. "Well, you better not try to release them or anything!" she snapped. "I'll have Columbia Records come down on you like a shitload of bricks!"

"Is this the reason you invited me down here?" I asked her. "Paid for my ticket, invited me backstage? Because you wanted me to give you those tapes? Well, you can just *forget* it!" I was beginning to feel sick to my stomach.

The dressing room telephone rang and Elliott snatched it up. "It's your mother, Barbra," he said nervously.

"Tell her to go fuck herself!" Barbra snapped.

As Elliott spoke *sotto voce* into the telephone, dragging it around the room in his hand, Barbra turned to me.

"Look, all I want—"

"I know what you want, Barbra," I said. "You want a discount on your whole life. You want everyone to give and give and give to you, and not have it cost you a red cent. That's the reason you've never acknowledged me, never talked about me in any interview. You're afraid I'm going to send you a *bill*. For One Career: Payment Overdue. Just what price would you put on *that, Bar-bar-a?*"

In all the time I'd known her, I had never before seen Barbra look so completely nonplussed. With a pounding heart, I wheeled around and slammed out the door.

In a white heat I strode down Broadway through the melting slush, toward the bus stop. God, I thought to myself, turning up my collar. What a delightful evening.

18

Happy Birthday, Barbra

I got two or three phone calls from Barbra in the beginning of
1992. On one of them, she was getting dressed for the evening,
simultaneously talking to me over the speaker phone from New York.
I don't know why, but I fantasized she had one of her famous, shapely
legs on an ottoman and was pulling on a long pair of black nylons.

"Listen, I wanna ask you something," she said at one point.
"You remember when we were working on the act together?"

"Of course," I said.

"I knew how to sing, right? I mean, you didn't teach me how
to sing. Did you?" she asked.

I had to smile. Was Barbra actually asking, in some coded sort
of way, if she owed me anything? I let her wait for a moment.

"No," I said finally, truthfully. "You always knew how to sing."

Later that year, I was quite pleased to receive an invitation to
her fiftieth birthday party at Jon Peters's house. It was like the
thank you I'd never received, all those years ago.

When we arrived, children were taking rides in front of the

251

house on a baby elephant, which was decked out in the most sump-
tuous embroidered velvet trappings. Inside, jugglers, magicians, and
fire-eaters performed act after act, to the amazed delight of children and their parents alike. Not surprisingly, since this was a Hollywood party and populated by people with massive insecurities,
the busiest table was that of a psychic reading the Tarot cards.

I looked around. There were famous faces everywhere. Meryl
Streep trudged across the floor of the elegant pavilion that had
been erected, a child dragging on each arm and a third hanging
from her neck. She looked like a poster woman for Mother Earth,
a walking blonde Christmas tree with her kids as the ornaments.
Warren Beatty and Annette Bening sat playing with their
daughter. Nick Nolte walked around looking exhausted and even
more disheveled than he did in *Prince of Tides*.

Then Barbra appeared. The last time I'd seen her was in England,
in 1969, when I'd come down to visit her on the set while she was
filming *On a Clear Day You Can See Forever* at the Brighton Pavilion.
There was something on my mind, and finally, in her dressing room,
I got the chance to blurt it out. I told Barbra how badly I felt about
the way we broke up. I told her I wanted to apologize and say how
sorry I was for the way I treated her. And although, as I went on, she
got a little embarrassed and terribly busy with some wardrobe pieces
laid out on a chair, I think secretly she was pleased to hear it.

And now, here she was again, standing in front of me. Her hair,
her face, her lipstick were honey-colored. Her dress was honey-
colored. She looked like she'd been dipped in a beautiful, gold-
flecked pot of honey. Our first face-to-face meeting, after all those
years; what would, what could we say to each other? She smiled
graciously at me...and crossed her eyes! I smiled, and crossed
mine back. And when she came over to say hello, to kiss me, give
me her hand, and meet my life partner, James, I noticed she had
cut her trademark long fingernails.

"So, where did you two meet?" she asked James.

"In London," he replied in his marked Scottish brogue. "We were both living there."

"Oh, so you're Irish?" Barbra asked sweetly.

"Scots," James said.

Barbra and I talked a bit, then she said, "Listen, excuse me, I have to go be with the children. I'll catch up with you later. Have some food," she called as she walked away over to a bunch of youngsters. "It's good!"

While we were chatting to each other that afternoon, time reeled backward, and she seemed suddenly like the teenager I'd known in 1960. And somehow I felt that our relationship, our feelings for each other, our hopes and dreams and wishes had all come around, full circle.

As I watched Barbra float around the room, watching a magician perform tricks with the cups and balls, greeting guests, chatting with friends, kneeling down to play with children, I wondered, what she would think . . . what would she think if I wrote about our time together?

As James drove us home after the party, my mind kept coasting back to the past, to the sixties, back to Barbra and all the amazing accomplishments she had achieved since we were together: two Oscars, two Emmys, eight Grammy awards, ten Golden Globes, the Tony, countless gold and platinum albums.

Then, suddenly it was 1963 and my mind scudded to a halt. There I was, in a Broadway theater at last. I had gotten my own first real, important job. After knocking around in summer stock, off-Broadway revues, and nightclubs, I had landed the understudy to the lead in the first national tour of *Stop the World, I Want to Get Off.* The musical had opened in New York a few months earlier, so our entire company rehearsed in the theater, right on the Broadway show's set.

Tony Newley, *Stop the World*'s writer, star, and director, was an affable, randy little cockney, very friendly, open, and approachable to all of us. One late afternoon, after we'd knocked off rehearsing for the day, he invited a small group of us into his dressing room. As we all stood around sipping glasses of white wine, I remember the feeling of uneasy dread that crept over me when Tony said he "wanted to play an album by this really *fabulous* performer, this *wonderful* singer who, I think, is going to become one of the greatest stars of all time." I just knew what was coming. Tony produced *The Barbra Streisand Album,* which had just been released, and popped it on his dressing room phonograph.

The needle fell into the first groove, "Cry Me a River," a song I'd never heard Barbra sing before. I looked around me. Even on a recording her voice was working its magic. The stars of our company stared at Tony's record player as if they were willing Barbra to physically appear. The album sleeve, with its striking, beautiful photograph of Barbra, and the album title printed in its classy, calligraphic font style, got passed around.

"Remarkable, isn't she?" Tony smiled, looking around the room proudly as if, just by buying her album, he'd made some kind of proprietary investment in launching this incredible new talent. Barbra's voice glided out of the loudspeaker, just as it had only three years earlier when she'd recorded her first tape in my apartment. So much had happened so fast. It seemed like a century ago.

> Now you say you want me
> Well, just to prove you do
> Come on and cry me a river
> Cry me a river
> I cried a river over you.*

*Arthur Hamilton, "Cry Me a River." Copyright © 1953, 1955 (copyright renewed) Chappell & Co. (ASCAP) and Momentum Music (PRS). All rights administered by Chappell & Co. All rights reserved. Used by permission. Warner Bros. Publications U.S. Inc., Miami, FL 33014.

As Barbra keened in frustration, anger, and the grief of lost love, the words and her deep feeling stabbed at me. I felt as if I'd been slapped across the face with an open palm. I knew exactly who she was talking to: me. It was our story she was lamenting, our failed relationship filling her with fury.

I looked around at my fellow actors enjoying the record, and felt like I wanted to die. How could I explain to them my part in the story of Barbra, tell them what the singer they were listening to meant to me? And would they have believed me if I had? And what difference would it have made to them anyway? Overcome with sadness but desperately trying not to cry, I backed out of Tony's dressing room door and staggered down the hallway, through the pass door into the theater. It was empty, with that atmosphere of anticipation empty theaters have, except for a solitary cleaning woman, dolorously pushing an upright vacuum cleaner along the strip of carpet at the back of the stalls. I slumped into a theater seat and buried my head in my hands.

Long ago, my father said to me, "Experience is the best teacher, but it's very expensive."

I think Barbra and I both learned from experience: all love affairs end in disappointment.

19

Payday on May Day

$\mathcal{A}$ s everyone knows, "Mayday" is the international distress signal. Well, May 1, 1997, was a personal Mayday for me.

I was deep in the literary equivalent of a slave ship: editing my text all day and night, the deadline delivery date of the manuscript was only a few days away, and I hadn't heard back from Marty Erlichman. I had been pestering Marty since January to ask Barbra for permission to use some quotes of hers in my book, extracts from letters and postcards she had sent me from her very first club dates out of town, in Detroit and St. Louis, back in 1961. I'd written Marty in January, then again in February and March. Now April was over and finally, after many back-and-forth phone calls and faxing xerox copies of Barbra's letters as well as the complete chapter in which they would appear, early in the evening on May 1, my telephone rang.

"Hello, Barry?" said the Voice. "This is Barbra."

This, I thought, is really weird. This was starting out exactly like the phone calls I got in 1992. 1 took a big breath. "Barbra *Who?*" I asked.

"Streisand," she replied. What followed was a conversation which so electrified me that, an hour later, when it was over, I ran upstairs to my desk and made copious and detailed notes, before it had the chance to fade.

When we first started talking, Barbra sounded easy and re-laxed, and I thought I heard a soft sound, like lapping water. But she didn't waste any time. She told me she was upset that I was writing a book. She didn't like any book that had ever been written about her because they didn't really tell the truth.

We talked about yet another Streisand biography that had just hit the bookstores.* Barbra hadn't read the whole thing, but what she minded was that the woman who wrote it gave me credit for "her whole creation."

Then Barbra said, "You know, I've always said in print, I lived with Barry Dennen, he played me this incredible music. He played me Ruth Etting, he played me Edith Piaf...."

"Listen," I said, "I know you really hate all these goddamn biographies that get everything wrong."

"Yes!" she exclaimed. "Listen to this: this woman says I took the IRT subway into Manhattan. I didn't take the IRT, I took the IND!" she fulminated.

The truth, as Barbra saw it, seemed to be a faithful, detailed re-production of the facts, exactly as they happened. Well, that might work for solid, incontrovertible data, the minutiae of everyday life, but what about the evocation of remembered human interactions, complicated motives, ambiguous emotional states? Barbra felt the truth was in the details, but I suspected the devil was.

---

*Sheldon Harnick, the famous lyricist of *Fiddler on the Roof,* had recommended this particular biography to Barbra. "You'll like it," he said. Barbra replied, "Sheldon, if *God* wrote my biography, I wouldn't like it."

"You know what you should do, Barry? You should say, this is my recollection of the events, this is my version."

"I do say that, Barb," I said. "That's how my book begins."

"'Cause, you know, your memory of it may not be the way it really happened. It's like the Telephone Game," she said.

I immediately remembered the Telephone Game from childhood birthday parties. You sat in a circle and the person at the top whispered a funny saying into the next person's ear and so on down the line, all around the room. Somehow when the phrase got to the end, it was invariably mangled, unrecognizable, and usually pretty funny. Out of nowhere I remembered the poetic British name for the game: Chinese Whispers.

There was that soft, splashing sound again. I wondered if she was washing the dishes; somehow, I doubted it. Suddenly Barbra's voice brought me back. "I mean, do you talk about me wanting to be an actress?" she asked.

"Of course I do," I said. "That's how we approached all your material. Like an actress."

"'Cause this woman says you taught me how to sing and it's just not true," Barbra said, sounding very hurt.

"Barbra, nobody had to teach you how to sing. You always knew how. What I did was pick and shape material for you."

"Do you say that in your book?"

"That I shaped material for you?"

"No, I don't mean that. Do you say that good thing you just said, that nobody had to teach me how to sing? I had a natural talent."

"Of course I do, Barbra. I'm not out to take anything away from you."

"Because it's pretty horrifying to read that I'm your creation, and you taught me how to sing."

"Barbra, please...please..." I begged. She was sounding so distressed and injured.

259

"It's so insulting to me."

"It's terribly insulting," I agreed.

"I always said, you know, Barry Dennen came up with the whole idea of 'Who's Afraid of the Big Bad Wolf?'—I gave you all the credit, Barry. You know that."

Well, I did remember a time early on in her career when Barbra neglected to mention me. But I didn't want to get into that now. She was being so open and vulnerable to me, and besides, I figured it was youthful insecurity on her part and I had forgiven her long ago.

"Ya see, in that chapter you sent me, on page 225. I don't remember you saying 'I picked a song for you' and me saying, 'You did?' 'Cause I always remember telling people about you playing all this extraordinary material for me. You know, living with you was like a touch of God, not only as a relationship, but it was such an amazing thing, that you had this collection of records, and good taste, and everything."

"Thanks, Barb," I said, touched. "That means a lot to me."

"So, why do you have to say stuff like that?" she insisted.

"Because you *said* that to me, Barbra. You came back from Detroit with a blank memory. It was like I'd never done anything for you. Listen, I think you were just trying to be independent, stand on your own two feet."

"But Barry, let me ask you something. What I remember is that you were bisexual. You were gay, right?"

"Yes. I was gay." This was a new tack. I wondered where all this was leading.

"And I moved out of your apartment because I came home on New Year's Eve, or something like that, and there was this black guy in your bathroom."

For a moment I was totally speechless, for me a rare condition. Then I managed to sputter, "Barbra, that's not what—that never happened."

"That *did* happen, Barry. There was a black guy in your bathroom. Why do you think I moved out? I mean, are you gonna talk about being gay in your book?"

"Yes, I am going to talk about my being gay, but—"

"Well, then, why don't you talk about that guy who was there on New Year's Eve?"

"Because I don't know what you're talking about."

"Don't you remember? This was a very mulatto-looking black guy. When I walked into the apartment and saw you with that guy, I knew you were still gay. For some reason I thought that maybe I could change you. Before you went away there was some sexual stuff going on between us. And I thought, this could go somewhere when he comes back. But when you came back—I think it was New Year's Eve—I found you with a black guy and I thought, holy shit, so I moved out."

"Where were you?"

"I'm in my bathtub." Barbra had thought I said, where *are* you. Of course, she was in her bathtub. Where else? That explained all that splish-splashing I kept hearing.

"No, no, I don't mean that. Although that's kind of interesting. Why weren't we together, if it was New Year's Eve and all?"

"I don't know, but I remember that it was very painful—it's the only time I ever saw you with a guy."

"Barbra," I protested, "I thought our breakup went like this: I went home to California to see my folks. You bought all this lox and bagels, 'cause you thought I was coming back. And then I stayed out in California a second week. Without calling you. So you ate up all the food—"

"That's not the important detail. The important detail is, I finally figured out I had no future with you because you were still … gay."

"Well, I see we remember it differently," I said. God, this was

261

making me uncomfortable. How could I completely block out of my mind something so crushingly traumatizing to Barbra? How could I forget bringing home a black man and Barbra walking in on us? I was getting really confused and upset. And what about Schulenberg's version of the story? He told me emphatically that Barbra and he ate through all the food together, and how distressed she was, and Bob had a memory that was crystal clear. I had to change the subject, if only so I could breathe for a moment. "But, listen," I said, "what do you think? Can I use the quotes?"

"What's the point, Barry? I mean, I don't want to be in a book. What is this book about—your life? Or just me in your life?"

"Well, it's about our time together."

"Tell me, why do you feel you need to write a book? Is it just for the money?"

Now it was my turn to feel a little insulted. "No, it's not *just* for the money. I think it's a really interesting story. I think a lot of young kids are going through what we went through. Sexual confusion. Trying to find out who they are, what they want from each other."

"Uh-huh," Barbra said, sounding very unconvinced.

"And trying to hack out their careers, and make it at the same time. I think it's a very modem dilemma. And anyway, it's my story, too."

"Did you write me any letters?" she said, suddenly changing the subject.

"Yes, sure, when you were in Detroit."

"Isn't that funny? You saved all my letters."

"Of course."

"I don't have any letters from anyone."

"I sent you copies of the letters you sent me, by fax, a couple of days ago."

"Yeah, I saw them. Most of them look like my handwriting. Some of them don't, but they're probably mine."

"Oh, come on, Barbra, I wouldn't pull a stunt like that. Forging your old letters."

"I know, I know you wouldn't but I'm honestly telling you why I said I gotta move out. And it was seeing you with the black guy." Oh, God, she was back to that again. She just wasn't going to let it go. Christ, I must have wounded her to the depths, all those years ago.

"I believe you. I believe you. I don't have any memory of this at all, but I believe you."

"Uh-huh."

"You know, I probably wouldn't *want* to have any memory of this because it's so, well . . . embarrassing."

"Uh-huh."

"And . . . hurtful."

"Yeah."

"To you. Of course it would be. I mean, I'm kind of a little flushed just listening to you tell me about it."

"Yeah."

"But listen, you know, I apologized to you a long time ago for my behavior then. . . ."

"Yeah."

"And I hope you believe me. I was very, very much in love with you, with my heart, and I just couldn't make the rest of my body go along and do what I wanted it to."

"Yeah, I know."

"But I adored you. I mean I just . . ."

"I know."

"Do you really know?"

"Yeah, I remember, you came and told me when I was making *Clear Day*, right?"

"Yes. In England. In Brighton," I said.

"In Brighton."

"Yes."

"And it was kind of nice to hear you say it, because that was a very painful time for me."

"It was a terrible time for both of us."

"And I was so young, I think I was seventeen."

"You were just a baby."

"Yeah. But I don't hold a grudge."

"Well, that's good."

"You know, you didn't mean to be…" she stopped and let it hang in the air.

"No, I *didn't* mean to be. I really didn't mean to be. I really thought I could make it work. You know, I spent the next twenty years trying to go straight. I got married in England, I had affairs with a lot of women."

"Really?"

"I still love women, I love being around them, I love their company…."

"Are you married now?"

"No, no, no."

"So what were doing all that time? What happened to your being gay?"

"Well, I am gay, Barbra. What I'm trying to say is that I fought it and fought it. I wanted it to be different. The first person I really wanted it to be different for was you."

"Yeah."

"I really did. God. I was married for eighteen years."

"Eighteen years?" she exclaimed.

"Yes."

"Were you faithful to her?"

"Absolutely. I never laid a hand on a guy. But you know something? I still looked at men when I walked down the street. Listen, I'm sorry to keep harping on about this book, but the bottom line is, I wanted this book to be funny, and charming, and to show a human side of you which, I think…well, I would like people to see that about you, I would like people to see that you are just a warm person, you know, a real, live human being, who does everything that we all do."

"You know," Barbra said with a sigh, "All these books, I usually read the first chapter, and this woman is talking about stuff she never could have seen, like she's a fly on the wall. Like, get this, when I opened at the MGM Grand, she says the stage manager handed me a cigarette and I took a few nervous puffs. There's only one thing wrong with this picture: I don't smoke."

"I remember that."

"So, you know what I mean, it's ridiculous."

"I've seen you puff on a cigarette, though."

"So, anyway, I—what did you say about that?"

"I've seen you puff on a cigarette."

"Ya mean, here and there."

"A little here and a little there."

"Yeah, every once in a while."

"Every once in a long while."

"Actually, I smoked when I was ten and stopped when I was twelve. And I certainly wouldn't take up smoking the night I'm first going to sing for a paying public. I mean, it's just absurd. And I'm kind of sick of it, I'm sick of hearing all this negative crap."

"I don't think you'll find my book is negative at all. You know, I wanted to show the funny side of you, and the sexy side, and lots of real, nice stuff. I'm not out to make you look foolish, exploit you in any way, or make you look mean."

"Do you remember doing a tape of me singing 'Sleepin' Bee' and we sent it to an agent, and the agent lost the tape?"

"No. When was that?"

"I'll save that for *my* book, Barry," Barbra said slyly.

I could hardly suppress a chuckle. "You little devil," I said, then added, "I wonder if Eddie Blum still has that tape of 'Day by Day'?"

" 'Day by Day'?"

"The first time you came to my apartment, to use my tape recorder, you came with Carl Esser. Do you remember any of this?"

"Yeah, I remember Carl Esser. I met him in acting class, or something."

"No! He was in *Insect Comedy* with us."

"Oh, he was in *Insect Comedy*, right, right."

"He and I were the snails, at the end of the show. You and I were the butterflies and the moths."

"Did you know, I went with Madeleine Albright to see a version of *The Insect Comedy*? She's from Czechoslovakia."

"That's right, she is."

"And I said, we've got to go. She wanted to see it, and I said, you're not gonna believe this, but I was *in* this play a million years ago. Go ahead with what you were saying."

"Well, I was just saying that you sat down and recorded 'Day By Day' and—"

"How does 'Day by Day' go?"

I couldn't believe it. Barbra Streisand was asking *me* to sing something to *her*! So I sang, "Day by day, I'm falling more in love with you....remember?"

"Vaguely, I'm not sure. I thought I made a tape of 'Taste of Honey' that first time, or 'Sleepin' Bee.' "

"No, it was 'Day by Day.' It really was."

"I don't think so."

"I promise you, it was. I ran into Carl Esser years later on a movie. We were both acting in it."

"Yeah...."

"And I had a trailer and he didn't. So I invited him in and we sat down. He said, 'Do you still have that tape of "Day by Day"?' "

and I said, no, I only had one tape recorder so I couldn't make a copy of the tape that we sent off to Eddie Blum."

"Yeah."

"So it's lost, and it's a shame because it was beautiful. And that was the tape that did it. I sat you down and I said, Barbra, you have the best voice I've ever heard, you have to sing. And you tried to wriggle away from me, and I said no, no, no, you *have* to do this."

"Why did I sing 'Day by Day'?"

"I think it was the only song that you and Carl both knew."

"Did he play the guitar?"

"That's right, Carl played the guitar."

"But did you know that I've been singing since I was five, on the stoops of Brooklyn? That I was the kid on the block with the voice? I mean, do you think that the only reason I sang was because you told me to?"

"I think that I gave you the security and the support and the confidence that you needed to be able to go out there and do it, yeah."

"I think you and Bob were great at that time, but—"

"Wait a minute," I bristled, "are you telling me you think you would've become a singer if you'd never met me?"

"Sure. I only became a singer because I couldn't get work as an actress."

"That was because of *me*! *I* was the one who made you do that!"

"How did you 'make' me do it?" she flung back at me.

"I talked you into it! I absolutely convinced you to do it! I went on and on and on at you until you agreed to go across the street and sign up for the talent contest. I wouldn't let you go. You absolutely fought me every step of the way!"

"Why, didn't I think I had a good voice?"

"No! That wasn't it. You were insecure. You had a wonderful voice, I kept telling you over and over until, I think, you finally believed me."

"Then tell me something: how did you know I could sing?"

"You came over and used my tape recorder."

"Why was I singing, though? You see what I'm saying, why was I making a tape?"

"Because Eddie Blum said he wanted to hear a tape of you singing, that's why."

"Why? Why did I do that?"

"Why did you do what?"

"The point is, I must have sung for you, or told you I sang before that or you wouldn't have said, make a tape."

"I didn't say, make a tape."

"Who? Who said it?"

"You were trying to get the part of Liesl in—"

"*The Sound of Music.*"

"That's right. And you sent that crazy photograph of your self—"

"Right."

"With the veils and everything."

"Yeah, that terrible photograph without a smile, right?"

"Without a smile, it was very serious, and Eddie called you in because he wanted to see what kind of a kook would send in a picture like that."

"That's right, that's true."

"I'm glad you agree with something," I said. "When he met you he started to talk to you, he was captivated by you. And then somehow or other you started to talk about singing. Maybe you sang something for him—"

"Oh, okay."

"I don't really know about that because I wasn't there. But you called me up—"

"—and said, do you have a tape recorder?" she finished the sentence for me.

"No, you *knew* I had a tape recorder because I told you about it in *The Insect Comedy*," I said. If she was going to nit-pick down to the very last nit, so would I.

"Right."

God, I thought. Getting Barbra to believe me is like walking uphill with a two-ton boulder.

"I told you I had this great Ampex stereo tape recorder that my dad gave me as a gift. So you called me and said, Eddie Blum wants to hear a tape of me singing. Could we do it on your tape recorder? And I said, oh sure, all right, come down. I thought you were crazy. I had no idea that you sang. I knew nothing about any of this."

"Right."

"So you came down to my house with Carl, you made the tape, and Carl had to leave, but I kept you there and I hammered at you. That's when I started to play records for you. And I absolutely wore you down. You kept saying no, no, no, I'm an actress, I'm an actress."

"Well, that could be right, that could be right."

"It *could* be right? It *is* right."

"It could be right."

"It could be right," I repeated sarcastically. "Thank you, very much."

"Well, it could be."

At this point Barbra's phone made a suspicious little beep. It occurred to me that possibly she was taping our conversation.

"Anyway, you know, Barry, I can't stop you from writing anything. I can't stop anybody. I'm not going to sue you. I think you're entitled to your memory of me."

"Well, thank you. It's something that I treasure, actually."

"I mean, did your publisher say I could sue you if you put this out without my—"

"Sure, if I publish your quotes without your written permission, you could take me to court for invasion of copyright, or whatever they call it. Infringement of copyright."

"Why don't you do it another way, then? Why don't you paraphrase it without my quotes?"

"I've already done that. I've got a paraphrased version ready, if I need it. But what's so wrong about quoting you? What's so wrong about giving this to me? I've never asked you for anything, Barbra. I've never even asked you for a concert ticket, nothing."

"I would have given it to you, Barry. If you'd ever called me and said I can't get tickets to your concert, I would have said here's two of them."

"I'm too proud."

"Well, I mean, I would have."

"I know, I know, you probably would've. I believe you."

"I actually would have. I take care of all my friends, ya know."

"I believe you."

"I mean, I haven't seen you in how long?"

"Well, the last time I saw you was at your fiftieth birthday party."

"No, you didn't."

"Barbra, where is your memory?!" I said, astonished.

"Wait a minute. You were at Jon Peters' house?"

"You invited me."

"That's right, that's right, I remember now."

"Oy, you're scaring me!"

"Wasn't that fun?"

"It was wonderful. You invited me and my boyfriend, James, whom you met."

"I met him that day?"

"My life partner. Sure, you met him. We've been together fourteen years."

"Wow."

"Yeah."

At this moment Barbra's telephone started to make another beeping noise.

"Is this a recording you're making?"

"Yeah. I am. So whaddya think of that? Wait a minute, Barry. I'll be right back." And the phone went dead. At that moment James walked into the kitchen.

"James," I said, "tell me I'm not going crazy. We did go to Barbra's fiftieth birthday, didn't we? Remember, the elephant and everything? I didn't dream that, did I? I mean, she's saying..."

"She just doesn't remember," James said. "Or she's trying to *Gaslight** you," he said, and left the room. Suddenly the phone clicked into life.

"Hello, Barry? You there?" With a churning whoosh of bath water, she was back.

"Are you at the far end of your bathtub—is that why I can't hear you?"

"Well, I'm tryin' to get some cold water in here."

"Anyway, what is the point of all this?"

"The point of all this is I have to think about whether I want to give you the right to use my quotes."

"Well, would you please make up your mind by Monday, 'cause that's when I have to send in my manuscript."

"Do you know how raped I feel when people write about me?"

"Oh, Barbra, don't say that. I'm not out to rape you."

"I know, but, again, you don't remember the black guy, Barry. That was like—"

"But *you* don't remember the things I'm telling you. You don't remember them and then you go, oh! Wait a minute. Yeah, yeah, could be."

Gaslight (1944) is the famous George Cukor film in which Charles Boyer uses subtle tricks and mind games to drive Ingrid Bergman insane.

"No, no, let me explain that to you, 'cause that's quite different. The thing is: who did the tape, Liesl, *Sound of Music*. That's factual stuff. I know it sort of happened but I don't know exactly when or in exactly what order. And when I'm writing my book, I'll have to talk to you about it, too. But my point is, there are moments in your life—we wrote a song in *Yentl* called 'There Are Moments You Remember,' you know, all your life. And there are moments I will never forget."

"And that's one of them."

"And that's one of them. Seeing you with that black guy, and being so shocked by the truth of it, you know?"

"Well, I imagine, if that really happened, it would be very shocking."

"I'm just telling you that you don't remember that, and that was one of the emotional moments that are indelible in my memory."

"I'm not saying I disbelieve you. All I'm saying is I've never had an attraction to black people, sexually. I'm not racist or anything. It's just that I've never found myself attracted. So I'm finding this a little—funny to remember as the truth, but I'll try to go back in my memory."

"He was a very pale black man, looked like a mulatto, ya know."

"Well, maybe so. If you say it happened, I believe you. I know you wouldn't lie to me about something as important as that."

"I wouldn't."

"Of course you wouldn't. But—all right, look. I don't know what to tell you. If you want to let me use these quotes, that's fine. If you don't want to, that's okay, too, because I'll paraphrase them, as you say."

"Well, ya know, here's the thing: I look at this book sent to me by Cis Corman, not by the publishers or the author, God forbid, 'cause they're guilty about it, ya know?"

272

"Oh, I see."

"Well, how about in the first chapter the woman who wrote this book says that I sing a song by Sondheim called 'There's a Place for Us.' She doesn't even know it's called 'Somewhere.' By the time she gets to the end of the book it becomes 'Somewhere.' Very inept, inaccurate, shoddy research, and a vicious kind of tone, I thought."

"I thought so, too. I wrote a long letter to her, and Marty asked me to fax him a copy."

"Somebody told me it got a review in the *New York Times* that claimed that she wasn't vicious *enough* about me."

"Oh, please. Why do people hate you—" I stopped myself. I could have bitten my tongue out.

"Why do they, Barry?" She asked me this terrible question so plaintively, it broke my heart.

"Look, this is something we talked about in one of those 1992 phone calls. I don't know if you remember."

"No."

"But you actually asked me, why do people hate me, and I got so upset when you said that. I said, Barbra, people don't hate you and you said, yes they do."

"Well, no, when I went to the Academy Awards with my love, you know, James Brolin—"

"Listen, by the way, congratulations!"

"Yeah, isn't that nice?"

"It's more than nice."

"I was upset that the end line of your chapter read, 'We both realized that all love affairs end in disappointment."

"But you're not having a love affair, you're having a love."

"Oh, I see what you mean, you and James are a love, not an affair."

"Of course! And you and *your* James are a love, not an affair. I do believe that. All love affairs do end in disappointment, but a love—a love lasts, and grows, and changes."

"But I was telling you about the Academy Awards, and I do realize I have a lot of fans and a lot of people love me. A lot of people love me. I'm thrilled about that. But why is the press so negative? I guess it's because they're jealous and I can't really understand the nature of jealousy. I mean, if I see something great I can feel a little pang but I don't want to *kill* it, I don't want to destroy it. I want to say, isn't that great, and it makes me want to do better."

"Jealousy is a hateful emotion. It's like guilt. It doesn't do anything good. It's just a rotten feeling. It kills a relationship."

"I'm into gardening. I have eight hundred rose bushes. I was at a cactus nursery today."

"Barbra, you found out. That's the way to live, to stick your hands in the earth."

"Well, I don't stick my hands in the earth, yet. I just say, I wanna buy *that* rose and *that* rose and *that* rose and I want to plant it here and there. And I'm learning how to cut them properly, above their five leaves and that kind of thing."

"Isn't it satisfying?"

"Yeah, we grow our own organic vegetables."

"You are so lucky. Listen, I don't know if you're going to remember a lot of the things I write about in the book—going out to the Brooklyn Museum and—"

"But I've only seen one chapter."

"Well, of course. I didn't even expect you to call. I certainly wasn't going to send you a whole book and say, oh, would you mind sitting down and reading three hundred pages for me, and tell me if they're correct?"

"I don't have the time for that!"

"Exactly. But listen, whether you decide to give me these quotes or whether you don't, what I want to say to you is this: I love you dearly, I am not out to injure you in this book. I decided to do it as a book that was about a young love, which meant more to me than I can possibly express. And I thought, okay, all right, if Barbra doesn't like it she's just going to have to find it in her heart to forgive me."

"Well I do, I do, you know, it's amazing, when someone touches your life, you always remember them. And that was a very important time in my life."

"That was a very important time for both of us."

"You know, the power of the printed word is so strong, Barry. Marty read some book about me and he said, I learned something I never knew about you. And I said, what's that? He said you moved to Manhattan and you continued to go to high school from Manhattan. You commuted to Brooklyn. And I said, what are you *talking* about? I graduated in three and a half years. In January I moved to Manhattan. You think I would commute to Brooklyn to go to school? Why would you believe that? Because it's in print. You see, he believed it, and he's my manager."

"Of course. The minute it's in print it takes on authority."

"So what I'm saying is, Barry, you have to understand: this is your reality. You must phrase it that way. Why don't you even say, you talked to me, and I said, 'Well, I don't remember it this way, I remember it like that.' Someday I'll write about it myself. It's an interesting thing, isn't it? But again, it's the Telephone Game."

"It's the Telephone Game and it's memories."

"Yeah."

"It's fascinating. What people remember and how they remember it. You know, you get ten people together who were at a dinner party ten years ago. And you sit them all down and you ask them, what is your memory of what happened that evening? Everybody's memory would be different. Everybody's."

The mystery of memory, I thought. Chinese whispers!

*   *   *

Two days after our conversation, Marty Erlichman called to tell me that Barbra was uncomfortable letting me use her quotes in an unauthorized book that she hadn't even read. I didn't argue. She had a good point.

When I was a kid in the Daniel Boone Grammar School in Chicago, and doing my best to deflect the aggression aimed at me by the bullies in the playground by distracting the other children with marionette shows, funny monologues, acting and singing, the very clever teacher who wrote the parody lyrics for our school shows* told me an interesting story: in one of the Balkan countries, a bride-to-be was presented with a basket of tangled twine. How she dealt with it, her approach to unraveling it, was the clue to what kind of a wife she would turn out to be. Would she throw the basket down impatiently after hours of struggling with it? Or simply give up immediately and walk away? Or would she persist, and patiently make her way through the colored threads, and untangle it all?

In some ways, in writing this book, I feel like I've been stubbornly working at knots and untying strings, trying to untangle a confusion of feelings and motives, to tell my story truthfully, as I remember it. And now here is Barbra, telling me that I've got some things all wrong, that she remembers them entirely differently. Well, maybe that's basically what we human beings do in our relationships: remember them differently.

There is a mystical religion that believes that when you die, before you can move on to a higher plane, you must spend some time in a kind of limbo, a sort of spiritual movie house, where your entire life, year by year, day by day, moment by moment, gets

*The only pastiche lyric she wrote that I can remember was based, coincidentally, on "Happy Days Are Here Again," and it went: "*Boone* School *Show*time's *here* again..." It's uncanny how the themes of our lives interweave and counter-cross. Who would have thought that nine years later I'd be living with the woman who would make that old song into a worldwide hit all over again?

played back to you so you can see it for what it really was, grow in wisdom, and learn from your mistakes. If there is such a place, perhaps only then will Barbra and I, and all of us be able to look back on our own pasts truly and clearly, and say, "Oh, *that's* what happened. *That's* what all that meant."

But even then, I'm not sure if Barbra and I would agree on what we'd just seen.

Afterword

*T*here's a popular arts program on television that interviews famous actors, writers, and directors in theater, film, and television. The last question they always ask their guests is, If you met St. Peter at heaven's gates and he asked you what good you had done during your stay on the earth, what would you answer?

I would say, "I helped give the world Barbra Streisand."

And what would I hope St. Peter would reply?

"Come in."

Acknowledgments

$\mathcal{F}$or the generous gift of their time, talent, and taste, the author is grateful to everyone who helped make this book happen, particularly and alphabetically: Paul Bartel, Eddie Blum, Pat Broeske, Rafe Chase, Shaun Considine, Lorren Daro, Phyllis Diller, Marshall Efron, Marty Erlichman, James Gavin, Bobb Goldsteinn, Dorothy Hart, Harald Holcomb, Mitchell Ivers, Jane A. Johnston, Miles Kreuger, Terry Leong, James McGachy, Marianne Meyerhoff, Eugene O'Connor, Joan Rivers, Bob Schulenberg, Ruth B. Sherwood, Treva Silverman, David Solomon, James Spada, Bob Stone, and Lucy Chase Williams.

And a special thanks to Miss Barbra Joan Streisand, without whom this book could not have been written.

For more information about this book, contact our Website at: http://members.aol.com/bazdennen. You can e-mail Barry Dennen at: bazdennen@aol.com.